THE BIRTH OF SOLIDARITY

THE BIRTH OF SOLIDARITY

The History of the French Welfare State

FRANÇOIS EWALD

Edited by Melinda Cooper and translated
by Timothy Scott Johnson

DUKE UNIVERSITY PRESS
Durham and London
2020

Cover designed by Matthew Tauch
Typeset in Minion Pro by Westchester Book Group

Library of Congress Cataloging-in-Publication Data
Names: Ewald, François, author. | Johnson, Timothy Scott, translator.
Title: The birth of solidarity : the history of the French welfare state / François Ewald ; translated by Timothy Scott Johnson ; edited by Melinda Cooper.
Other titles: Etat providence. English
Description: Durham : Duke University Press, 2020. | Includes bibliographical references and index.
Identifiers: LCCN 2019032720 (print)
LCCN 2019032721 (ebook)
ISBN 9781478007715 (hardcover)
ISBN 9781478008231 (paperback)
ISBN 9781478009214 (ebook)
Subjects: LCSH: Social security—France—History. | Welfare state—History. | Accident insurance—France—History. | Social legislation—France—History.
Classification: LCC HD7175 .E9313 2020 (print) | LCC HD7175 (ebook) | DDC 344.4403/2—dc23
LC recordavailableathttps:// lccn.loc.gov/2019032720
LC ebookrec ordavailableathttps:// lccn.loc.gov/2019032721

Cover art: Béthune (mining disaster in the La Clarence mine), September 5, 1912, the public in front of the mine. Press photograph/Agence Rol. Courtesy Bibliothèque nationale de France. ID/Cote : btv1b6921232c.f1; https://catalogue.bnf.fr/ark:/12148/cb404588579

This book received a publication subsidy from Duke University Press's Translation Fund, a fund established by Press authors who donated their book royalties to support the translation of scholarly books.

TO MICHEL FOUCAULT

CONTENTS

TRANSLATOR'S PREFACE

TIMOTHY SCOTT JOHNSON

It is now over thirty years since François Ewald's history of the origins of the French welfare state was published in its full form and twenty since it reappeared in the abridged form translated here. If belated, this translation will allow a new audience of students and scholars to appreciate a work that has already been influential in not just French history, but also economic history, political theory, and legal history. In some ways, this delayed translation highlights the aspects of the history that may now appear dated. For instance, the history told is a purely metropolitan history, with no reference to France's imperial existence or the role the empire played in the development of modern welfare state funding and functioning. Nonetheless, the history told remains theoretically insightful, uniting aspects of legal, social, political, and intellectual history under one framework. Despite being a history primarily of nineteenth-century France, the questions and themes covered are still very much relevant to our modern world: labor relations, statistical risk analysis, insurance guarantees and regulations, the state as a source of security, and population management. Insofar as the welfare state is still an institution to be repudiated, defended, or reformed, our world is still informed by the logics Ewald relates.

Born in 1946, Ewald traversed many of the most important moments and movements in the intellectual and political history of postwar France. He was first drawn to the existentialism of Jean-Paul Sartre, was politically active in the wake of the 1968 student and workers' rebellions, and became an assistant to Michel Foucault at the Collège de France, adopting many of his ideas. For this reason, this translation will be of interest to intellectual historians as well. Ewald's unique journey from postwar radicalism to state bureaucrat has been documented elsewhere.[1] So far, to most Anglophone audiences, if Ewald's name is recognized, it is as one of the editors of the many posthumous collections of Foucault's texts and lectures. This history of the genesis of welfare state thinking in France shows Ewald's own study of government techniques of power that Foucault popularized, matching the breadth and critical insight of Foucault's best work.

For the most part, the text of this translation is as it originally appeared, but I have added several notes. These notes are meant to add some context for statements and allusions that would have needed little or no explanation for French readers in the 1980s, as well as references to lesser-known thinkers and terms Ewald discusses. In some instances the citations Ewald originally gave were incomplete, inconsistent in format and style, or inaccurate. Sometimes citations appeared in the first longer book but not the shorter second one. None of the inaccuracies are major, but are rather likely due to the haplography inherent in analog research and reference. The digitization of many of the sources cited has allowed me to rather easily check the references given and track down others left out. Where a change has been made, I have provided a note explaining the change and, where appropriate, an alternate translation corresponding to the original citation and text. A number of the texts Ewald discusses and cites are classics of political theory. Where a standard translation exists for these quoted passages, I have mostly adhered to that text. In some instances, either the stylistic choices of those texts' translators or the slight differences produced by triangulating translations between multiple languages, as in the case of German texts Ewald cites in French translation, I have either amended the standard translations to fit with the style of the rest of Ewald's text or translated those passages anew. Any changes to published translations are flagged in the notes.

In addition to notes on sources, historical figures, and references not readily obvious to a younger English generation, I have added notes specifying the logic behind particular word choices, including wherever my own interpretive license might deviate from a strictly literal translation of the text. A number of translation choices bear special note. By and large, the general social, political, and economic transformations Ewald's history presents are mirrored in other nineteenth-century Western states. However, some of the terminology specific to the nineteenth-century French context sits slightly askew with modern English terms. The French word *patron*, for instance, is generally translated into English as "boss" or "employer." I have chosen to render it simply as *patron*, since "boss" would imply a level of informality not reflective of the formal and hierarchical relationship Ewald sketches; *employeur* as a French term emerges toward the end of the nineteenth century as a distinct term more neutral than *patron*, and one meant to avoid the latter's specific social implications. The same choice goes for all of *patron*'s variants: *régime du patronage* (translated as "regime of patronage"), *patronat*, etc.[2] Likewise, there is often little to no differentiation between translations of *bienfaisance* and *charité*, both often translated into English as "charity." However, with the rise of the industrial patron in the nineteenth century, older charitable practices change in their social character. Ewald reinforces this by reserving *charité* for older, early modern practices and *bienfaisance* for the newer modern practices. Therefore, *charité* is translated as "charity" and *bienfaisance* as "benevolence" or "benevolent aid."

Two French words with particular philosophical importance pose their own issues: *dispositif* and *objectivation*. As it stands, there is no direct standard equivalent for *dispositif* in modern English. When referring to a physical object, the English words "device" and "facility" are usually accurate. However, Ewald, like Foucault, uses the word in a more figurative manner, referring more to conceptual and social arrangements and dispositions than actual material artifacts (these latter bear the imprint of the former). *Dispositif* in these contexts refers to the various immaterial (concepts, prejudices, ideologies) and material (institutions, administrative practices) arrangements that reinforce power relations. Some Anglophone historians, such as Stephen Kotkin, who, like Ewald, were influenced by Michel Foucault, approximate *dispositif* with the word "apparatus."[3] The choice is also common in many translations of Michel Foucault's works. This, however, I think still has too material a connotation in English. Further, there is a separate word in French to designate apparatus—*appareil*. As a solution, I have simply translated *dispositif* as "dispositive." My hope is that this choice clarifies the specificity of the term and does not obscure it. Similarly, I have chosen to translate the French word *objectivation* as "objectification." In some contexts the French word *objectivation* might appear to mean what "conceptualization" implies in English. However, following Foucault, Ewald uses the term to specify when an object or event is qualified in a precise manner, out of a range of possibilities. So, as Ewald's study shows, accidents could be interpreted and analyzed in a number of ways, including as dangers or unnatural phenomena. But among the different interpretations available, the insurance system that emerged toward the end of the nineteenth century will specifically *objectify* the accident as a risk.

I would like to thank those who aided me in the translation process. First and foremost, a good measure of gratitude goes to Melinda Cooper for careful readings of the translation as well as for advice on legal terminology. The final version of this translation owes much to her input. Martijn Konings, too, read over the manuscript, offering helpful comments. François Ewald also helped clarify key issues regarding the terms and concepts he employs. Any and all inaccuracies or errors, of course, rest solely on my shoulders. Finally, I would also like to thank Michael Behrent for introducing me to Ewald's work many years ago. This translation most certainly would not have existed otherwise.

RISK, INSURANCE, SECURITY
EWALD'S HISTORY OF THE WELFARE STATE

MELINDA COOPER

François Ewald's *Histoire de l'état providence*, published here for the first time in English, offers an arresting historical account of the birth of the welfare state in France. The book traces the slow and laborious process by which a liberal juridical regime of fault and personal responsibility, embodied in the 1804 Civil Code of the French Revolution, was displaced by the hitherto unknown technology of social insurance and how this technology provided the blueprint for the twentieth-century welfare state. It shows how the apparently mundane problem of workplace accidents assumed monstrous proportions as the nineteenth century wore on and how the sheer scale of injury, on a par with the massification of industry itself, eventually overwhelmed the capacities of liberal jurisprudence. The book, in Ewald's words, aspires to be three things: a social history of the welfare state, a philosophy of law, and a sociology of risk.[1] Together, these three perspectives give shape to a genealogy, in the Foucauldian style, of social security—the idea that the multiple accidents befalling citizens in and beyond the workplace can be collectively accounted for and managed through the selective redeployment of the much older practice of insurance. As such, the book's interest extends well beyond the specific history of the French welfare state, whose trajectory was reproduced in slightly different form around the world, to throw light on the general process by which risk was first identified as a target of power and subsequently collectivized in the form of social insurance.

Ewald's magnum opus was born out of a collective research endeavor inspired by his thesis supervisor, Michel Foucault, and nurtured in the context of a private reading group made up of Foucault's doctoral students. The tone was set by Foucault's Collège de France seminars of the late 1970s, where he first drew attention to the problematic of "security" as it arose in the large commercial cities of eighteenth- and nineteenth-century Europe. Here he identified a form of power distinct from both the politicotheological framework of sovereignty and the normalizing focus on bodies he had explored in his study of the prison, *Discipline and Punish*.[2] It was in the eighteenth century, Foucault suggested, that states were for the first time confronted with the problem of managing and regulating the circulation of people, merchandise, and money, at a distance and by approximation, and in the process, began to apprehend their citizens in statistical and probabilistic terms—that is, as a population rather than a sovereign body or collection of subjects.

The subsequent shift in focus from territory and bodies to population demanded an entirely new mode of governing. Where "sovereignty capitalizes a territory" and "discipline structures a space and addresses the central problem of a hierarchical and functional distribution of elements," "security will try to plan a milieu in terms of events or series of events or possible elements, of series that will have to be regulated within a multivalent transformable framework. The specific space of security refers then to a series of possible events; it refers to the temporal and the uncertain, which have to be inserted within a given space."[3] In this particular passage, Foucault focuses on the aleatory and probabilistic dimensions of population science, the forms of projection that attempt to discern the possible, future events that might befall us; elsewhere, he shows how this horizon of events becomes knowable at an aggregate level through the collection of statistical data and how this demographic information opens up the possibility of *normalization*, the prediction or production of population-level equilibria. In Foucault's words, the "mortality rate has to be modified or lowered; life expectancy has to be increased; the birth rate has to be stimulated. And most important of all, regulatory mechanisms must be established to establish an equilibrium, maintain an average, establish a sort of homeostasis, and compensate for variations within this general population and its aleatory field. In a word, security mechanisms have to be installed around the random element inherent in a population of living beings so as to optimize a state of life."[4] These technologies originally derived from the practice of commercial insurance, and yet they were widely and increasingly adapted by states throughout the eighteenth and nineteenth centuries as a way of managing population risks.

The elements were there for a genealogy of social security, but as was often the case with his seminar series, Foucault soon abandoned the problematic of security in favor of newer interests, leaving behind a profusion of tantalizing, half-finished research projects for others to work with. Several of the students in his private seminar took over where Foucault left off and went on to develop much more extensive studies into the history of social insurance. Much of this work began on commission, when the French Labor Ministry approached Foucault's partner, the sociologist Daniel Defert, to deliver a series of studies on the history of workplace accidents and their management.[5] Defert then contracted a handful of Foucault's students, including Ewald, to help conduct the research. The first report, submitted in 1977, bore the title *The Socialization of Risk and Power in Companies: History of the Political and Juridical Transformations Permitting the Legalization of Professional Risks* and announced the arrival of a concept, social insurance, that would soon become central to the research endeavors of Foucault's students.[6] Building on this excavation work, Foucault's students went on to publish a series of major monographs dealing with the history of social welfare and its correlative concept of risk. Jacques Donzelot's study *The Invention of the Social: Essay on the Decline of Political Passions* appeared in 1984.[7] In 1993, Giovanna Procacci published her doctoral thesis under the title *Governing Misery: The Social Question in France, 1789–1848*.[8] And although he was not a student of Foucault's, the sociologist Robert Castel contributed to this collective research enterprise with the 1981 publication of his *La Gestion des risques*, a study on the displacement of "dangerousness" by "risk" in the management of psychiatric patients.[9] But it was undoubtedly Ewald who delivered the most sustained and important inquiry into the problematic of social security as the guiding framework of the twentieth-century welfare state. Indeed, Ewald claims to have been the first among Foucault's students to have identified the importance of the concepts of social insurance and risk and the first to have illuminated the complex trajectory from commercial insurance to the twentieth-century welfare state.[10] Ewald's doctoral thesis, "Risque, assurance, sécurité," focused precisely on this trajectory. The thesis was defended in 1986 and published in book form the same year, with the title *L'État providence*. A shorter, more concise version, titled *Histoire de l'état providence*, followed ten years later, and it is this version that we have chosen to translate here.

It was in the course of his work for the French Labor Ministry that Ewald came across a piece of legislation—the 1898 law insuring workers against industrial accidents—that would completely reorient his research interests over the next decade. The law came into being after half a century of fractious court battles pitting employers against workers over the question of who should pay for workplace injuries. As the century progressed, it became increasingly obvious that the Civil Code of 1804 was unable to accommodate the sheer scale of the problem. For most of this period, the legal system appeared to be weighted against workers. The configuration of accidents as a problem of tort law meant that workers needed to arraign employers before the courts if they wanted to seek redress for workplace accidents. This in itself posed a significant obstacle to workers who struggled to find the means to cover expensive court proceedings. But more than this, the very rationality of tort law proved inimical to the management of workplace accidents. The tort law provisions of the Civil Code entailed a highly restrictive understanding of civil liability according to which the personal fault or negligence of the employer had to be proven before compensation could be awarded for damages. In many cases, the chain of causation linking the worker, the employer, and the machine was much too diffuse to merit any personal assignation of responsibility, thereby precluding the award of damages and leaving workers with no means of assistance. The need to determine fault or negligence in order to justify compensation all too often proved a hopeless endeavor in the midst of multiple chains of command and a complex industrial machinery.

Toward the end of the century, the courts strove to redress the balance by extending the scope of negligent behavior and pushing at the limits of causation. Matters came to a head in 1896 when, in the landmark Teffaine case, the Cour de Cassation or Appeals Court ruled that employers should be held liable for any injury caused by things in their possession.[11] Referring to article 1384 paragraph 1 of the Civil Code, the court ruled that French law did in fact recognize some notion of strict liability, implying that fault no longer needed to be proven for the employer to be impugned.[12] All of a sudden, the balance of powers seemed to have shifted in favor of workers, and the scene was set for a flood of litigation. Instead, the French Parliament stepped into the breach and proposed an entirely new mechanism for dealing with the problem, one that would dispense with the courts altogether and save both employers and workers the effort of engaging in lengthy litigation. With one stroke, the 1898 law on workplace accidents overrode the juridical framework of the Civil Code and replaced it with a statutory regime of socialized insurance: workers would now be automatically compensated for "professional risk," encompassing both accidental injury and work-related illnesses, and employers were instructed to create insurance funds to finance the costs. The state, via the use of mandated insurance funds, would now take charge of compensation and thereby ensure workers of adequate and timely redress in the event of an accident. The uncertain and costly route to compensation via the courts was replaced by a system of socialized security that would dispense with the need to adjudicate responsibility and prove fault. The same principle would later be extended to a multitude of other risks, from unemployment to old age.

With the passage of this law, Ewald discerns the birth of a new technique of power—"normalization"—and an entirely new kind of legality—"social law." As the operative logic of the welfare state, "normalization" denotes the redistribution of risks within the limits of the nation and (we might add) the family wage.[13] "Normalization," in this context, no longer refers to the disciplinary standardization of bodies and minds around an anatomical or psychological norm but rather refers to the pooling of risks in the interests of social protection. This practice, Ewald contends, will give rise to an entirely new body of law—one that is embodied in the administrative corpus of workers' compensation statutes, social security legislation, occupational health and safety laws, road safety rules, manufacturing standards, and product regulations. Where Foucault refers to the same developments as indicative of a broad process of "juridical regression," Ewald offers a rather more nuanced picture of the "evolving status of law."[14] At stake here, he notes, is not the marginalization of the "juridical" as such (which Foucault at times seems to conflate with the sovereign mode of power) but rather the displacement of an essentially liberal order of private law, embodied in the tort and contract provisions of the Civil Code, by an entirely new order of law, which can be usefully characterized as "social" and solidaristic.[15] American legal scholars refer to a similar transition from nineteenth-century contract and tort law to twentieth-century administrative law.[16]

As Ewald's history reminds us, the framework of social law was very often promoted by social reformers and business interests as a way of containing the threat of revolution. It would later be denounced for the very same reason by some but not all Communist unions.[17] And although Ewald himself at times seems to confirm this reading, elsewhere he offers a more complex picture of workers, employers, and the state locked in an ongoing battle to define the terms and scope of social insurance.[18] As Ewald notes in the final passages of his monograph, the 1898 law was at best a "Pyrrhic victory" for employers because it left the door wide open for an expropriation of social insurance practices by the union movement. By the end of the nineteenth century, social insurance had become "the form, the instrument, and the stakes" (chapter 9) of political struggles between workers, employers, and the state.

This observation would be borne out by the subsequent history of workers' struggles, although Ewald himself does not pursue his investigation beyond the primordial moment of 1898. In the late 1920s, for instance, Communist, Socialist, and Catholic unions locked horns over the question of whether to support a new social insurance initiative on the part of the state and, if so, with what margin of control by the unions.[19] In the late 1930s, the leftist Popular Front embarked on an extraordinary program of social legislation, hoping ultimately to implement a worker-controlled national insurance fund and pension scheme. This ambition was cut short by the collapse of the Popular

Front in 1938, but it would be implemented, on less favorable terms, by the technocratic government of the post-Liberation period.[20] Later in the twentieth century, the availability of a relatively generous system of social protection was widely blamed for the social unrest and stagflation crisis of the 1970s, when workers were able to push up wages in a context of high unemployment. The French sociologist Michel Crozier was one of three international contributors to the Trilateral Commission's 1975 report, *The Crisis of Democracy*, which identified overly generous welfare programs as a source of social revolution.[21] And with the arrival of persistent unemployment and structural changes to the labor market in the 1980s, new social insurance movements for the long-term unemployed and performing artists have sprung up outside the traditional trade unions.[22] In short, it would be difficult to nominate any significant moment in twentieth-century labor history and beyond, when the question of social insurance was *not* in play. Social insurance never proved to be the antidote to revolutionary struggle that nineteenth-century social reformers (and perhaps Ewald) had hoped for.

From the Accident to Risk

Ewald's approach to the question of liberalism is an unfamiliar one, oriented more toward the question of security than wealth and property rights and guided more by the legal history of tort than contract law. Dispensing with the habitual focus on the sovereign subject or the possessive individual, his first insight is to suggest that the problematic of the accident plays a constitutive, even providential, role within liberal philosophy. With the decline of theological doctrines of fate, he observes, liberalism not only recognizes the inevitability of the accident as a fact of life, common to rich and poor, but actively celebrates its role in adjudicating differences of fortune. Thus, Ewald discerns a distinct moral philosophy at work within liberalism. According to its terms, we are all equally subject to the uncertainty of fate, yet we are individually differentiated by our ability to respond to and capitalize on this uncertainty. The blows of misfortune may be beyond my power, but I alone bear responsibility for anticipating and preparing for them. In this way, the accident serves as a test of foresight and prudence; by revealing an individual's willingness and capacity to confront the inevitable misfortunes of life, it also decides his or her worth. "Each is, should be, is supposed to be responsible for his or her own fate, life, destiny" (chapter 1). But for this reason also, the actual distribution of misfortune appears as an irrevocable judgment and an expression of natural justice—an act of God. According to this conception of things, poverty can only be a mark of personal failure, just as wealth represents the natural reward of those who have exercised foresight.

As a moral philosophy of the accident, Ewald claims, classical economic liberalism finds its exact juridical translation in the Civil Code provisions on civil liability. The French Civil Code of 1804 contains two categories for understanding the problem of civil liability—contract and tort law. Contract law recognizes liability when a defendant has failed to observe implicit or explicit obligations specified in a contract, while tortious liability arises in cases where general rules of conduct, imposed by statute, regulation, or case law, have been breached. Given the way in which work accidents were treated in France, Ewald's specific focus is on the Civil Code provisions on tort, in which fault and personal responsibility play a determining role. Article 1382 of the Code specifies that "any act of man which causes damages to another shall oblige the person by whose fault it occurred to repair it." In other words, the plaintiff must prove a direct line of causation between an individual act and a provable injury to establish a case for civil liability. In order to be awarded compensation, the plaintiff must convince the court that someone is at fault, although the fault in question can extend from deliberate acts to cases of imprudence or lack of foresight. Thus, article 1383 specifies that "one shall be liable not only by reason of one's acts, but also by reason of one's imprudence or negligence."

But beyond this homology between economic liberalism and tort law, Ewald also identifies an intellectual affinity between the liberal philosophy of the accident and the calculus of probability. It is hardly surprising, he notes, that both forms of reasoning emerged around the same time. Both understood the accident as subject to a kind of natural lawfulness: left to itself, it was assumed, the apparent disorder of free wills and chance encounters would generate an order of its own. It is ironic then that the workplace accident would ultimately test the limits of liberalism's capacity to govern. As workplace accidents took on industrial-scale proportions as the nineteenth century progressed, both the moral doctrine of personal responsibility and the juridical doctrine of tort law proved inadequate to the task of governing industrial relations. Tort law may have been sufficient for dealing with accidents as long as the relationship between the plaintiff and the defendant was one of direct personal dependence, as in the domestic household or the small artisanal workshop. Here at least it was possible to establish direct causal relations between the act of the defendant and the wrong suffered by the plaintiff. But as work shifted to the industrial shop floor, it was often impossible to assign fault for any one incident. By mid-century, the accident of unknown cause had emerged as an apparently insuperable obstacle to the proper compensation of workers. Unless it could be attributed to a precise causal agent, the accident was legally equivalent to an act of God, without recourse or hope of compensation. As a consequence, the worker very often ended up assuming the costs of his or her own welfare, even when the injustice of the situation was patently visible.

A first solution to this problem came in the form of paternalism, the uniquely French system of patronage that was conceived as a means of alleviating the peculiar social insecurities generated by liberalism without empowering the workers against their masters. Famously outlined in Le Play's *La Réforme sociale en France* (1864), the social economy of paternalism represented a corporatist and socially conservative attempt to remedy some of the crude injustices of the industrial workplace. This it hoped to achieve by recreating the imagined dependencies of the feudal household in the context of large industry. Emerging in the first few decades of the nineteenth century, the system of patronage replaced the liberal understanding of the labor contract as a simple exchange of commercial services with a morally charged relationship of mutual obligation. The term *patron* was itself a self-conscious reference to the paterfamilias of the feudal household economy: no longer a mere contractor of services, the *patron* was imagined as a benevolent master responsible for both the labor and well-being of his workers and dependents. The trade-off was strategic. The *patron* agreed to take sole charge of his worker's welfare, relieving him of the burden of personal responsibility, but in exchange prohibited any kind of solidaristic alliance among workers and any kind of state intervention in the workplace. The paternalist welfare regime was astonishingly ambitious: it extended from the care of injured and retired workers to the construction of schools, clinics, and parks for the worker's dependents. Entire factory towns such as Creusot and Mulhouse were built on the paternalist model and thought to be immune from worker unrest. But the failure of this model became clear when a massive strike broke out at Creusot in 1870. Paternalism, it now seemed, was not capable of stemming the tide of worker discontent.

Another solution, arising within the case law of the courts, was to push tort law to its limits and extend it well beyond the original intentions of the Civil Code. In this way, the French case law of the late nineteenth century ended up recognizing the concept of strict (that is, no-fault) liability for "things in one's possession." Hence, an employer in possession of a complex machinery could in principle be rendered liable for workers' injuries through the mere fact of ownership. But although this solution had the merit of widening the scope of legitimate injury, it didn't dispense with the slow and costly process of litigation.

As such, the extension of strict liability to workplace accidents signaled the exhaustion of tort law itself as a reliable means of dealing with the risks of mass manufacture. The sheer regularity of workplace accidents overwhelmed the heuristic of fault, suggesting as it did that accidents were not rare or exceptional events but rather simple facts of industrial life—regular, routine, and to be expected. In this context, it no longer made sense to conceive of the injury as an accident, a punctual event interrupting the normal laws of nature; rather it began to assume the qualities of a statistical regularity, an event whose likelihood could be calculated in probabilistic terms—that is, as a function of risk. More than this, the phenomenon of the industrial accident seemed to suggest that most causes were too complex to be known or blamed on any one individual. The incorporation of muscles, metal, wood, and stone into a complex automatic machinery meant either that no one was responsible for any one incident or that all were potentially responsible for the accidents suffered by others. In any event, the question of assigning fault was now redundant. If the workplace injury was both a normal part of industrial experience and a risk factor referable to a statistical series rather than a punctual accident, then it needed to be managed in a routine and collective fashion. At this point, French legislators turned to an instrument that many employers were already using as a means of covering the costs of court-awarded damages to injured workers—that of insurance. Having originated as a commercial innovation, insurance had acquired an increasingly social function in the course of the nineteenth century. When they ratified the French law on work accidents of 1898, French legislators completed this evolution by assigning to the state the function of insurer of last resort and designating workers as the holders of a collective insurance policy vis-à-vis the state. This was the first step toward the development of social insurance—the idea that the state should underwrite the ensemble of "social risks" incurred by its citizens, ensuring the general social security of its policyholders in the event of economic loss.

The route from commercial to social insurance was by no means preordained. As Ewald reminds us, the speculative logic of insurance was for many years much more prominent than its potential actuarial functions. From its first widespread commercial use in fifteenth-century Genoa, insurance was much more closely associated with games of chance and wagers than with the virtue of collective foresight. The first insurance contracts were negotiated between traders, who were looking for a way to hedge against the danger of cargo loss, and merchants, who anticipated that profits were to be made by exploiting the need for financial protection among a sufficiently large population of clients. Tellingly, the word "risk" derives from the early modern Italian *risco* (reef), which in turn references the ever-present danger of shipwreck that confronted traders in their travels to the New World. The word encapsulates the technical innovation of early insurance contracts, which drew on the established probabilistic logic of gambling but applied it for the first time to the practical question of how to compensate for economic loss while making a profit. The concept of risk thereby acquired a very specific meaning at the interface of the economic and the mathematical: more than a simple calculus of probability, it came to designate the future likelihood of an event as it related to a specific stock of capital. And more than a punctual accident or roll of the dice, risk was understood to be collective by its very nature, since the insurer's calculus was based on the intuition that profits could be made only as long as risk was shared. Hence, the three features of risk as defined by Ewald: risk belongs to the future, yet is calculable in probabilistic terms; risk is always collective in nature, a quality of populations; and risk translates all loss into a capital loss.

A further step toward social insurance was made with the development of social statistics in the nineteenth century. Here the sociologist and mathematician Adolphe Quetelet (1796–1874) played a key role. Quetelet, whom Ewald sees as a much more perceptive analyst of the social than Auguste Comte, set out to develop a systematic theory of the "average man," using the combined methods of probability theory and statistics and applying them to historical data on all aspects of human behavior. His treatise on social physics brought to fruition a project that had been foreshadowed by Condorcet and Laplace but that hitherto had floundered on the paucity of available statistical data.[23] When Quetelet began this work, he had few resources to draw upon other than the mortality tables used by life insurance companies. Later, he was able to collect much more extensive population-wide data from state administrators on birth and mortality statistics, criminal prosecutions, and disease. Quetelet himself was instrumental in pushing for the establishment of government statistical bureaus and standardized practices of state data collection through his work with the International Statistical Congress.[24] This process of bureaucratic scale-up would prove invaluable to the project of social insurance. Only once the state had developed the means to consult longitudinal data on its own populations was it able to make reliable predictions about the demographic future and thus take on the role of social insurer. The availability of vast, standardized pools of demographic data made the technique of insurance amenable to the needs of the state and turned what was often a speculative undertaking for both insurer and insured into a sound actuarial practice. Insurance would henceforth be reimagined in solidaristic and actuarial terms as a form of mutual protection and would give rise to the idea that "social security" should form the horizon of state intervention.

In France as in many other countries, the promulgation of a first law on workplace accidents led, within a few decades, to a gradual broadening of social insurance to include provisions for old age and illness, along with an extension of coverage beyond the worker to his dependents. This trajectory, as Ewald points out, was one that would be replicated by countries across Europe, sometimes considerably earlier and sometimes much later. As is well known, Imperial Germany was the first to introduce a comprehensive system of social welfare in the 1880s, when the conservative chancellor Otto von Bismarck pushed through a series of laws insuring against workplace accidents, sickness, and old age in an effort to stave off the threat of socialism. Louis-Napoléon Bonaparte had advanced a similar proposal in France as far back as 1850. At the time, however, the political landscape in France was not ripe for such large-scale interventions on the part of the state, and it was not until 1898 that a first form of social insurance—namely, workers' compensation—would be adopted. Some three decades later, on April 5, 1928, and April 30, 1930, France implemented a social insurance system extending beyond the workplace to cover the multiple risks of old age, sickness, maternity, death, and disability.[25] After World War II, William Beveridge set the stage for the creation of the postwar welfare state in Great Britain: his report *Social Insurance and Allied Services* (1942) called for the creation of a universal welfare system financed by taxes and eschewing all invidious distinctions between the working and nonworking poor. Rising to the challenge, France followed suit. France's law no. 46–1146, passed on May 22, 1946, created a universal system of social insurance combining elements of the Bismarckian (contribution-based social insurance) and British (universalist) welfare state and guaranteeing all French people the right to "social security."[26]

In North America, too, the prehistory of the New Deal state lies in the late nineteenth-century encounter between the industrial accident and classical tort law. John Witt, whose *Accidental Republic* traces a North American history of industrial accidents in many respects parallel to Ewald's history of France, explains how in the American context, the pervasiveness of the free labor doctrine and employment at will made the transition from tort law to social insurance particularly difficult.[27] Like the French Civil Code, the American common law of contract and tort held that the parties to a contractual exchange of service had entered into a relationship at will and were therefore liable for any harm that might befall them in that context. Only if fault or negligence on the part of the employer could be directly proven was it possible to lay a charge against him. Here, as in France, the problem was that most industrial accidents could not readily be attributed to a single causal agent. As the jurist Oliver Wendell Holmes remarked, the peculiar conditions of industrialization appeared to have created a special kind of legal category—"the nonnegligent victim of nonfaulty harm"[28]—for which tort law had no answer. Workers at first responded to this conundrum by creating their own forms of mutual aid and cooperative insurance. Based on the principle of voluntary participation, these institutions offered them some hope of compensation without derogating from the principles of self-ownership and contractual freedom. With the scale-up of industry in the early twentieth century, however, and with the rise of a doctrine of scientific management, a new generation of managers resorted to the technique of collective workplace insurance as the most efficient means of dealing with the problem. This capitalist-welfare regime of social insurance moved from the shop floor to entire industrial sectors before it was enshrined in workmen's compensation statutes across multiple American states. With the passage of the Social Security Act in 1935, the workmen's compensation model was extended to old age and unemployment, and social insurance became the guiding principle of the New Deal welfare state. As noted by Witt, not only had many of the architects of the Social Security Act, including Franklin Roosevelt, cut their teeth on workmen's compensation, the actuaries who were hired to flesh out its details "had introduced their techniques to American audiences largely through descriptions of the seemingly inevitable onslaught of industrial accidents."[29]

What the English-language literature nevertheless brings to the table—and what is entirely absent from Ewald's account—is a sense of the selective nature of risk protection under the early social insurance state. The question of how to prevent, redistribute, and compensate social risks was from the very beginning predicated on the conception of the white workingman as full-time breadwinner and "contributor"—hence deserving recipient of risk protection. The insurance protections offered to other workers were typically much more partial and conditional, if not entirely absent. Some four decades after the publication of Ewald's monograph, we now possess a vast literature on the gendered and racial boundaries of the mid-twentieth-century British, American, and French welfare states.[30] Importantly also, this literature helps us to understand how the expansion of social protections that took place in the 1960s and '70s, often under the impetus of new social movements, was a central focus of the subsequent backlash against *welfare in general.*

After Social Insurance?

Ewald's *History of the Welfare State* has had an unusual reception in the English-speaking world. It is the only significant monograph produced by Foucault's students to have frontally addressed the role of labor in the formation of the welfare state, and it is one of the few outputs of this circle to have remained without translation.[31] Arguably, however, it is Ewald who has inspired some of the most nuanced and fruitful English-language investigations into the relations between risk, law, and governmentality.[32]

Today, many will be interested in Ewald's work precisely because of the intervening history of sustained assault on the welfare state. Ewald's *History of the Welfare State* was published at a time when the right was intensifying its ideological attack on the welfare state, in France as in the United States, although the actual erosion of postwar social rights would arrive somewhat later in France.[33] What has become then of the project of social insurance? There are few clues to this question in Ewald's subsequent oeuvre. Although Ewald has consistently explored the rise of new understandings of risk and new techniques of risk management, particularly in relation to environmental disaster, there is no hint in his later work as to the evolution of the welfare state after the publication of his magnum opus. From the very first edition of *L'État providence*, Ewald observed that the project of social security had perhaps reached its limits with the rise of new postindustrial and environmental disasters such as Chernobyl and global warming. Reprinted in English translation as "Two Infinities of Risk," this chapter (not included here) warned that the new generation of ecological risks could not be managed in the same way as the industrial and social risks of the mid-twentieth century.[34] By virtue of their diffuse, cross-border, and often self-replicating qualities, such risks were radically unknowable, resistant to the probabilistic logic of prediction, and thereby uninsurable. The framework of (national) social insurance appeared to have reached a natural and technological limit. But what does Ewald make of the parallel claim that the welfare state itself has exhausted its usefulness, a claim that was becoming hegemonic at the time Ewald was completing his book?[35]

To understand this latest chapter in the history of social risk we need to look to other theorists. In his *Great Risk Shift*, the American sociologist Jacob

Hacker attributes the growing insecurity of the American worker to several decades of neoliberal reform intent on undoing the multiple social protections built up since the New Deal. The assault on social insurance, Hacker tells us, was inspired by the neoliberal critique of "moral hazard"—the idea that too much social security would encourage irresponsible behavior and generate "perverse effects" among its beneficiaries.[36] First popularized by the Virginia school public choice theorist Mark Pauly, the "moral hazard" argument resuscitates the classical liberal idea that we should all assume personal responsibility for the multiple hazards of everyday life, from workplace accidents to unemployment and illness, and assigns a new value to the private law of tort and contract.[37] Drawing on Hacker's general insights, a number of scholars have traced the specific impact of the Chicago school "law and economics" tradition on both the discipline and practice of law. Pat O'Malley, in particular, who has done much to extend Ewald's project in English, traces the rise and fall of social insurance principles in administrative law and the recent return to fault-based principles of personal responsibility.[38] Thomas McGarity explores the political implications of this shift, pointing to the multiple ways in which neoliberal policy actors have managed to undermine the consumer and environmental protections built up after World War II.[39] These are just some of the most pertinent studies to have taken up Ewald's project at the point where it tapers off.

The intellectual inspiration behind this attack on social insurance would have been familiar to Ewald.[40] In France in 1978, Henri Lepage published his *Demain le capitalisme*, a book that methodically introduced French readers to the various schools and intellectual currents within American neoliberalism. In the Collège de France seminar series that he delivered in 1978 and 1979, Foucault drew extensively on Lepage's exegesis of the new American liberalism to present what he saw as a new diagram of power. Foucault was in no doubt that the arrival of a neoliberal mode of government, seemingly confirmed by the election of Margaret Thatcher in 1979, represented a watershed moment in the history of postwar liberalism and a turning point in his own thinking. Faced with an articulation of power that was more concerned with the expression of difference and the incentivization of choice, he observed that the concept of the "norm" and the practice of "normalization" were perhaps no longer as pertinent or as all-encompassing as they had once been.[41] The point was reiterated by Ewald in a retrospective essay on Foucault's late work.[42] If risk had become "uninsurable," the concept of the social norm was itself in decline.

Today, the question of Foucault's political and epistemological relationship to neoliberalism is the subject of intense controversy.[43] Ewald's own trajectory from Maoist militant to Foucauldian scholar and finally to state bureaucrat has been well documented.[44] After failing to receive a post at the École des hautes études en sciences sociales, Ewald moved out of academia into the French Federation of Insurance Companies, where he became close to such figures as Claude Bébéar, the founder of AXA, and Denis Kessler, former vice-chairman of the MEDEF (Mouvement des entreprises de France), France's premier federation of employers. In the early 2000s, Ewald, with his intimate understanding of welfare state history, served as adviser to the MEDEF during its campaign to roll back French social protections.[45] It was during these years that Ewald revised his own perspective on the politics of risk: having meticulously demonstrated the failure of the classical liberal politics of the accident in his doctoral thesis, Ewald could now be found exalting the romance of uninsured risk and the limits of social solidarity. In a 2000 interview reflecting the state of his thinking on the question of welfare, Ewald remarked that "with salaried employment, we created a general status of dependence. Today, we are faced with the question of whether we have gone too far in this direction. For in practice, people try to maximize the protection they've been given; they arrange their situation and status so that they can make most use of the assistance they receive. Protective institutions have created forms of existence in which the weight of what insurers call 'moral hazard' can become preponderant. For example, is Social Security only a form of sickness insurance or rather an incitement to turn a myriad of life events into sicknesses?"[46] Here, Ewald's unselfconscious reference to the "moral hazard" argument marks a 180-degree turn from his earlier critique of liberalism.[47]

But whatever Ewald's later retractions and volte-faces, the value of his history of the welfare state remains undiminished. Here Ewald does not shy away from the power struggles that pitted workers against employers. Nor does he hide the fact that the politics of social insurance could be multivalent, sometimes harboring the threat of worker revolt, sometimes reclaimed by employers as a shock-absorber of conflict. Insofar as the neoliberal agenda takes "social insurance" as its primary target of attack, Ewald's history constitutes an invaluable lens into our present.

PART I

The History of Responsibility

To begin this history of responsibility we require a date and a problem.

The date is the moment of the birth of two fundamental texts, the 1789 *Declaration of the Rights of Man and of the Citizen* and the 1804 Civil Code. The Constitution of October 4, 1958, that still holds sway over France, in a manner that is reproduced in each of the Constitutional Council's decisions, situates our juridical origin in 1789.[1] And the Civil Code, despite the numerous projects for revision that have been advanced, remains the medium through which French common law expresses itself. One might regret this, denounce the hypocrisy of such a situation, or recall the importance of the law's transformations that have taken place since 1804, but the Civil Code remains the unavoidable reference of juridical judgment.

The problem concerns public aid: assistance to the poor and homeless. It is symbolic of the social contract. If I have entered into a contract with someone, or if I have committed a crime, it is self-evident that I am juridically obligated. In contrast, when it comes to the poor, any obligation for me to relieve poverty can only be found in the social contract itself. This is so true that the problematics of assistance directly lead to the principles that preside over relationships of obligation.

One must therefore retrace the question of the relationships between liberalism and poverty, between liberalism and the labor question, topics about which everything has already been said.

Nineteenth-century liberalism is the long martyrology of the working class, the horrible "laissez-faire, laissez-passer," the story of an avid *patronat* that could profit from exploiting men, women, and children with no limits.[2] It is a page of history we will have—or at least will almost have—turned, thanks to the heroic struggles of the working class, to the French Republic, to the emergence of a democratic government and the adoption of social regulations.

All of this is certainly true. It will nevertheless be noted that this type of discourse gives more attention to exploitation and workers' misery than what, in a sense, was liberalism's positive form. These judgments only concern liberalism by inference. One judges the cause, liberalism, on the basis of its specific effect: the misery of workers. For this reason, it is better to speak of association than to speak of causality. The association is based on the fact that pauperism is a form of poverty tied to industrialization and that it arose when the principles of liberalism were dominant. This temporal contiguity has been transformed into a causal relationship that is itself transformed into a relationship of necessity. Liberalism defines a politics that necessarily produces the misery of the greatest number.

Our position will be sacrilegious. It is not because we profess liberalism (which would be nothing dishonorable, for that matter), but because, upon examination, there is nothing scientific about this judgment of liberalism. It is moreover those "judgments of history" that attest less to reality than to the ideological battles through which we constitute reality. It is easy to follow this judgment of liberalism at the beginning of the twentieth century among the "social reformers" and its official institutionalization with the advent of the Third Republic. It is one of those rationalizations that allow for a politics to create the past according to its own needs. If there is no reason to accept the liberal judgment of liberalism, then there is no reason, either, to adopt attitudes that have been historically justified as antiliberal. Both need to be placed in parentheses.

The preceding themes lead one to imagine that liberal practices with regard to workers are scarce. In fact, these practices are numerous: juridical practices governing contracts for services and civil liability,[3] benevolent aid practices, patronage, philanthropy, and the use of savings banks, relief and retirement funds, and insurance companies. The goal is to envision these practices in their positivity, from the point of view of their *rationality*.

But what sort of calculus or strategy do they obey? To what sort of objectification do they correlate? What is it that unites their articulation or defines the principle of their combination? In a word, what is it that constitutes their common field of rationality? Though the condition of workers has been scrutinized in its minutiae, the question of liberal rationality has been little studied, despite the fact that, after two centuries of permanent critique and accusation, it remains our fundamental political reference.

A political rationale may be examined from one of two points of view: as a rationality of *program* or of *diagram*. In the first case, one studies the rationale from the point of view of the practices it commands or forbids, from the way in which it problematizes its objects, from the form of these practices and the calculus from which they proceed. In the second case, one seeks a transversal view, to extricate from within what might constitute the schematic arrangement of their disposition, the dream of their adapted operation. The term "diagram" comes from the passage in *Discipline and Punish* where Michel Foucault shows how dispersed disciplinary practices—relating to education, production, military training—had found within Jeremy Bentham's "panopticon" the simultaneously general and simple principle of their operation.[4]

Two broad characteristics can be ascribed to a diagram. It is first of all an abstract machine.[5] It is the complete opposite of a utopia. It is not the dream of another world, but rather this world in the imagination of its pure rationality. It is the blueprint, the figure of the perfect functioning of a social machine. It is through the diagram of their operation that institutions of diverse natures might communicate with one another. It is through the panopticon, for instance, that a school communicates with a prison, a prison with a factory. A diagram is an exchanger.

The second characteristic of a diagram is the principle of its self-regulation. The invention of the panopticon is the invention of a machine that does not need anyone to make it work. The central tower of the Benthamite prison can be empty. The effect of its visibility is not reduced on the prisoners. The panopticon is a machine whose operation requires no other energy than that of the individuals to which it is applied. It can therefore function indefinitely.

It is perhaps a political dream. It is certainly a liberal dream. Its will is to arrange the social machine in such a way that it has no need to be governed, or to be governed as little as possible. One hypothesizes that it is possible to formulate the liberal diagram and that, in the imaginary of this well-governed society, meaning a society where governmental activity will naturally tend to limit itself, the principle of its regulation is called *responsibility*.

CHAPTER 1

Civil Law

General opinion understands liberalism as great license accompanied by a series of prohibitions. The great license is affirmed by the revolutionary principle of free labor with its prohibition of workers' guilds and master crafts, of corporations and the old division of labor. It is accompanied by a series of prohibitions that are meant to be applied to all, although in practice they are applied to workers. The Le Chapelier law banned all forms of association among laborers, among masters, and between masters and laborers, with the double purpose of avoiding the reconstitution of corporate bodies and of preventing the creation of intermediary bodies between the citizen and the state.[1] The rights of assembly and coalition were prohibited for masters as well as workers, but, practically speaking, more for the workers than the masters.

Formulated in terms of obligations, liberalism defines a regime where the duties of society are limited, according to the formula of article 2 of the 1789 Declaration of Rights, to "the conservation of the natural and imprescriptible rights of man," liberty, property, security, and resistance to oppression. For their part, the duties of citizens are limited to not harming others, not infringing on citizens' rights, not disturbing their pleasure, and not restraining their liberty. Refusing to endorse any positive duty to loyalty, fraternity, or solidarity, the regime of liberal obligations was both simple and impoverished, even frugal. As Karl Marx said, it was the regime of "cash payment."[2]

It was also a regime so strict that it would be forced to retreat when faced with the consequences of its own principle: "The doctrine of laissez-faire, whose laws forbid any form of legal aid or recognition of economic rights toward the victims of a chaotic economy, exposes society to a level of abuse that makes some kind of corrective indispensable. This corrective was charity, benevolent mutual aid."[3] Confronted with its own effects, the liberal regime was forced to correct, amend, contradict itself. Charity—benevolent aid, the ensemble of the philanthropic moral duties the rich have toward the poor—would be formulated as a supplement. They rigorously contradicted the logic of the system, but they were necessary to temper its callousness and assure its survival. They were last resorts that ideally would have been used sparingly but that social reality had made indispensable. The duties of aid and benevolence attest to the contradiction between the liberal utopian dream formulated by the economy and the needs of politics.

This presentation of the liberal regime of obligations—reducing duties to rights with benevolent supplements in order to keep the ensemble from falling apart—matches well the schema one usually uses to situate the actors in this history. On the one side there is bourgeois rigorism, harshness, and rapacity, and on the other there is the workers' misery and struggle that compel the bourgeoisie to make a small effort, but only with its egoistic interests in mind. Yet one may doubt how much historical truth there is in this. From the outset, this is because a system as negative as the one we have just described could never function positively. Nor could any reasonable political theorist conclude that social function could be reduced to this. Finally, this schema corresponds neither to effective liberal practices nor to the numerous texts where these practices are formulated, reflected upon, and rationalized.

Law and Morality

What then emerges from these texts of Jacques Turgot, François de La Rochefoucauld-Liancourt, Jean-Baptiste-Joseph Delecloy, Tanneguy Duchâtel, Jean-Baptiste Say, the Baron de Gérando, and Adolphe Thiers that continually speak to one another, where one finds this question so fundamental and symbolic of the social contract, the question of aid? Principally, three things emerge: (1) that there are plenty of other social obligations besides those that can be juridically sanctioned, such as all duties of moral assistance and benevolence; (2) that these duties are not merely necessary correctives—that on the contrary they are at the foundation of the social order and constitute its base; and (3) that legal or juridical obligations proceed from them, are based on them, and constitute their inevitable consequence.

"The poor have uncontestable rights to the wealth of the rich. Humanity and religion make us duty-bound to relieve the sufferings of our peers," wrote Turgot, in the same article, "Foundation," where he condemned the idea of a right to aid.[4]

If the liberal authors were thus unanimous in their critique of the idea of legal charity, of the legal obligation to provide aid to the poor, they were far from condemning the principle of aid, since with the same unanimity they also affirmed its need. The only thing that was rejected was the idea that duties to assist the poor in society would correspond to rights of the poor. The liberal question was not, "Must we or must we not provide assistance to the poor?" Whether this assistance must be provided, individually or collectively, was never contested. From both humanitarian and political standpoints, everything confirmed the necessity of this assistance. The liberal question was one of *law*: what could be the juridical system of these necessary services? Are these services based on law and, if so, on what law?

Put another way, liberalism was not a politics that would reduce social obligations to only those that could be juridically sanctioned. Rather, it was mediated by a complex system of obligations to arrive at two bases, or two elements, by distinguishing and joining two types of social, moral, and juridical obligations, "justice and charity," to use the words of Victor Cousin.[5] The responses to the two following questions explain liberal reason. How were rights and duties articulated in the liberal economy of obligations? And, above all, how were the respective spheres of each delimited? The first question concerns the relations between law and morality. The second question essentially concerns tracing the limit between these two types of social obligations.

The answer to the first question was found in liberal philosophy. Liberal philosophy accorded a simultaneously historical and logical priority to society over positive law, which is to say a law sanctioned by a statist constraint. Civil society exists prior to political society. Humans live in society naturally and form society from multiple relations of exchange and affection. The natural law question of the origin of society has no place in liberal thought, since the social bond is from the beginning not of a legal order, but rests on a sociology, a psychology, an economy of passions, interests, and sympathy.[6] Liberals never thought that a society could exist solely on the basis of a code, on juridically sanctionable obligations. A society whose only bond was juridical would immediately dissolve. Surely, the greatest error and the greatest injustice that one might commit toward liberalism are reducing its system to its positive laws.

Of course, collective life would not be possible without the consideration of a group of obligations that are simultaneously moral and social. Juridical doctrine combined them under the title of a natural law whose requirements were characterized by a vagueness and generality that might easily make them appear timeless. There is little chance of discovering any society where these laws are not respected and little chance that a social obligation might escape from the abstraction of its categories. Thus, classified under natural law are duties toward God, duties toward the self (to conserve and perfect one's own life), and duties toward others. These last not only comprised a duty not to harm others, but also and above all the entirely positive duty that invites us to treat others the way in which we would like to be treated, a duty that corresponds to those primitive sentiments of sympathy, pity, and benevolence, which directly place us in relation to others and which express the primitive mechanism for relating to others.[7]

Civil law has no other source or foundation than positive law itself, the law of the legislator: it consecrates the principles of natural law, giving them a constraining force. More precisely, positive law only endorses certain natural obligations, because not all of them can be received in positive law. According to an often-reproduced formula of Jeremy Bentham, law and morality have the same center, but they do not have the same circumference.

Put another way, the liberal position on law did not differ from its predecessors or successors in the content of the social obligations it pronounced—these were the same ones that seem to have been repeated since time immemorial—but through the manner in which juridical liberalism traced the *dividing line* between rights and duties. The difference between liberalism and its other was not in the recognition or the misreading of certain rights and duties. Nor was it in their formulation, but in the recognition of the limit between what might be a right—and thus productive of collective constraint—and that which must remain a moral duty, stemming from individuals' free wills. In short, the question that allows us to think the identity of liberal reason is not the question of the content of rights and social duties, but the question of the limit between what may and may not be a right, the question of *the criteria of juridicity*.[8]

The Liberal Limit

Juridical liberalism was known for having placed the criteria of juridicity very high or very low, depending on one's point of view. In effect, out of the ensemble of natural duties, liberal juridicity did not recognize anything as juridically punishable, apart from the duty to respect one's engagements, except the duty *to do no harm to another*. The denial of any juridical sanctions regarding a positive duty toward other persons characterizes juridical liberalism. Liberally speaking, the idea of a right to assistance is a sort of contradiction in terms.

In order to justify such a rigorous division, liberal theorists developed a two-part argument. The first part of the argument, which related to the critique of practices of assistance, consisted of denouncing the perverse effects of charity. The aim of assisting must be that of liberating the poor from poverty, but charity does not cure poverty. Charity maintains poverty, "making" people poor by giving them a reason to be poor. The thrust of the argument is to denounce the inefficacy and contradiction of the practices of legal charity: provide the poor with rights and you will have poor people. This argument, to the extent that it argues a posteriori, does not allow us to grasp the rationale behind the liberal limit.[9]

Liberals also developed another series of arguments, formulated more positively according to their position on legal-moral relations. These were not arguments about context, concerning the economic appropriateness of such and such measure taken or to be undertaken; rather, since they expressed liberal reason, one might say they were arguments of pure reason.

An initial argument consisted of explaining that insofar as benevolent obligations are moral, they should not be made mandatory. Morality excludes constraints, or else it ceases to be morality. Virtue and devotion cannot be forced. As explained by Alfred Jourdan, "The pure moral law, devotion, self-denial, must not be the rule of society. These are things that society must not command or impose. It is for the best. Supposing that devotion or self-denial were obtained by force of constraint, they would lose all moral value."[10] The argument claimed that too great an expansion of the juridical sphere would menace the existence of morality. Law and morality reciprocally limit one another and are distributed within social obligations according to a differential principle. But the argument begged the question, having already assumed the necessity of an economy of obligation divided between law and morality. The argument drew its consequences from an already-formed division between law and morality. Something relating to the moral order cannot be of the legal order. Perhaps. But why should the domains of law and morality be identified in this way at all?

A second argument returned to the framework of the contract. Consider what Jean-Baptiste Say tells us: "To speak rigorously, society owes no assistance, no means of subsistence to its members. By uniting through association, individuals are supposed to provide for all aspects of their livelihood. Any person who enters society with no resources would be required to make a claim on the resources of another member; the latter would want to know under which authority such a burden is imposed and it would be impossible to demonstrate any. If one cannot form a duty for one citizen it cannot be imposed on a second, a third, or the whole of society. Such is the severity of the law."[11] In a way, this argument complemented the preceding one. It situated itself on the other side of the liberal division. The first insisted on the contradiction between wanting to combine morality and legal constraints. The latter explained the juridical logic: there are no noncontractual laws, and laws presume equivalent exchange. The poor person who takes without giving falls outside of the law. No legal obligation answers the poor person's plea. But just as with the preceding argument, this one, too, begged the question. It reached its conclusions by taking for granted the limit between legal and moral obligations.

The third argument explored a politics of right. The way in which liberal economy thinks the relations between equality and inequality leads it to view the existence of social inequality as a politically positive fact and to accord a structural function to the benevolent relationship. "Between various social classes, divided by the whims of fate with an unevenness that at first sight is so revolting, charity is the most powerful mediator. It reestablishes harmony, unites the rich and the poor, and transforms an odious superiority into protective guardianship and generous support."[12] The relationship of benevolence to society is one that cannot be legislated without being destroyed: "The rich, who see benevolent aid as nothing more than a burden, look to lighten its load, so that there are taxpayers for all taxes. They become obstinate, cruel, greedy. The poor, strengthened by the rights that the law assigns them, become fierce, violent, hateful."[13]

Beyond a certain limit, the law, as an instrument of pacification, foments war, provokes hostility, and nourishes antisocial passions. Similarly, the distinction between law and morality does not only correlate to a conceptual difference. It hearkens back to a political economy of obligations and their distribution. It has a constitutional function that is contradicted by the idea of the rights of the poor: "To recognize the poor's right to alms is to authorize the seizure of alms by force. It is tantamount to annihilating the right to property and marching toward communal wealth. Whoever seizes their wealth can neither be found guilty nor justly punished. One cannot at the same time punish the theft committed by a needy person in misery while also according them a positive right to aid at the expense of the rich. Either the law is not a real law, or it constitutes the poor as co-owner of the stolen property, and no one can be a thief for using that property. Thus, the idea of the rights of the poor shakes the bases of the social order, as it prevents the action of the sentiments of peace and concord!"[14]

But if this argument explains the political and constitutional stakes of an appropriate delineation of the limit of obligations, it does not, however, account for its liberal delineation.

A fourth argument, developed by Frédéric Bastiat, approaches the heart of liberal rationality:

> Does the law, considered from the general and theoretical point of view, have as its mission to uphold the limit of preexisting reciprocal rights, or better, to directly make people happy by provoking acts of devotion, self- and mutual sacrifice? What strikes me in this latter system is the uncertainty it casts over human activity and its results. It places society before the unknown, the unknown that by its own nature will paralyze the system's forces. One knows that justice exists and where it exists. It is a fixed, immutable point. Everyone knows what to expect when the law takes justice as its guide and acts accordingly. But fraternity—where is its fixed point? What is its limit? Its form? Apparently, it is infinite. In its definitive form, fraternity consists of making a sacrifice for another, to work for another. When it is free, spontaneous, and voluntary, I understand and applaud it. I especially admire the type of sacrifice that is total. But when one places the principle that fraternity should be imposed by the law at the heart of society, which is to say, in proper French, that the redistribution of the fruits of labor should be made legislatively, without regard to the laws of work, who can say to what degree this principle will act, under what form the whim of a legislator might dress it up, in which institutions a decree might incarnate it from one day to the next? Now, I ask, is it possible for a society to exist under these conditions?[15]

To place fraternal duties within positive law is to set in motion a chain reaction that threatens the very existence of law. First, this is because these supplementary rights can only be gained through the sacrifice of the primitive rights articulated through contractual exchange. According to Pierre-Joseph Proudhon's formula, "Give me the right to work and I will give you the right to property."[16] In addition, this is because these rights are indeterminate. Fraternal obligations have neither rule nor measure. Their definition, in any event required for them to become positive law, can only be arbitrary.

Furthermore, they are indefinite, indeterminable, limitless: to go beyond the liberal limit is to begin a process of multiplying juridical obligations, a process whose end cannot be predicted. To the extent that these numerous rights do not themselves contain the principle of their own definition, they depend on the whims of the legislator or the game of majority rule. Therefore, going beyond the liberal limit produces a constitutional effect: law loses its sovereign position; it is no longer what binds the will of the legislator and lends it the appearance of the law. The juridical recognition of fraternal duties implies the reversal of the relationship between law and politics, legality and opportunism. It subordinates law to the political.

The argument developed by Frédéric Bastiat does not solely concern various consequences tied to the misunderstanding of the real distinctions between rights and duties. It contains the principle of a distinction between law and morality as well as another definition—one that may not cover rights but at least covers those obligations that might receive a legal seal of approval. Those obligations that contain their own limits, whose extension can be deduced from an examination of their concepts, belong to the field of law. Thus, we arrive at the problem of juridicity: how does one define these self-limiting obligations?

"The laws," explained Jean-Étienne-Marie Portalis, "can be nothing without morality. But not everything that concerns morality can be governed by laws. A legislator who wishes to understand in his law code everything that belongs to morality will be forced to confer on those who execute its rules an overly arbitrary power. He will believe he has protected virtue. He will have only established tyranny."[17] As one might predict, the principle behind the liberal separation of law and morality is found in a way of thinking about the relationship between constraint and liberty. This contains the necessity of a division between law and morality. The proposition is not of the philosophical order: it does not refer to an idea of liberty as a characteristic of human nature. Rather, liberty appears as the correlate of a properly managed juridical constraint. It results from a certain abstention from law, which, if it is not respected, provokes a sort of inversion of signs and makes the law an instrument of tyranny.

The problem of the liberal limit is in a way a problem of pure logic, a problem of the principle of noncontradiction: to determine a system of constraint founded on liberty in such a way that its consequences do not destroy it. How do you base a constraint on liberty while also preserving it? The liberal position rigorously distinguishes law from morality. Even better, it makes the coexistence of conflicting liberties dependent on this distinction, and thus also on the limits of the juridical. It is by virtue of being able to distinguish between two orders of social obligation and to delimit their respective spheres that a free life is possible within society. The generation of law from a selection or limitation from a sum of natural obligations should itself operate according to the principle of the coexistence of liberties.

Thus, one cannot say that law is defined by obligations that are incomplete because they remain outside of our consciences. Rather, we must see within this alleged incompleteness the condition of possibility of a regime of obligations that, unlike orders or commandments, does not imply any hierarchical relationship among its components. The distinction between law and morality, the necessary limitation of law, its exteriority, do not call its incompleteness into question. These are the regime's qualities, not its faults. It is only under this set of conditions that the "complete constraint" that characterizes law might cease to be thought of as a coercion somehow constricting liberty from the outside. On the contrary, because it protects liberty from all other restraints, this complete constraint should be conceived as its condition of possibility. Thus, from the outset law is not what guarantees civil liberty, but rather what constitutes it.

This means that for the liberal the problem of law is not to determine what one must desire. It consists not in an itemization of ends but in the discovery of criteria that allow one to decide which obligations might be the object of a collective constraint. The problem of law is not to be found in the researching of rules of conduct that may and must be juridically sanctioned—because they are just and good, necessary or timely. These are the result of social practices that constantly arise from and appeal to new information. The formulation of a new rule of conduct may only proceed from experience. It may only be constructed a posteriori. Its study arises from a sociology. Law (understood as the principle of separating obligations), the definition of a criteria of juridicity, depends on an a priori deduction. If the law should not proceed from experience, it should at least permit experience to evaluate it. The law does not state what should be done. It does not state what is just. Rather, it is about setting down the conditions on which something like a rule of justice is possible, which obligations may be justly imposed.

What then could law be? Kant responds: "Law is therefore the sum of the conditions under which the choice of one can be united with the choice of another in accordance with a universal law of liberty."[18] Thus the criteria of juridicity find their place in the *universalization* of a constraint that at the same time remains a condition of its liberty. Its principle lies in the idea of *reciprocity*, which is to say, ultimately, in the idea of *equality*. The universal, this same universal that legitimates the idea that the generality of its objects defines the competence of the legislator's will, is the criterion of juridicity to the same extent that, as in article 1 of the 1789 Declaration of Rights, liberty and equality are placed in reciprocal relation.[19] The law does not tell me what I should do—even if positive law collects and recounts a set of rules around which I should obey under threat of penalty. The law only makes me verify that the action I foresee respects the principle of the coexistence of liberties.

The rule of universalization that defines the juridicity of a maxim or of an obligation should be understood in two senses. First of all, it establishes that there is no action that I might envision that might claim to escape its jurisdiction. The principle of universality has the same *extension* as the juridical order: as far as the space that it controls, the empire of law obeys the principle of "all or nothing." The idea of a legal lacuna only makes sense if one forms it through the absence of a precise rule for grasping an unprecedented situation. It does not make sense from the juridical order's point of view, because what defines a constraining order as juridical is first of all the universality of its application. Put another way, the law does not grasp the entirety of my existence, but my complete intersubjective or social existence.

Having pretense to totality in extension, the law is limited *in comprehension* by the same law of universalization. Constraint is only juridical if it prevents something from being an unjust obstacle to liberty, or rather whatever fails to respect the principle of the coexistence of liberties. "Therefore if a certain use of liberty is itself a hindrance to liberty in accordance with universal laws (that is, wrong), coercion that is opposed to this (as a *hindering of a hindrance to freedom*), is consistent with freedom in accordance with universal laws, that is, it is just."[20] Juridical constraint is never primary or immediate. Rather it is, so to speak, reflexive. It exists less on the order of action than that of reaction, or of legitimate defense.[21]

Likewise, if the juridical doctrine might without great inconvenience envision, from its own technical standpoint, a code or regulation as a set of instructions or codes of conduct, these statements only make sense as legal statements to the extent that they react to an actual or potential situation that implicates the principle of the coexistence of liberties. A juridical statement puts forth not a code of conduct but a rule for judging conduct, a rule that aims to evaluate the conduct from the point of view of a universal law of liberty and to decide if the use of constraint might in this case be just, which is to say necessary.

It follows that the law cannot in itself compel one person to help another. It could only do so if not helping would be deemed an attack on liberty. This is certainly not possible, since it concerns an abstention. The law cannot force me to do good on behalf of others.

The liberal position with regard to a right of the poor may well have been tied to the needs of an economic policy; it also rigorously obeyed a certain legal policy. Its policy was to set up law not as an exercise in constraint but, on the contrary, as that which should limit constraint, to fashion from the law the critical question posed to any matter of legality or any possible regulation. The law can only be limited, or else it annuls itself. *Not everything can be a matter of law.* The inflation of the law, the multiplication of rights, far from being the sign of a conquest or recognition of law, is rather a threat to law. In other words, it is a problem to "want the law." It is in the principle of law's necessary limitation and in the drawing of this limit with reference to the three ideas of universality, equality, and liberty that we find liberalism's specific contribution to the question of law.

This legal position was singularly constraining. It functioned as an insurmountable barrier until the end of the nineteenth century, when the doctrine of solidarity, instituting a sort of priority of contractual relations over the will of the contracting parties, would make it possible to think about a right of the poor based on the ideas of reciprocity and exchange. The strength of the liberal position on the law stems from the fact that it is purely rational. It is defined in such a way that, though the times and circumstances may change, the liberal limit will remain, like reason, identical to itself. It is such that it does not depend on anyone's good will to decide what is and is not a matter of law. It is not only a constitutional rule that is imposed on the majority but also a supraconstitutional rule that constitutions must respect in order to be constitutions of liberty. If one had to situate it in Hans Kelsen's hierarchy of norms, it would precisely occupy the place of a fundamental norm.[22]

The Liberal Diagram

The liberal position on the law renders it unable to recognize a right to assistance of any kind. Stated positively, this means that *no one may burden another with the weight of their existence, the blows of fate, or the misfortunes to which one may have fallen prey*, except in the case where they may have been caused by someone who has infringed the supreme law of the coexistence of liberties: do no harm to another. In other words, *each is, should be, is supposed to be responsible for his or her own fate, life, destiny*. Adolphe Thiers will recall this sentiment in the aftermath of the Revolution of 1848: "The fundamental principle of every society is that each man is charged to provide for his needs as well as those of his family, through the resources he has acquired or passed on. Without this principle, all activity in society would cease, because if a man could survive by counting the work of another as his own, he would happily rely on it to deal with life's cares and difficulties."[23]

The general principle of responsibility is less the recognition of a natural human quality that the law would happily endorse than a principle of objectification and judgment of conduct tied to the liberal position on the law. Thus defined, liberty forbids placing the burden of your fate on another. Its objectivity is not one of nature, but a type of rationality in which liberals saw the diagram of a well-ordered society, one that contains in itself the principle of its regulation and its continual perfection.

The principle of responsibility is mediated by a relationship between humans and nature in such a way that all that happens to me, whether good or evil, must be counted as an inevitable consequence. Responsible for myself, I cannot blame anyone else for my failures. Even if these failures are also the result of circumstance, other people, or a difficult obstacle, I am fundamentally responsible for them. It is I who failed to take notice of a certain element. It is I who sinned through my ignorance. It is I who failed to understand the laws of nature or who did not know how to use them. In every case, always, and without exception, *it's my fault*. I am the unique and definitive point of reference for all that comes my way. "To err is human," says the adage, in order to excuse either the error or the human. Liberal philosophy precisely converts all error into fault. Better yet, liberal reason is only rational on the condition that it counts all error as fault.

Liberal reason defines a certain way of handling the causality of events according to *moral* categories. This is its defining characteristic. There can be objective causalities, a nature, and social laws, but these can never excuse an action by claiming it is one of their effects. It is incumbent on each person to understand and master these processes. The liberal might adopt Roger Vailland's libertine maxim: always be the subject and never the object, always be active and never passive.[24] Liberal reason is a general function of moral improvement. It submits all activity and all conduct to a moral jurisdiction. The cause of evil is always moral: it stems from individuals' moral corruption. And, because the liberal worldview is a moral view, the liberal sees no other salvation from the different social evils than a surfeit of moralization.

1. In 1884, the great legal writer Joseph-Émile Labbé could still write, "Responsibility is the most perfect regulator of human actions." The principle of responsibility rests on a way of managing causality that allows an individual to think the self-regulation of conduct and activities. To the extent that no individual can blame someone else for his or her own failures and misfortunes, because each should consider his or her self their sole cause, failures and misfortunes will become the undefined principle of their own modification. The principle of responsibility thus offers itself as a universal converter of evil into good, without soliciting the resources of an external constraint. It is presented as a principle of progress and perpetual individual and collective development.

   The principle of responsibility allows one to view social life according to the model of harmony. In liberal thought, the idea of harmony does not indicate a balance between humans and the world. The problems of evil and insecurity penetrate liberal reason completely. Rather, the idea represents an agreement between different spheres of activity and the different ways of classifying behavior. The liberal idea of harmony is that morality might play in concert with the law, and the law with the economy, so that, far from contradicting each other, the guiding principles of each of these spheres refer to and mutually reinforce each other. The concept of fault is charged with assuring harmony. It has universal value, whether economic or juridical. It is an exchanger, something through which economic conduct is at the same time moral. Through it a juridical sanction corresponds with remorse.

In order to serve as the great regulating social principle, responsibility tolerates no middle term. Its validity demands the greatest rigor. It is liberty or the absence of liberty. The smallest transgression will jam this beautiful mechanism and ruin the whole of the framework [*dispositif*].[25] To allow an individual to give up his or her responsibility, to let him- or herself be supported by another person, would at the same time be an economic, moral, and political mistake. It would mean destroying the very principle of the social order, undermining the very basis of individual and collective betterment. Thus responsibility provides not only the principle of the liberal diagram, but also the regulating principle of its programs: to always ensure that people find in themselves the principle for correcting their behavior. The less individuals are able to offload their fate onto others, the better things will be; and if things are still not very good, it is because there is still not enough liberty.[26]

2. The principle of responsibility provides the rule of liberal judgment concerning poverty. The causes of poverty are not to be found anywhere other than in the poor themselves, in their moral dispositions, in their will. *Poverty is a way of behaving.* It must be analyzed and combated as such. The poor alone are responsible for a state from which they alone can remove themselves. In a society constituted according to the principle of liberty, poverty gives no rights; it confers duties. The poor may elicit pity, but they are no less responsible for their misery, their destitution, their fate.

Perhaps. But one only knows how to be responsible for that which depends on one's will. Yet the poor person, henceforth condemned to work, as worker or proletarian, is doubly dependent: on the size of the person's salary and the thousand causes of unemployment that threaten it. "He risks falling into indigence from the moment an accident comes to increase his needs or diminish his resources. In effect, a host of incessantly active causes tend to give rise to these accidents through disease, injury, the intemperance of the seasons, war, political disturbances, work stoppages."[27] To guarantee workers against so many possible outcomes that do not depend on them and that make their situation as precarious as it is uncertain, is this not the duty of a government that resolutely claims to respect the rights of humanity?

From the outset, if these risks cannot be attributed to the one who endures them, then neither can they be attributed to society. They fall under the domain of fate, fortune, chance or mishap, destiny: "There are accidents of indigence the same as there are accidents of theft, fires, floods, shipwrecks, epidemics."[28] Their existence, their eventuality, and the threat they pose to us are inscribed in the fundamental relationship between humans and nature: "We are brought back to the supreme question of human destiny, this singular mixture of necessity and liberty, of power and servitude, of fault and misfortune."[29] Far from being the attribute of only a certain group of people, they are the lot of all; they attest to the veritable equality of all before fortune.

Precariousness, instability, uncertainty are so many characteristics of our life in this world. To attain security is a requirement of liberty. *Thus, security cannot be a right, only a duty.* Its attainment is the sanction of a struggle, a combat, the exercise of a virtue, the liberal virtue *par excellence: foresight*. "Among the first rank of virtues sits foresight, which is nothing but the control exercised over our own fate."[30] Correlative to liberty, foresight is the virtue through which humans cease to live from one day to the next and come to understand the future, thus leaving the immediacy of the state of nature. It is through foresight that one is able to overthrow the relationship of dependency that primitively binds us to nature, to be liberated from fortune's whims, to win one's autonomy and sovereignty. It is foresight's presence or absence that explains the inequality of "fortunes." Wealth and poverty share an origin in liberty. The poor may be rich by the same virtue that has enriched the wealthy. Thus, guaranteeing one's security can only be the affair of each person. To want to place one's responsibilities in the care of another is to abdicate one's freedom, to renounce one's human character, to want slavery.

It should be added that the institution of society in no way permits one to offload this duty onto society. In placing at each person's disposal a set of instruments that restrain fortune's reach, society increases the weight of our responsibilities in equal measure. "Fortune's share diminishes, that of human powers increases. Such is the march of humanity." There is no escape route for the poor; the "march of humanity" tends toward the inflation of responsibility.[31] In other words, in the liberal world there are no *victims*. First of all, in the sense that the fact of suffering a misfortune does not give you a right to anything. It is furthermore in this sense that the victims themselves, whatever sentiments of pity and compassion they might inspire, are always supposed to be in control of their own destiny. Of course, this does not mean that no one is ever struck by misfortune. Who would want to claim that? Rather, no one is allowed to be constituted as a victim, which is to say in passive submission to fate, and to be made dependent upon others.

3. The principle of responsibility designates a rule of judgment that is at the same time a rule of justice. This is because liberal reason sees the natural distribution of goods and evils as just, because it takes what exists for what should exist. There is thus no need for society to correct nature, no need for a social justice opposed to nature's justice. Legal responsibility consists only of putting things back as they were. It does not correct; it reestablishes and restores. This sentiment of a natural justice supposes that the only causes that affect us are another person or natural causes. There is thus no properly social causality. Consequently, society has no need to artificially establish justice, which is to say to correct itself.
4. The principle of responsibility, finally, is at the foundation of articles 1382–86 of the Civil Code that define the law of civil liability. Liberal political economy assigns to law, and in particular liability law, a decisive function in social regulation. It is its duty to establish the just separation between these two constitutionally valuable principles: that no individual may place his or her own burden on another and that no one may harm another. It is up to the law of civil liability to delimit the respective spheres of application of these two principles, which represent responsibility's positive and negative poles. The law of civil liability is the guardian of the liberal division.

Article 1382 of the Civil Code posits that "any human action, which causes damage to another person, obliges the person at fault to repair the situation."

If one is to believe the Civil Code's preparatory studies and the earliest commentaries, this formula was presented with a certain obviousness. "Every individual is guarantor of his own affairs; this is one of the first maxims of society," recalls Bertrand de Greuille in his report to the Tribunate, before concluding that the provisions concerning civil liability "are all drawn from reason, wisdom, natural equity, and the sturdiest principles of morality, essential bases for good and lasting legislation."[32]

However, the concept of *fault*, implicated in the Constitutional Council's principles, is far from having the precision that might be expected from such decisive provisions. The jurists speak of it as an "indefinable" concept. Doubtless, it has a discriminatory function: not all damage is caused by fault; fault should remain the exception, otherwise it ceases to be fault as such. Doubtless, it supposes responsibility can only belong to an adult endowed with reason, which is to say individuals capable of predicting the consequences of their actions, and deciding in light of this foresight. But this does not suffice to clarify the criteria for fault-worthy behavior. One must, as they say, construct a model, a system of references. Yet, the concept of fault does not itself clearly construct any.

In fact, the difficulty does not reside in the absence of such a model. The principle of responsibility provides one. The difficulty resides in the model itself. Its source derives from the decisive distinction between *causality* and *attribution*. It was not sufficient for someone to have caused damage in order for that person to be judged responsible. It still had to be demonstrated that the damage was caused through that person's fault. To reduce the attribution of damages to the simple concept of causality would in effect amount to suppressing the same idea of responsibility. Social life is such that we unintentionally keep harming each other, that one cannot achieve one's own satisfaction without resulting in harm for others. It is an unavoidable consequence of the principle of liberty, in particular the freedom of work and industry and the competition they produce. It was a common criticism that competition guaranteed that some people would harm others with impunity. Wanting to punish all causes of damage would amount to suppressing, along with competition, the very principle of a government based on liberty.

The concept of fault designates a rule for the selection and administration of damages. This rule should make it possible to reduce the conflict that the liberal principle of responsibility sets up between the constitutive idea of liberty (a liberty that the law should guarantee) and the necessary reparation of damages caused to another. The concept's extension and its juridical understanding are caught between the double need to restrain its application, so that the principle of responsibility works at capacity, and the need to spread its jurisdiction, so that no wrong is left unpunished. In matters of civil liability, the slightest faults should be penalized. The concept of fault that appears in article 1382 of the Civil Code designates a principle for determining the just allocation of the definitive burden of damages between authors and victims. This has to be done in such a way that no one can take advantage of a juridical opening—allowing an individual to shift the weight of his or her own burden onto someone else—while at the same time ensuring that every infraction of the principle of coexistence be penalized. The concept of fault thus does not signify certain types of conduct or behavior that could themselves be called blameworthy. It is a principle for the distribution of rights whose rule is found in the principle of responsibility itself. The concept of fault only acquires its meaning in reference to the liberal division. Article 1382 states that its reasoning must serve the rule of judgment in order to solve the necessary conflicts of liberties. Not only does fault coordinate the economy, morality, and the juridical, it expresses the juridical through the political. This is not to say that fault turns the law into a political instrument, but that fault is at once the expression and the guardian of liberal rationality itself.

Articles 1382 to 1386, which define civil liability, may be few in number, and they might not enjoy an exceptional place within the structure of the Civil Code, but they have both a pretension to universality and a predisposition to extend it. It was the task of these articles (as well as the courts systematically soliciting them) to decide upon the myriad legal conflicts arising from the conflict of liberties.

Policy

This is the legal argument: whatever the circumstances that led an individual there, whatever reasons might excuse him or her, a person must always be judged according to liberty and will, as if that person were solely responsible for his or her fate. It is in this way that each person knows how he or she will be judged; it is also how each person should judge him- or herself in relation to the liberty of others. Liberals have located the condition of possibility for objectively judging one's self according to the principle of responsibility. This is what defines legal judgment.

But, it bears repeating, liberalism cannot be reduced to its pronouncements and laws. Liberal policies regarding civil security are not only, nor even principally, legal policies.

Liberal philosophy may well found the possibility of juridical judgment on the premise of equality: this does not imply that liberals are blind to the facts of inequality. On the contrary, inequality is at the heart of liberal reflection. Inequalities are natural, unavoidable, and irreducible. They are part of the order of creation, which is composed of variety and diversity. Inequalities are necessary for social progress, as rewards and punishments for each person's good and bad behavior. Finally, they are providential: constitutive of the social bond, they are foundational of society's very existence.[33] So, not only should we not avoid inequalities, we also cannot wish for them to disappear. Their existence is a sort of political good that we must know how to manage. In the existence of inequalities are also found the possibility and necessity of an art of liberal governance.

Indeed, if foresight is truly the fundamental virtue a person can possess in relation to themselves, the one that allows a person to liberate themselves from their primitive relation to the world and its accidents, the one that allows a person to actualize their liberty and achieve their dignity and respectability, then *benevolence* is the primary social virtue. We cannot go without an innate and instinctive form of the social bond, the root of sociability. In it society discovers one of its foundations: "The human creature may not, in a host of situations, be self-sufficient: the weak need the support of the strong; old age, physical infirmity, and morality call for constant protection or immediate assistance. This necessity is one of society's foundations. It reveals the purpose behind humanity's call to the state of society where services are exchanged and forces allied, where a community of interests forms itself. Thus, familial bonds arise from the weakness of children, women, the elderly. Thus, welfare's sacred relations arise from misfortune. Unequal conditions produce effects analogous to the distribution of ages. Differences in destinies determine a way of forming alliances between men."[34] Society has two origins. On the one side interest moves us to combine our forces with our peers. On the other, pity, commiseration, and compassion move us to help them in their misery. The social bond has a dual nature. One aspect concerns relations of interest, founded upon the principle of equal and equivalent exchange. Its juridical form is the contract. The other aspect concerns relations of assistance, aid, and mutual relief, founded on the inequality of abilities and conditions. Alongside the law that says *do no harm to another* is the feeling of commiseration that commands us to *do unto another as you would have them do unto you*.[35] The social order has a dual foundation. In principle an individual affair, responsibility makes it a duty for each person to provide for their needs on their own. It is up to benevolence to go beyond contractual relations, to connect inequalities, to unite and reunite what would otherwise remain hopelessly separate. Benevolence serves an indispensable political function of socialization. It is up to benevolence to reunite those with divided interests, to connect those that contractual exchange alone would keep dispersed.

But benevolence has a more precise function. It is the indispensable instrument that will allow the poor to become legal subjects once more. It is necessary to allow the poor into the cycle of foresight. The reason for this is that if the poor are poor through their own fault, through their own lack of foresight, they risk being trapped in an endless cycle where lack of foresight engenders poverty, which itself will induce a lack of foresight. There is a need for a benevolent intervention that provides the poor with the ability they lack in order to escape their fate. This need operates on the principle of liberating the poor. It is also what provides it with its limit, object, and form. Indeed, benevolence, based on foresight, should be limited. "Philanthropists, who wish to ameliorate the condition of their peers, always remind the poor their destiny is in their own hands. . . . Never forget it: the greatest good you can do for the working classes is to teach them to do without your help."[36] Benevolent practices must contain the principle of their own end, since they are a relationship based on "guardianship."[37] The exercise of benevolence cannot take on a continual, definite, permanent form. Always ready to intervene when necessary, its action should always be discrete, intermittent, and discontinuous. It should be of such a nature that the poor could never count on it. Therefore, benevolence cannot take a legal form. This is for two reasons. The first is that, once it becomes legal, it will relieve the poor of their duties toward themselves and lend them a false sense of security, since it will discharge and exonerate the weight of their own faults by transferring it to those who were able to plan ahead. This would be contrary to all justice. But secondly, if benevolent aid became a right it would destroy the principle on which the benevolent relation works, the relationship of mutual affection that should connect the benefactor to the one receiving the benefits. As we have noted, to make benevolence a legal obligation is to turn a condition of peace into a cause for war. Benevolence cannot take an administrative form either. In essence, benevolence is always antithetical to state function. "As for state establishments, compared to benevolence, they do not produce the same moral effects as private charity. Moreover, they fall prey to the same ordinary inconveniences of every administrative regime: taxes, functionaries, all sorts of carelessness in the distribution of aid."[38]

Benevolence belongs in essence to an individual and individualized relationship. It is only thus that benevolence will distinguish the truly impoverished from the fakes, those who merit assistance from those who only seek to take advantage of the assistance offered them. As a form of socialization, benevolence cannot be universal, helping the poor en masse as a population. It takes the poor one at a time, according to the specifics of each individual case.[39] Moralization is its mode of action. What benevolence is supposed to produce is a *conversion*: convert the poor in their relationships with themselves, the world, and others. Benevolence converts the poor to the laws of the economy, reminds them of the duties they have toward themselves, returns to them the feeling of their own dignity, shows them that they hold their fate in their hands. Benevolent practice should take the form of a lesson. It is an education.

In this way, in liberal security policies, two things are required of benevolent practices. Being politically as well as socially necessary, one must encourage, develop, multiply these practices as much as possible. Yet, they can never be made mandatory, nor can they be given a constant and guaranteed form or an administrative presence. That which makes them necessary forbids them from being obligatory. The numerous social institutions that arose in the nineteenth century—savings banks, mutual aid societies, public insurance firms, patrons' institutions,[40] childcare centers, asylums, company stores, workers' housing and gardens—developed according to this program of interclass alliances and moderation of inequalities.

We cannot understand the paradoxical presentation of the liberal approach to aid, this strange mix of necessity and abstention, this manner of obligating without constraining, if we do not situate it in the long history of assistance and charity.[41] Liberals hesitate; they do not dream of putting limits on practices of assistance. They wish to reform them. They look to define a policy that would be commensurate with the considerable problems of poverty existing at the end of the Old Regime, and one that would not end in failure like its predecessors. As the importance of the philanthropic movement as well as the many works dedicated to the problem attest, the liberal attitude is certainly not one of withdrawal, disinterest, or disengagement. Rather, it crystalizes a new experience of poverty, a new "pathos of misery," a new sensibility. Far from relegating poverty to the periphery of the social body, on the contrary this sensibility places poverty at its center, and for a long time.

The early modern period, after the Reformation, secularized the problem of poverty. While they had not lost all of their religious dimensions, with the presence of the poor, charitable works took on a resolutely social meaning. Poverty had become a problem for society, which, as such, fell under state policy.

In the second half of the eighteenth century, the philanthropic movement pursued this long movement toward the secularization of poverty that the French Revolution would definitively accomplish. The poor no longer attest to God's presence on earth. They are no longer the sign of a disorder that needs to be reduced. Theirs is the drama of everyone on this earth—if not right now, then eventually. The situation of the poor, so common, provoked the formation of societies, first to provide aid, then to prevent poverty. The opinion of the Baron de Montesquieu, Jean-Jacques Rousseau, Jacques Turgot, and Jacques Necker was unanimous: "The state, which owes all the citizens an assured sustenance, nourishment, suitable clothing, and a kind of life that is not contrary to health."[42] Established in this way, poverty becomes its own source of social obligations. Any initiative, whether public or private, individual or collective, must be inscribed in a program of social policy that is unified, rational, adapted, and concerned about its effects. Benevolence takes the place of charity.

The socialization of poverty transformed both the status and the system of aid policies. Assistance is one of the fundamental duties of society. The obligation to assist the poor rose to the constitutional level.[43] It was thereafter inscribed in various declarations of rights and constitutional preambles.[44] Poverty no longer attests to a moral disorder that demands to be punished. Poverty is from the outset the privileged site where society discovers its truth and grows conscious of its duties. The poor are no longer prompts to a guilty conscience. They call attention to the necessity of a form of government action whose aim is no longer to punish or reprimand a segregated and dangerous population. In effect, its space of action extends across all of society, because the true aid we may bring to poverty is its prevention: "Lending assistance to the poor is without a doubt a most sacred and imperious duty. But the duty to prevent poverty is no less sacred or necessary."[45] This is an immense task that delocalizes government action and gives it a generalized authority, particularly in economic matters.

The program of assistance is organized around one principle and two categories. The principle consists of placing work at the center of the aid relationship. The plight of the poor does not relieve them of their social obligations. On the contrary, it makes work an obligation. "If the poor have the right to tell society, *let me live*, society has the right to respond: *give me your work*."[46] Such is the contract. It implies a double division at the heart of poor populations: between the poor and the beggars. On one side are the true and the false poor, and on the other the abled and disabled poor. Only the disabled, people whose condition prevents them from working, may claim assistance from society without providing anything in return.

In this way assistance became "the foremost social duty, regardless of its recipient, as that is the basis on which societies are held together, the living bond between men, the link that is most personal and yet the most universal as well. But eighteenth-century thought hesitated over the concrete forms this assistance should take."[47] Indeed, the social obligation we have recognized was plagued by a fundamental legal ambiguity. What is the juridical regime that the reciprocal relationship between the poor and society should obey? Must one speak of a right of the poor based on a *right to work* for the able poor and on a *right to life* for the others? Or is it based on an "unlimited aptitude to be assisted" to which no rights correspond?

Some, like the Abbé Beaudeau, did not hesitate to speak in terms of rights: "Our fundamental axiom is that the truly impoverished have a real right to demand what is truly necessary for themselves."[48] Others, like Turgot, who had nevertheless created charitable houses during his time as bursar of the Limousin region, despised this right. And the Revolution, while institutionalizing this new policy on poverty, would also lend weight to its internal juridical ambiguity. The same La Rochefoucauld-Liancourt, who, as rapporteur for the Constituent Assembly's Committee on Begging, declared that "society should provide support for all of its members who might lack it," seems to have actually understood it as a governmental obligation to organize assistance as a vast public service unified under state control. The Convention reiterated such a program when it included article 21 in the new Declaration of Rights: "Public aid is a sacred debt. Society must offer assistance to unfortunate citizens whether in helping them secure work, or assuring the means of existence to those who are unable to work."[49] *Public aid is a sacred debt*—an entire republican tradition appealed to this formula as a formal recognition of a right of the poor. Be that as it may, it does not specify whether this "debt" corresponds to a specific right that the poor may claim against the state. The Revolution bequeathed this ambiguity, along with the problematic of assistance, to the nineteenth century. Such ambiguity is intrinsic to an obligation whose simple formulation does not define any recognizable right. Its content is not definable a priori: it depends on circumstances, available means, accumulated wealth, and the state of the economy. The rights of the poor establish a variable, experimental, and adjustable kind of claim. It would be contradictory if these rights had a limitless claim. In the economy of the law, the status of these rights is therefore singular. Specifically, their dependence on the political is inscribed in their very formation. Even though the game of the different declarations of rights was supposed to have established the necessary subordination of the political to the juridical, the idea of a general duty of assistance with its own constitutional status introduced the considerable anomaly of a self-generating source of juridicity endowed with unlimited authority.

The liberal program of civil security participated in the same kind of problematic; the recognition of a general duty to assist that should bring together the efforts of the state with those of individuals. It therein proposes a resolutely nonjuridical version of this duty: the social obligation with regard to the poor founds a kind of *politics*. But it cannot be translated into a legal form without contradiction. The same goes for work assistance. Creating a right—thus, a right to work—would flood workhouses with a population whose presence could be due to a real lack of work or selfish expectations. The idea of a right to work contradicts the obligation to foresight, a condition of a right to aid, just as it contradicts the principle of a liberty of work. While the right to assistance should have a contractual form, the right to work would compel one party to give without reciprocation. And what is not viewed as an extraordinary instance of aid will quickly become the norm, one that, disturbing the natural course of the economy, will certainly have the perverse effect of multiplying the need for more assistance.

The liberal interpretation of this obligation to assist has other, more positive reasons behind it. Liberals have sufficiently repeated that law annuls duty. Yet they think that morality has an eminent political function and consequently must be allowed to claim its rightful field of action. Liberals could not conceive of social relationships as only juridical or economic. In a well-ordered society, one must be able to express human sentiment. One must be allowed to exercise the virtue of benevolence. However irreducible the presence of the poor may be, it is there to allow the education and development of this civic virtue.

It could be said, almost paradoxically, that if there truly is a liberal obligation to assist, it derives not only from the gruesome pain of those who suffer, but also from the passion of those who witness the suffering, who find it intolerable and who, as an expression of their very humanity, want to put an end to it. If, despite all of this, we can speak of a right to life, then it must be located just as much in the care provider as in the person receiving care. The liberal idea was that the virtues of humanity and benevolence should not only be encouraged, but that it is the "right" of the person who wishes to aid someone in need, one that the state cannot prevent as the result of its own administrative workings. And this was because its exercise is a privileged mode of human realization itself, which implies that a person who fails to satisfy this need will be condemned to remain incomplete. There was thus an ethical dimension to benevolence that attested that the liberal philosophy of poverty had not broken from the religious significations once invested in charity. Liberally speaking, if there is a "right" to assistance, there is also a "right" to assist that must be claimed against the state—a right that might truly be a natural right, since it contributes to human perfection.

To say, as others have, that liberalism dreams of an end to politics is thus completely questionable. The liberal diagram, ordered around the principle of responsibility, proposes, like all diagrams, a system of self-regulation. Despite this, however, it does not eliminate the need for governmental action. On the contrary, it provides the basis for this action. Certainly, its program is not to be found in the treatises of political economy or law where one finds the formulation of the liberal diagram, but in the abundant literature concerning the problems of aid, benevolence, and charity, which deal with the management of inequalities. This confers on policies of civil security, policies of aid, and policies of poverty a central place in the formulation of liberal politics. This is to say that the social constitutes an essential preoccupation of liberal politics, one that concerns the management of social bonds or the social contract. In fact, liberal politics are a social politics.

Liberal political economy is thus much more complex than the bit of political economy summed up in the phrase "laissez-faire," itself reduced to the stance "do nothing." It is not a matter of being unaware, in the name of rights, of the fact that inequalities exist. It is a specific manner of expressing rights in relation to inequalities, as inseparable and mutually dependent. Practices of *inequalities* and practices of *equality*, as before, obey a twofold regime of obligations—moral obligations for the first and juridical obligations for the second. The liberal limit was drawn so that these two regimes of practices did not overlap or infringe on each other, both being equally necessary for the good social order. Only the law enjoyed the double privilege, epistemological and practical, of finding its jurisdiction based on the same reasoning as the liberal division itself and being able to ensure its proper administration.

Rigorously drawn from a purely rational point of view, the liberal limit contained two great sources of difficulty. The first resided in the legal administration of the principle of responsibility and the conflict between the rights and liberties that it set up. Without a doubt, fault had the merit of flexibility and malleability. It is a principle of allocation that, in accordance with its function, must be as sensitive to ideological movements as to short-term political needs. This also made it a poor guardian of the liberal division. By doing more than blindly endorsing the liberal division, by overextending it, fault would provoke a conflict between law, concerning responsibility, and right, as impunity conferred to liberty. The law of responsibility expresses the juridical through the political in such a way that, if in theory, politics must submit to the juridical, in practice the juridical must be sensitive to political needs, or else it would degenerate into pure fiction. Therein resided the difficult problem of finding an equilibrium between the twofold necessity of maintaining the identity of the juridical, which cannot change without entering into conflict with itself, and of avoiding an excessive juridical rigidity that would compromise its regulatory function.

There was another source of difficulty coming from the other side of the liberal division. Liberal reason forbade the legal recognition of the ensemble of moral obligations to aid, benevolence, and assistance that were nonetheless so politically necessary for the proper functioning of the liberal order. Liberalism required the satisfaction of the very moral duties that it was unable to turn into obligations. The more it reduced the sphere of the juridical, the more it demanded of morality, virtue, devotion. Hence the permanence and insistence of its moralizing programs, the intensified appeal to good will and sentiment. This was liberalism's practical paradox: its objectification of liberty led it to deny itself the political instruments it most needed to ensure its existence.

The juridical experience of the nineteenth century was marked by the development of this twofold difficulty, the exacerbation of the conflict between juridical reason and policy imperatives. The limit liberalism drew soon appeared juridically unsatisfying and too politically constraining. The history of fault was one of its inflation, the staging of the opposition between law and right, and its progressive replacement with the concept of *abuse* as the more just and adequate principle for distributing rights. And the call to liberties would turn out to be sufficiently disappointing for liberals to accept (in spite of their principles but as the only means of maintaining the liberal order itself) that the juridical sphere had to be extended to include moral obligations. This double displacement of the liberal division produced such perverse effects that it soon led to the abandonment of the liberal diagram itself.

CHAPTER 2

Security and Liberty

Liberal philosophy certainly did not think the relationship between humans and nature is a harmonious one. On the contrary, human beings and the world are radically opposed. Liberal freedom placed humans as sovereigns of the self, as final causes that may never admit to being caused. Of course, nature, the world, and other human beings affect the liberal individual. The liberal individual is not inexpressive or without feeling. He must account for himself, his passions, his weaknesses, and everything beyond his control in order to adapt, make use of chance, combine resources, and master adversity. But none of this can ever diminish the excessive privileges of his will. Whatever may come, victory or defeat, he can attribute his place in the world to himself alone. Defined by such a proud liberty, condemned to strive to meet the highest of standards, the liberal individual exists at once without pretext or excuse.

This liberal position on liberty objectified everything beyond it in the name of insecurity. Because freedom has withdrawn into itself, ranged against the world, the world becomes menacing, unpredictable, and dangerous.[1] The liberal individual only knows how to guarantee his or her own situation through the powers of resolve and will. No fortune is to be taken for granted, and misery has no assigned limit in life. "Evil exists," explains Frédéric Bastiat, who gives evil a decisive function in his *Economic Harmonies*: "Deny evil! Deny suffering! Who can? We must forget that our subject is man. We must forget that we are men ourselves. The laws of Providence may be regarded as harmonious without them necessarily excluding evil. It is enough that evil has its explanation and its mission, that it checks and limits itself, that it destroys itself by its own action, and that each suffering prevents a greater suffering by repressing the cause of suffering."[2] In liberal philosophy evil played the role of a prime individual and social motivation, the role of a prime cause that is irrepressible, irreducible, and inexhaustible. It is a role that, feeding off freedom and ignorance, pushes each and every activity to indefinitely pursue its own perfection.

Evil, in liberal philosophy, occupied a providential function. It is not a question of trying to definitively eliminate evil—not because this would be an impossible task, but because it would be wrong. Evil, insecurity, suffering, misery had a function in the liberal order. They had a "mission" to provoke their own eradication. Of course, not everyone would survive. But the spectacle of their fate was a sort of natural lesson addressed to freedom. The goal of the liberal state was certainly not to ensure a secure existence but to ensure safety, which is something completely different. Safety is the guarantee of rights.[3] Liberal philosophy placed freedom and insecurity in a reciprocal relation; the one lived off the other. "The possibility of evil is the inherent condition of freedom."[4] Evil is in the order of things; it is not to be combated for its own sake, lest this sacrifice additional freedom. It is better to wish for evil than the loss of freedom. Evil, suffering, poverty might be lamentable; they are not in themselves unjust. And only injustice calls for social intervention.

To be more precise, liberalism was tied to a particular experience of evil that took the form of *the accident*. Liberals identified the causes of evil the same way they would accidents. This is notably the case with poverty.

The definitions of rich and poor were so essentially identical that poverty itself could only ever be an accident, and the rich could only be distinguished from the poor to the extent that they had managed to prevent and bypass a constitutive misfortune. The accident was the form of evil tied to the liberal objectification of freedom. The Baron de Gérando explains, "From the moment where man becomes the arbiter of his destiny, he must submit to the consequences of his errors and his faults. From the moment of man's emancipation, the usage of his liberty is exposed to one thousand accidents. He is only emancipated under the condition of conducting himself wisely, of redoubling his efforts and confronting the obstacles before him. He is injured while working; while sailing he is exposed to shipwreck; by acting he enters into a struggle against a host of obstacles. To act is to vanquish: victory constitutes his honor, his merit, his necessary condition, and for which his individual strengths do not always suffice."[5]

The accident was not merely one form of misfortune among others. It was the general form of adversity. Accidents referred to an experience of evil where, deprived of all substance or essence, evil takes an atomistic, individual, multiple, discrete, and dispersed form. Present everywhere, accidents have a real presence but no being. Without a physical form, they exist on the order of the encounter. Accidents are also fleeting. They never last longer than an instant. They resonate with ideas of conflict, shock, collision, and hazard, with good luck and bad luck: ungraspable, and always unseen and unpredictable, accidents are the only type of event that truly threatens liberal freedom. This freedom was always caught between the need to predict and prevent and the knowledge that it is impossible to definitively reduce the unpredictable and unavoidable.

One may hypothesize that the experience of the accident, which, since the eighteenth century, constituted the dominant experience of evil, displaced this other experience that essays on theodicy expressed and tried to explain: how an infinitely benevolent God might have willed evil into existence and given it a place in his providential plan. The Lisbon earthquake (1755) brusquely put an end to these speculations. While intellectual and popular circles in Europe viewed the world through the theses of optimism, the destruction of Lisbon suddenly appeared as not only without justification, but above all as unjustifiable. Kantian reason and Voltaire's poem *On the Lisbon Disaster* soon articulated the indecency of confronting the pain of victims with any justification of their misery. Both condemned, along with metaphysics, the constitutive vanity of all projects of theodicy.[6]

Thus at the end of the eighteenth century the world withdrew into its lonely empiricism. Faith and knowledge were definitively separate. The accident was a laic and secular form of evil that corresponded to the new relation between humans and the world.[7] On the one hand, there was the idea that the whole of nature obeys natural laws, that the "system of the world" is saturated with a positivism that leaves no place for evil. Excluded from being, evil may only appear as accident at the crossroads of different natural orders. It breaks no laws, since it obeys laws of its own. On the other hand, there was sociological individualism and the idea that nature, having emancipated humans, prompts us to be lawgiving entities. The numerous versions of the state of nature had as a common matrix the double theme that humanity's entrance into society is an accident of history and that it defines a space of coexistence that, as the figure of the state of war attests, is from the beginning a field of generalized accidentality.[8]

It is not a coincidence that from here on the developments of a rational art of conjecture and prediction, under the form of probabilistic calculus, would mirror the developments of liberal philosophy—not that we might reduce the one to the other, but because each was found in the other as support and instigation. The new calculus made it possible to conceive of the techniques and institutions that make liberal politics practicable by dedicating its efforts to the virtues of prediction. Beyond that, probabilistic calculus made it possible to positively demonstrate that freedoms without exterior guidance and left to themselves are nevertheless subject to laws of their own. The new calculus proved that governing through freedom did not necessarily imply disorder and that it was even the only natural way to govern.

As a result, history, as history of freedom, was able to replace the older theodicy. Divine politics was supplanted, as in the case of Immanuel Kant, by a "natural design" manifested by statistical regularities: "Individual human beings and even entire peoples give little thought to the fact that they, by pursuing their own ends, each in his own way and often in opposition to others, unwittingly, as if guided along, work to promote the intent of nature, which is unknown to them, and which, even if it were known to them, they would hardly care about."[9] It is by freedom, and not by constraint, that nature, in human affairs, achieves its ends. As a correlate, through the conflicting freedoms provoked by the existence of evil, conflicts, wars, and the "unsociable sociability of men" might be thought of as taking part in nature's plan, as having a positive providential function: to help ensure that these evils eradicate themselves.[10]

In this way, demonstrations of probabilistic calculus conformed to and verified the fundamental schema of liberal sociology. This same schema, that of the unconscious conspiracy of freedoms, is at the foundation of Bernard Mandeville's *Fable of the Bees*, the theme of Adam Smith's "invisible hand," and Frédéric Bastiat's *Economic Harmonies*. Even in the greatest apparent cacophony, this conspiracy contributes to the best of all possible orders without even willing it. Reduced to its guiding principles, this schema, by giving birth to an order of purely unpredictable encounters among individual atoms, may be described as one of generalized accidentality. From the accident—meaning pure freedom, chance, inferior primitive freedom—this schema forms the very basis of social order.

Paradoxically, even though liberal philosophy objectified the causes of insecurity in the general form of the accident, one of its obstacles was the reality of accidents. This is because, with industry, accidents would take on elusive characteristics.

The liberal diagram of responsibility, just like its legal endorsement through articles 1382–86 of the Civil Code, was not conceivable without certain presuppositions about the reality of harm that may result from the competition of behaviors and activities: in particular, that social life will not be naturally harmful. These presuppositions were due to the ideas of fault and crime that the law used to redress them. Contained in the juridical idea of fault was the notion that faulty behaviors are not routine. And as attested by the Civil Code's preparatory studies, its authors were convinced that punishing fault would allow for all social harm to be redressed. It had to be assumed that the competition between individuals' behavior, rationally guided by interest, would not *normally* produce accidents. This is to say that competition would not result in accidents, in harm, without the contribution of someone committing a fault, one that would thereby become punishable. Apart from faulty behavior, presumed rare, a certain harmony reigns between the activities of each and every person. People would associate with each other, would take precautions against nature's dangers, and any troublemakers would be punished.

Yet in reality, industrial societies proved to be *normally* harmful societies, societies where harms are born from their regular functioning, and not from a momentary dysfunction. They were essentially harmful societies. The essential regularity of evil would appear at the core of industry. Workplace accidents and, more generally, the ensemble of accidents tied to conditions of work and economic life—what one would soon designate with the sinister term "pauperism"—naturally came to occupy the general form of the accident-event. They would force us to think *at the same time*, as reciprocal, complementary, and nonexclusive, the *normality* of individuals' (nonfaulty) behavior and the *regularity* of accidents in competition with this behavior.

It was an extremely difficult problem, since the social harms that *equitably* deserved reparation—the ones that did not come from nature, that pointed to an activity, a functioning—had to be dealt with. However, these same harms were not rigorously *attributable* to anyone. They did not emanate from a fault—is it faulty to create an industrial business, to use machinery, to establish railroads? Therefore, imputing social damages to someone according to the logic of fault (the only one available at the time) would mean turning a social activity that is profitable to all into a legally punishable offense.

Thus, between nature and man, from a certain quality of their competition, industry brought forth in the form of the accident a new domain of objects, neither human nor natural, but properly social. Here we find a mode of objectivity of the social that was very different from what derived from traditional juridical formulations based on contracts. Between the individual and the state, it would be discovered that "society" distributes goods and evils according to its own logic. And now the natural, individual attribution of benefits and costs does not quite appear just. One might justify inequalities, the fact that there are rich and poor, to the extent that the rich have earned their wealth and the poor, no less on their own, have earned their poverty. But to the extent that evils appeared to be distributed according to social laws that are relatively indifferent to the good or bad behavior of each person, the principle of liberal justice—that it is undesirable to contravene the natural division of goods and evils—was called into question.

Attenuating Circumstances

Liberal policy with regard to the poor was inscribed in the duality of foresight-benevolence. The idea was that poverty, henceforth emancipated from all forms of aid that would make poverty a rational behavior, would limit itself: the poor could only find in this emancipation from aid so many incentives to support themselves. The new economic and political order would have led the poor to look for the principle of their existence elsewhere than in charitable aid. Their own interest would make them prudent. The patronage of an enlightened, rational, and calculated benevolent aid would only assist (and in a temporary manner) this natural process. Savings banks gave this process its institutional organ. Until the end of the nineteenth century, when the first social insurance laws would emerge, civil security policies would remain in the grips of this duality between foresight and benevolence. They would be moralizing policies. But the calculus from which they proceeded was complicated, integrating a series of elements whose specific efficacy they failed to understand. The rationality for thinking about the government of the poor and civil security policy would accordingly be profoundly modified.

In effect, poverty would soon change its appearance. It had been combated under the guise of begging; it would now be discovered in the hitherto unknown, formidable, and menacing figure of *pauperism*.[11] Beginning in the 1830s, a multitude of inquests attested to the existence of this new evil,[12] describing it by its symptoms and manifestations, following its progress and showing its scope. Unless one was careful, pauperism carried with it the death of liberal societies. It had been thought that the principle of responsibility would allow pauperism to limit, select, isolate, and condemn itself. Instead it was discovered that these societies were pregnant with a poverty that, far from dying out, was instead expanding, holding society responsible, intensifying, and completely changing its nature.

Pauperism presented a phenomenon of poverty that could be described with three interconnected characteristics.

First of all, its expansion: one was dealing with a type of poverty that touched entire populations.

Secondly, its intensity: it acted like a durable, permanent poverty that perpetuated itself, multiplied, reproduced itself in space and time—an "epidemic" and "hereditary" poverty.[13] At the foundation of the politics of foresight, there was the idea of a fundamental equality between the poor and the rich, the equality of their will. Their inequality was an inequality of condition explained by the way in which each had directed his or her willpower: inequality was the result of a difference in behavior. With pauperism, social inequalities became differences in physical and moral constitution. Between the poor and the rich, the proletarian and the bourgeois, there was from now on a difference in nature that, collectively, separated them and opposed them as two social classes.

Finally, its origin: pauperism was not a form of poverty that came from the absence of work, but from work itself. Pauperism was the consequence of industrial labor. It accompanied industrialization, if not as its condition, at least as its consequence, the shadow it cast.

Thus emerged the idea of an economic, social, and political causality of misery. This was a dangerous idea, since, grasped in its radicalism, it came to relieve the poor of all responsibility for their state and to transfer this responsibility onto society, its principles of organization and functioning, making impoverishment an effect, a product, as we will say much later, of the "system." Admitted indiscriminately, it would lead to the repudiation of this system's two constitutive principles, those of property and those of liberty. It opened the door to socialism, to the organization of workers, to revolution. But it was susceptible to a more subtle manipulation: it distinguished between *causes* and *conditions* of workers' misery. Its causes would remain those that had already been identified: the lack of foresight on the worker's part, the demoralization, the perversion of the worker's will. Workers were responsible for the sufferings of their situation. Poverty remained behavioral. However, the conditions of the new industrial regime tended to produce it and to favor it: "It is easy to explain by lack of foresight the origin of misery, as with most of the evils that befall men. It is easy to use it to reproach the poor who become the victim. But this lack of foresight itself, from where does it come? . . . By dealing with the question, we discover that the poor are to be pitied more than blamed, that, if foresight is more necessary in their situation, it is also more likely to be absent."[14] This was a displacement, a remarkable bifurcation in the categories used to analyze poverty. Up to this point there had been a philosophy of misery, a metaphysics of poverty. Poverty had been understood in moral terms: it was a pure matter of will. Now one had to deal with a psychosociology of poverty. This was a new objectification of the poor. When one analyzed poverty in terms of morality, will, according to the principle of autonomy, was opposed to everything that it was not. It was defined as the capacity to be self-determining; otherwise, the circumstances in which it had to be determined might excuse the manner in which it could be determined. Now, on the contrary, the relationship of individuals to themselves and to the world, the relationship of the will to what the will determines, had changed. The individual's will—morality—was no longer opposed to what it was not—it depended on it. A relationship of complicity between persons and the world replaced the relationship of opposition. Persons and their wills are inscribed in the order of the world. They are affected by it. They endure its influences. Here we witness the birth of a pathology of liberty. The problematic of foresight was supplemented by a problematic of the *milieu*. The struggle against poverty could no longer only operate via the relation of one will to another will. The government of the poor would no longer reside exclusively in the intimate space of a management of conscience. From now on it had to reckon with the physical and material conditions that determined the behavior of the poor. It had to intervene in their milieu. Here we see the emergence of a new politics of poverty that would find one of its privileged points of application in the question of housing. What then appeared was a comprehensive reflection on the habitat of the poor, which ended up being blamed for the demoralization as well as physical and moral degradation of the workers. But this was not the only cause. The milieu also meant family life, workers' urban areas, and their promiscuity. Here we witness the birth of a problematic concerning the relation of the person to the environment, to space, an ecological problematic that Frédéric Le Play will develop under the name "social economy."

Of course, workers' poverty, their condition, continued to be understood using the categories of foresight. And certainly, the politics of workers' security would remain a politics of moralization. However, we could note a double displacement in the objectification of the worker and in the strategy of worker security. The poor, workers, would henceforth be characterized by their lack of foresight. This would be a primary, radical lack of foresight correlative to their living and working conditions—a lack of foresight whose origin indicated that workers could not get by on their own. To abandon workers to their personal freedom was to deliver them to this sort of economic and social determinism that would lead them quasi-necessarily to the torments of pauperism. The workers' liberty, in the conditions of the new industrial regime, needed *tutelage* from a patron who would protect and shield the workers from themselves.[15] The necessity of a policy of benevolence was reinforced, multiplied in its objects and its means. One discovered the need for a benevolent practice that was no longer tangential, intermittent, and patched together in form as it had been in the past, but permanent, constant, and regular. The profound lack of foresight now attributed to the worker meant that the previously imagined instruments for encouraging foresight were now considered insufficient and null. It was at this time that the savings bank lost its privilege as the institutional model for promoting foresight in favor of mutual aid societies. Institutions for promoting foresight would multiply, and new stratagems would be invented.

Henceforth, the poor could no longer be expected to reform their behavior; it would have to be steered, governed perpetually. It was necessary to give benevolence a social function, public and private. The politics of security shifted from a politics of worker foresight to a politics of generalized benevolence. Civil security was no longer only an individual obligation. It became a social obligation of one class with regard to another. Society's division into classes was recognized. The politics of foresight presumed the natural equality of the rich and the poor and that poverty was only ever an accident from which the poor could always escape if they so wished. The benevolent aid that was extended to them was organized around the principle of equality. It obeyed a logic of *fraternity*. With the new politics of security, benevolent aid became a necessary relation between two classes. Its logic was one of interdependence and *solidarity*. It no longer sufficed that government confined itself to asserting respect for the strict legal and contractual relations consecrated by positive law. Broader and wider-reaching functions were the government's purview: the government might, or even should, in order to better ensure civil security, transform certain moral obligations into legal obligations.

The problematic of milieu also implied a critique of the organization of labor in the factory and workshop. Alongside the economic, political, and social conditions that explained the lack of foresight, the demoralization and misery of the worker, there was room for a more precise allocation of responsibility: the way in which business owners utilized manual labor, the way they governed their business. Precisely in order for pauperism to not condemn the industrial regime (industrial society and its order), its individual responsibilities had to be identified. One had to presume that a different way of managing business would eliminate pauperism. Thus, the *patrons* had to be made individually responsible for the conditions of the workers they employed. They would no longer have to be only "masters," but "*patrons*." They would have to use foresight for themselves as well as their workers. They became responsible for the security of their workers. This responsibility was no longer based solely on their particular interest—a "moralized" worker was more productive than a demoralized worker—it was also based on a social interest. Here there was an obligation that doubtless remained a moral obligation, but it was equally a question of public order. If necessary, it would be made a legal obligation. Thus, the problematic of responsibility was profoundly transformed. A problematic of equal liberty was replaced by a problematic of unequal responsibilities, which was to be enforced by the law of March 22, 1841, governing child labor in factories.[16]

This law is often cited as a model of bourgeois bad faith. Rather than prevent the odious exploitation of children, one sought only to limit child overexploitation in order to save children for future exploitation.

This dimension, which is incontestable and actually explicit in the debate, does not exhaust the meaning of the law. Whatever the motives may have been that inspired its authors—and why its authors would legislate this phenomenon at this moment, a question that is really very interesting—the law of 1841 concerning child labor matters also, and perhaps primarily, because of the modification of the juridical and political rationality that it involved, the type of business analysis that it sanctioned, and the new security policies that it institutionalized. Without a doubt the law would not be applied much, if at all. And sociologists would see its inefficacy as a good reason to neglect it without pausing to ask if it had any side effects (which it certainly did).

But the event was elsewhere: in the same legislative act, an act that at the time could only mean rupture. Regulating child labor in effect touched on these two fundamental principles of the liberal order: freedom of business and the authority of the head of the family. The regulation in question assumed that these two quasi-constitutional liberties, left to their own devices, were not naturally regulated, that they needed to be directed and placed under tutelage. The debate around the law of 1841 was less concerned with the contents of the legislation to be promoted than the fact of knowing if such matters fall within the concern of legislative competence.[17] The debate did not oppose those who would like to do something against those who would be hostile to any measure protecting children. It revolved around the juridical status of the measures at hand. Did the matter at hand fall within the jurisdiction of a *law*, which, as such, could only articulate a new set of principles contradicting the fundamental principles of liberalism? Or did it fall within *regulations*, adapted to the circumstances and respectful of these principles?

Deputies and members of the Chamber of Peers were well aware of the constitutional stakes of the new legislation.[18] In the course of the debate the Duke de Broglie declared that this "law, whose aim is for the first time to restrain paternal authority and freedom of work, touches on society's greatest interests."[19]

"This is the first step we are taking on a perilous path. This is the first act regulating industry—industry that requires liberty to move forward," declared Gustave de Beaumont, while explaining that if refusing to take measures that are necessary by virtue of all that is said in their favor was impossible, it also had to be recognized that their legislative consecration inaugurated a new world. The measure conceived in favor of children contained a principle of infinite regulation. In the first place, as far as workers are concerned, arguments that were initially used to justify the protection of children would soon be used to campaign in favor of protecting adults and the working class. Secondly, as far as the labor relation is concerned, in the name of morality and hygiene they will grant the state a regulatory authority lacking ascribable limits.[20] In other words, the measure envisioned implied a modification of the juridical status of industry, its socialization: "We always place a factory in the paternal domain. This is a patent error. A factory that gathers together three or four hundred people is completely different from the interior of a family. It is an establishment that displays, through the very multiplicity of its workers, a more than private character in which public authority has the right to intervene in particular manner in order to ensure the conditions of well-being, hygiene, morality, and health of the children of the people who find themselves employed there."[21] Under all of these points of view, legislative regulation of child labor appeared difficult to reconcile with the great principles of liberal political economy.

The difficulty would be circumvented by bracketing the question. At issue here was a "special" question. It was only meant to combat "excess"—not to constrain liberty, but to give it the means to punish the "abuses" that threatened the very existence of its principles.[22] In other terms, license is not liberty. There is no liberty without laws, and, according to Montesquieu's formula, "Liberty can consist only in having the power to do what one should want to do."[23] Be that as it may, the fact remained that the liberal division was at the center of the debate and led to a rethinking of its contours. In effect, it was not a matter of placing a limit on child labor, deemed as necessary for the child as for the child's parents, but of combating the "demoralization" that might follow from it. It was a matter of finding a dispositive in which child labor would not occur to the detriment of children's development or instruction—in a word, their education. More generally, the object of the law was to prevent a "demoralization" that concerned the parents as much as the industrialists.

Morality was thus the real object of the law. The law would legalize moral obligations and at the same time displace the contours of the liberal limit.

In practice—and perhaps this was the most novel part of this regulation—legislators looked less to state a principle that as such was general, impersonal, and had a claim to perpetuity than to organize a compromise among three groups of interests while recognizing their legitimacy: the interests of the industrialists, who, for many reasons, such as training, justified the use of child manual labor; the interests of the family, who must not be deprived of their children's wages; and finally the interests of the children, of their development and their morality. This last interest now appeared in its connection to the previous two, and in particular in relation to the interests of the father, as a specific social interest that must be taken care of by the state—because only the state as it was constituted knew the child's interest. The law of 1841 introduced a new rupture. The law made the state the holder of an interest that is specific, positive, and very different from the interest that had been defined as safety. Actually, through the interest of the child, the state's interest became the reproduction and conservation of society, from the point of view of its material conditions (and no longer only from its constitutional conditions). Through the intermediary of children, the state established that it had an interest of its own—a public interest, no doubt, but one that could not be reduced to the general interest, because over time it opposed the interests of industrialists and fathers. The latter two interests are exhausted in the timeliness and immediacy of their satisfaction. It was up to the state to take control of the interest of the future. Foresight thus became a state function. In this division of tasks and time, what was also implied was a reinterpretation of the relations between the legal and political and a new source of political regulation, a regulation characterized by the fact that it would always have to be exercised indefinitely.

Thus was established a new form of rule that spread the law's jurisdiction to the center of the factory, and over the conditions of work, which is to say over the *patrons'* exercise of power. It was possible this form of rule could be used against the *patrons* themselves in order to control their management of labor.

Law and Contract

The collected jurisprudence concerning the responsibility for workplace accidents opened with two decisions from the Courts of Appeal of Lyon and Toulouse, delivered in 1836 and 1839, respectively, dealing with two analogous cases.[24] Two workers were employed by the same "master," and in the course of work one worker wounded the other. The latter worker claimed compensation from the master. The two courts of appeal rendered similar decisions.[25] The wounded worker had no standing to claim damages from the master who employs him on the grounds that "someone who consents to furnish salaried or informal assistance for any such work, accepts the chances that danger may present itself . . . , that the risks that may go along with the work are compensated, vis-à-vis the proprietor, through the salary particular to their type of occupation."[26]

The judges' decision rested on an interpretation of the contract for services that boils it down to the sole exchange of a wage for a service, an interpretation that this is the only legal obligation comprised in the wage labor relationship, and that as a consequence the existence of a contract for services suspends the applicability of the rules of civil liability law common to worker-*patron* relations. *In a certain way, the contract overrides the law.*

This interpretation of the contract for services, which in practical terms ended up depriving the worker who is victim of an accident of all juridical recourse, found its enabling condition in a contractual understanding of rights and the law that itself rested on the grand principle of liberal legal philosophy. The Civil Code brought into being a world of liberty where men, heretofore emancipated from all constraint, would know no other obligations than their own, where the constraining force of the law would have no other source and foundation than each individual's free will.[27] Only my will can obligate me, and I am only obligated as far as I have wished to be so. Similarly, the law only knows how to be contractual, and every obligation has to derive from a contract. And if the Civil Code recognizes the existence of informal engagements, these simply reproduce the social contract (the tacit contract presumed by the very existence of society) and replicate the principle (coextensive with all social life) that requires of everyone to do no harm to another. At bottom, criminal responsibility itself was only based on a contractual responsibility pertaining to public order, endorsing our contractual agreement to belong to society.[28] This doctrine was expressed in article 1134 of the Civil Code: "Legally formed agreements take the place of law for those parties that have formed them." From this follows the double consequence that, as soon as two persons are contractually engaged, they are presumed to have made the contract voluntarily and freely, and one can only judge their mutual obligations concerning the execution of the contract in light of the convention that binds them.[29]

In addition, like every contract, the contract for services engages two persons who have contracted (or more precisely who are supposed to have freely contracted) and, with full knowledge of the facts, who are supposed to assume the risks of their commitments. Through the contract for services, the worker "accepted" the chances of danger that might be entailed, and through the promised wage the master is freed of the work-related burdens that the wage earners have accepted.[30] The contract for services only deals with the solitary exchange of a wage for a service. The reparation of damages, however opportune it may be, is not within the contract's jurisdiction. In a word, we work at our own risk and peril.[31]

This doctrine of the accident as "individual risk" would be upheld throughout the nineteenth century by liberal economists and lawyers alike.

As a consequence, in the event of an accident, workers had at their disposal no legal recourse against their patron. Of course, as the Court of Lyon urged, workers might "solicit aid from humanity and from those who have employed him or who have profited from his services."[32] But this obligation, which corresponds to a moral duty, could not be sanctioned by a positive law and form the basis of a legal responsibility.

Thus, according to the doctrine in question, there could be no specific problem of workplace accidents. Work and its risks did not and should not enjoy any privileges: "Every act of life, however insignificant, implies a risk."[33] Labor's risks had no quality that should separate them from "humanity's risks": "This great professional risk of humanity, is that every human being is mortal and might lose their physical and mental faculties. Each and every one of us is vulnerable to suffering resulting from events over which we have no sort of responsibility. This is no truer for industry than any other branch of human activity."[34] Work may well entail particular risks for the person engaging in it. This is an objective fact that does not destabilize the relations between free wills. That work is conducted under particular dangerous conditions does not differentiate it from all of the other dangers that everyone must face. The fact of workplace accidents would not automatically imply the enactment of special obligations or particular responsibilities for one or another protagonist in the labor process. It should be resolved according to the principles of the common law of responsibility. Preventing accidents is a matter of prudence and personal vigilance. Protecting against their likelihood is a matter of individual foresight.

The doctrine of individual risk reflected the fundamental principles of liberal political economy. It "is logical, it responds to a sublime conception of human dignity. It makes man a kind of demigod, master of his own destiny, of his future, of the destiny and future of his loved ones."[35] It would nevertheless be abandoned. In the 1830s, one could, in effect, see in the analysis of workplace accidents a discrepancy analogous to the one provoked by the discovery of pauperism, at the same moment, in matters concerning poverty.

The worker's lack of foresight was, if not natural, at least understandable, explicable, and justifiable. The causes of accidents in which workers were injured, although still attributed to their negligence, were supplemented by an analysis of what made them so harmful: the lack of training, mindlessness of the job—in a word, the conditions of work. These entailed the responsibility of patrons: "The workers are men, and in this even we become culpable—we should say criminals—since our negligence exacerbates their fate. When science has yet to discover the means of protecting the workers from certain gases that alter their health and shorten their lifespan, the manufacturer who employs them and the state that protects them can only decry this state of affairs and all of their efforts should aim to eradicate or limit these effects. But when the means of protecting the workers exist, when, at little cost they can be established, then the manufacturer no longer has any excuse for the accidents that occur in his factory, and society has the right to hold him accountable."[36]

The Court of Appeals would quickly make this doctrine its own. Through a decision of June 21, 1841, it overturned the decision of the Court of Toulouse on the grounds that the existence of a contract cannot suspend the law's application, in this case article 1384 of the Civil Code. *The law overrides the contract.*

Against the thesis of individual risk, this decision practically declared that the *patron*'s obligations were not reducible to the simple exchange of a wage for a service; that apart from and above contractual obligations, the *patron* had to satisfy another type of obligation, one with public status—an obligation to provide security. The decision declared that the wage relationship could not be reduced to the mere existence of a wage; it is submitted to a dual regime of legal obligations that have neither the same sources nor the same foundations. By giving the injured worker legal recourse against the *patron*, the Court of Appeals recognized a right over the way the labor process was organized and administered. If workers, consistent with the contract for services, should provide services to a *patron* and place themselves at the *patron*'s disposition, they now enjoy some recourse over the way these services are carried out, over the conditions of labor and security in which they conduct their activity. Accidents were no longer simply objective risk, whose likelihood had been freely accepted by its victim; nor was the victim responsible for preventing and guarding against the accident through prudence and personal foresight. Accidents were no longer understood in the abstract form of a risk stemming from fate or fatality, good or bad luck. Now the cause of the accident had to be determined and sought in the will of the *patron*. Accidents were no longer a hazard that attested to the precariousness of the human condition. They became a fault: something that *should not* happen, something that depends on a *patron*—on his obligation to manage his workers' labor, on his vigilance to protect them from danger—so that it becomes impossible. The industrial accident took the form of a *workplace* accident, isolated and distinguished from the "risks of humanity." Inversely, labor, the industrial business, and its relations of production were objectified from the standpoint of accidents. The rules of the law of responsibility endowed *patrons* and workers with a new legal identity. The *patron* was no longer simply the person who pays a temporarily contracted laborer according to the laws of the market. The *patron* was the person who was expected to ensure the worker's security. Workers might demand security from the person who employed them; they were individuals whose security depended on another person and not only on themselves. In other words, what the law of 1841 did for children, this decision from the Appeals Court did for adults.[37]

In the years 1830 to 1840, liberal reason was thus distinctly transformed. The analysis of the pauper's poverty as the cause of workplace accidents allowed for a new way of managing responsibility to appear. If people must always be regarded as governing themselves freely, then now the liberty of some was supplemented by a game of circumstance that limited liberty's free play, perhaps going so far as to determine their liberty. If liberty remained truly equal for each, circumstances were such that there were inequalities in responsibility, therefore an imbalance that must be considered in the juridical judgments as well as in the definition of social policies. A modification of the social rule of judgment took place. To be precise, the novelty did not consist in the discovery of some pathology of liberty, in which there are circumstances, inherited traits, and an environment, where there are patterns and motives that might account for the manner in which a free choice is made. What was new is that some of these elements would inform the rule of juridical judgment. They broke through, as the specialists say, the threshold of juridicity.

When, in 1836 or 1838, the judges dismissed the injured worker on the grounds that the contract for services implied that he had taken account of the risks of his trade, they were not so blind. Their judgments did not imply that they had ignored the actual inequality between the master and the worker nor that they had been indifferent to the man's distress or that of his family. Rather, their judgments attest to the way they felt their judgment to be constrained—the manner in which they thought they had to judge some behavior in order for the law to fulfill its regulatory function. These judgments do not point to the judges' inhumanity (what would have been even more inhuman is for the judges to be able to judge according to their own sense of humanity); they express a type of rationality. And this supposed that juridically one had to judge behavior as if it were free, as if each individual were responsible for his or her own fate. Patterns, motives, excuses: none of this could be legally recognized or inscribed in the rationality of juridical judgment. There was a set of factors that was neither juridically opposable nor admissible. What changed in the 1830s was that facts that were hitherto excluded from the law would find their place, be recognized, and be accepted. In a word, we witness a modification of the relations between fact and law.

It is not a question of saying that, for the first time since the French Revolution, the law took account of the fact of inequalities. Both the law of Germinal, Year XI (April 12, 1803), the first act of our current labor legislation, and the Civil Code already contain clauses recognizing, in terms of wages, the fact of inequality between contracting parties. In both cases, the problem was that of imagining a dispositive that would make it possible to implement wage relations based on liberty. Workers, in the majority of cases, were penniless. There was no risk that they might neglect their engagements and speculate on or exploit the labor market through their mobility. A dispositive had to be found that could serve as guarantee to workers, even if it was external to the contractual economy: it was found in the old corporate institution of the *livret*.[38] In the same way, article 1781 of the Civil Code, considering that wage rates are mostly promised verbally, sought to avoid the trickery and disputes that testimonial proof would tend to promote when it came to wages.

In a way that differed from established practices, the practices of inequality introduced by the law of 1841 concerning child labor, like the Court of Appeals decision concerning workplace security, did not seek to render an existing juridical dispositive more practicable: they modified the dispositive itself, not in its approach but in its principles. The measures of 1803–4 sought to prevent a speculation on the law that would disable the idea of freedom of labor. They were not contrary to the general principles of the law. They were rather the condition of possibility of law within the sphere of work. The measures of 1841 shifted the boundaries of liberal limit: they extended the sphere of the juridical and curtailed the space of morality. And the expected effect of deregulation did not fail to materialize. The legal instantiation of the *patron*'s obligation to provide security would generate a conflict of responsibilities that in the long run challenged the possibility of locating the regulating principle of society in the concept of responsibility.

CHAPTER 3

Noblesse Oblige

"The *patron* owes his workers something other than a mere wage."[1] "The *patrons* of Elberfeld are careful not to subordinate salary questions to the simple law of supply and demand. They are persuaded that the security given to the worker concerning daily bread is, for the factory, a condition of success as urgent as the perfection imparted to technical and commercial operations."[2]

With regard to his workers, the *patron* enjoys extensive power; he regulates their salaries, guarantees their subsistence, and the fate of his business exerts a powerful influence on the destiny of the families employed: in a word, as Alexis de Tocqueville said, "The *patron* increasingly resembles the administrator of a vast empire." Due to the very fact that he plays this role and that he is entrusted with this power, the *patron* is bound by a correlative duty. The Socialists of the Chair[3] in Germany call him: "A functionary appointed by the collectivity for the creation and implementation of the nation's means of production." Remove from this definition the disturbing germ of bureaucracy and statism it might contain, and there yet remains this idea of the social function, a *patron*'s social duty. The social duty is the counterpart and, one might even say, the ransom of social entitlement. One used to say, "noblesse oblige" [nobility obliges]. We must expand this charming motto to include those born with fortune's gifts, talent, beauty, and intelligence. "All superiority obliges." All superiority must atone for itself through the devotion to social duty.[4]

All of these formulas repeated the principles of the *patronage regime*, which is to say the set of rules of conduct that the *patronat* (at least those of the *grand patronat*)[5] claimed to be suitable for governing industry and that form, in opposition to "political economy," the doctrine of "social economy." If Jean Charles Léonard de Sismondi provided its first theoretical formulation in his *New Principles of Political Economy* (1819), we can agree to recognize that its first applications to the management of industrial businesses came from the *patronat* at Mulhouse. Systematized by Frédéric Le Play, based on his investigations of European workers, under the Second Empire the regime of patronage would become official doctrine and the social economy the basis of a program of *social reform*.[6] Under the Third Republic, the Unions for Social Peace and the members of the Society of Social Economy,[7] pursuing the work of the "master," would endeavor to expand their principles and defend them against the growing threat, coming from Germany, of state socialism.

Problem: the *patron*'s regime and the principles of social economy simultaneously defined a doctrine of the "labor contract"—stipulating, against the liberal economists, that the relations between *patrons* and workers are not reducible and cannot be reduced to the mere exchange of a wage for a service—and a politics of civil security making workers' security a *patron*'s responsibility. The *patron* should, in particular, guarantee workers' security in the exercise of their work and, more generally, guarantee a secure existence for workers.[8] This doctrine recalled the criteria that the courts would apply in matters of workplace accidents after 1841, a doctrine that moreover corresponds to the spirit of labor legislation inaugurated by the 1841 law on child labor. We may well conclude from this that the labor law functioned, beginning in the 1840s, in harmony with the principles of social economy and patronage. Here we would have further evidence that, in the nineteenth century, the law was on the side of the *patrons*. In practice, however, this doctrine would be used to condemn the *patrons*. These *patrons*, on the other hand, would develop *patrons'* organizations like so many other instruments meant to allow them to avoid fulfilling their juridical obligations, to bypass them, to evade both judge and the judiciary's interference in the relationships they would like to build with their workers. If the *patrons* denounced the principle of responsibility, it is nevertheless clear that the *patron*'s organization constituted a permanent and constant critical practice of liability law. The doctrinal homology should not conceal the conflict between practices.

This conflict does not attest to a contradiction between the manner in which the law conceived the *patron*'s responsibility and the way in which the *patrons* themselves understood it. Rather, it attests to the disturbance that was introduced—in the social management of responsibility—by the displacement of the liberal limit and the juridical sanction of moral obligations. The principles of social economy might well have been homologous to juridical obligations, even when the fact of their juridical sanction corrupted or reversed them, and would provoke a conflict of responsibilities. Spanning the nineteenth century, this conflict would catalyze the future debate around the responsibility for workplace accidents and injured workers, along with the allied, more general problematic of instituting a new social management of responsibilities, to be governed according to a new type of law—social law.

On the Government of Industry

The politics of civil security, from the outset defined as a strategy of individual foresight founded on the principles of equality, sovereignty, and the autonomy of wills, had shifted in the 1840s in favor of an inegalitarian strategy of generalized benevolence and indefinite moralization. The dream of a society where each person would only depend on himself, on his own will and liberty, the utopia of a society of foresight, had come and gone. In the conduct of this affairs, the *patron* now had to aim for the "moral and material amelioration" of his workers. He had to "patronize" them, which meant not only paying them for their labor but also shepherding them and governing them. These imperatives overlapped with a set of much older requirements, born of another political context, that of *industrialization*, with its governmental and managerial dimensions. On one side, the governmental program that guided France's industrial policies strove to offer *patrons* a framework favoring the development of their initiative while compelling them to conceive of their function as a public one: they had to ensure security, in every sense of the term, to the populations under their charge. The company heads, for their part, confronted with the problem of the creation of an industrial workforce, had to take into account, as a condition of production, a series of social elements, distinct from wage rates alone: the personality and needs of the workers they employed. The *patrons'* regime was born from the articulation of this double imperative as a way of reinforcing the one through the other.

1. First of all, there was a *governmental program*, elaborated and put to work in particular by Jean-Antoine Chaptal, Bonaparte's minister of the Interior from 1800 to 1804,[9] with, initially, the awareness of a new geopolitical fact: "The colossal power of England rests on the prosperity of its commerce; but its power will crumble the day when general peace will call on all peoples to compete with it."[10] Humanity had attained the "age of maturity," where the industrial regime, as primary motor that henceforth announced the duty to reign over the world's interests, was going to replace a "system of war," which up to this point had ruled over nations and the relations between them, and would impose "peace," both as its condition and its consequence.[11]

Thus industry was a national affair of public interest—an affair of the state. "Commerce, agriculture and manufacturing make up the nation's strength and wealth; the government may have only one end, to protect and encourage them."[12] The problem was to define an industrial strategy, which cannot be a general strategy, but rather one fitting the specific case of France, according to its history and geography, its status, its wealth, its strengths, and its weaknesses. The task of "direction" was up to the government. But this is precisely where the difficulty resided. Indeed, was it not the actions of previous governments, their willingness to manage industry, that had kept France from its rightful place in the world? "A government that wants to meddle in the means of production, to influence buying and selling, regulate transactions, can only hinder industry and damage its interests."[13] Similarly, it is not this particular, arbitrary, regulatory, and constraining direction that Chaptal discusses. France's place as the first manufacturing nation was inscribed in its nature; it was only a matter of freeing industry from the fetters and obstacles that had up until then hindered its development.

This liberation was the work of the Revolution. By abolishing the old manufacturing regime, by proclaiming the liberty of work and industry, the Revolution had set down the true principle for guiding the government of industry. "There is no government more favorable to the arts than the one that is free."[14] Is this to say, though, that governmental action should limit itself to this merely negative task? No. The principle of the freedom of industry should not have government abstention as a consequence; it is, moreover, necessary for the government to take a series of positive initiatives according to the terms that Chaptal repeatedly invokes, that government "protects" and "encourages" industry. Freedom of industry depended on the enabling action of government to suppress the administrative obstacles that might interfere with industry's free exercise. But government should also create the conditions that set industry in motion, that safeguard and support industry's existence. If initiative rests with industrialists, liberty is a function of the government. Hence Chaptal's creation, according to a "combined framework,"[15] of a dispositive where governmental action, the industrialists' initiative, and the labor of workers are destined to operate as a harmonious whole, in a system of mutual support.

This dispositive has two major characteristics. The first is a dispositive of *security*. There is no liberty without security, without guarantee:

this is the condition of its existence and exercise. Guaranteeing security is the task of a free government. This task obeys three directives:

a. Government should first of all "guarantee property" and, more generally, act in a way that guarantees all of the conditions of stability, duration, and longevity for the businesses of industrialists. Government must establish the conditions that ensure industry's success by reducing, within its sphere of action, the hazards and risks that might threaten industry. It is by guaranteeing industry's security that freedom of industry will produce its useful effects—with the proviso, however, that this liberty is not an end in itself but an instrument of government. This is the best means of accelerating industrial development and national power. The 1810 law on mines is a monument to this policy. Since 1791, mines were considered property of the nation. The problem: how to exploit the mines so that the nation reaps the maximum benefit? The 1810 law responds thus: by entrusting them in perpetuity to individuals. In the eyes of the legislator, the freedom granted to the mines' developers, along with the guaranteed possession of their concessions, do not represent the abandonment of national wealth to private interests but the best way of assuring that the nation derives the maximum profit from them. "The public interest is secure when, instead of seeing private interest as an enemy, it sees it as a guarantor."[16] Liberty, property, security may well be inscribed on the pediment of our constitutions. Nonetheless, they are government tactics. They impose themselves as the instruments of an art of governance. There is an essential element in this combination: the law. It is up to the law far more than the administration to guarantee security: "As for the rest, Napoleon would rather leave personal interest to its own devices than to establish surveillance over engineers. It is a great defect in a government that would like to be too paternal. Through overconcern, it ruins both liberty and property."[17] To govern according to the principle of liberty is to govern by laws whose principle characteristic should be permanence and stability. Law is the instrument that ties government to the liberty of the industrialist, the contract that guarantees property to the latter and to the former guarantees that it will serve the public interest.
b. But the government should not only guarantee the security of the industrialists and their property. It is also incumbent on government to

take charge of the problems of *public security* posed by industrialization. "The manufacturing industry has effected a total change in our morals, our habits, our relations."[18] There are two types of problems here: one of national defense, which, according to Claude A. Costaz, led the Duc de Sully to privilege agriculture over the manufacturing industry.[19] "According to him, there are very serious disadvantages to the multiplication of manufactures, above all manufactures of luxury goods, which provide the workers a pleasant and tranquil life but weaken the population; and, in this fashion, we might lack men robust enough to don military uniforms and resist the bellicose nations surrounding France."[20] There is also a problem posed by the collection of workers around industrial businesses. Chaptal had always regarded the great collections of workers as one of the most dangerous scourges attached to the progress of civilization. It is a problem of public security that is also a problem of territorial management, the location of industry, and the territorialization of workers. It should be resolved in favor of the countryside. It is a question of creating an industrial population that is not exclusively wage-earning and dependent on industry—which would have the double disadvantage of favoring insurrections in times of industrial crisis and exposing the industrialists to the whims of the workers—to combine the advantages of industrial labor with agricultural labor, to do it so that the industrialist profits from the qualities of the agriculturalist. This is the "alliance of industrial and manufacturing labor," which would be recognized by the special jury of the 1867 Universal Exposition as one of the essential practices of patronage.[21]

c. Finally, the government should take the *civil security* of workers into account. "In general, the workers live day to day, without dreaming of saving their wages to prepare resources for their old age and moments when sickness prevents them from working. . . . The effects of this carelessness toward the future are too unpleasant to not warrant the attention of the administration." It is the government's job to encourage, while also controlling, the creation of community relief funds and the multiplication of savings banks.[22] At the dawn of the nineteenth century, at a moment considered to be one of liberal hegemony, the politics of industrialization appeared as an autonomous regulatory force, beyond the scope of common law, as much as a politics of security.

Characteristically, from the outset this politics of security did not have a repressive aim. Above all else it incited. The security measures, whether they might concern the security of property, public security, or workers' civil security, were connected in such a way that they combined and mutually reinforced each other. It turned security into a mechanism of encouragement and an instigator of industrial development. Security belonged to the realm of tactics: to turn a difficulty or obstacle into an opportunity, into a reference point for future progress; to turn what would be a loss into a profit. And security belonged to the realm of combination: it always combines, articulates, mutually reinforces interests—private interest and public interest, the *patron*'s interest and the workers' interest. It unites them, makes them inseparable, and makes it so that the interest of the former finds its support in the interest of the latter. Paradigmatic of this politics was the institution that had for a long time been its symbol: the *worker's livret*.[23]

According to Chaptal's vision, the *livret* was a central piece of industrialization's dispositive. The *livret* would allow for the harmony between the boss and his workers that is necessary for the business' success to be established. By ensuring the stability of hiring, preventing frequent layoffs, connecting the worker to the business and the business to the worker, the *livret* would make it so that each would find his own security in the security that he procures for the other.[24] Doubtless, in practice, the worker's *livret* had above all been an instrument for policing workers. Doubtless, it had served to maintain the subordination of the workers to their patrons. It was no less a dispositive meant to combine the threefold interest of the *patrons* (the *livret* guarantees the stability of manual labor), the workers (the *livret* attests to their conduct and gives to the good worker the credit he deserves), and the state (from the point of view of the two imperatives of encouraging production and public order). This industrial politics can be summarized in three words: encourage, unite, and socialize. At the same time this all exists in the realm of a mechanics or dynamics of forces and resistances—forces that must be expressed in a way that is mutually beneficial and that does not slow down the three groups—and in the realm of a politics of space, socialization, and territorialization. It is mechanical and geopolitical.

The second significant feature of this industrial dispositive is the place that is given to the industrialist, to the captain of industry. He is the essential, central piece. The success of this politics of industrialization depends on his initiatives and the manner in which he governs his business. Hence the necessity for the government (a) to place and maintain industrialists in a state of permanent competition, to arouse perpetual emulation, to arrange a system of knowledge that would allow each to profit from the inventions of the others: the creation of the Society for the Encouragement of National Industry (1801), a regular institution of the Industrial Expositions; (b) to honor them, to give them the place that society owes them, to connect them to government, to connect their interest to the public's interest. Hence the proliferation of tactics that ranged from the visit, the direct contact between the government minister and the industrialist,[25] to the creation of the Council of Arts and Manufactures, an institution whose function was to guarantee communication between industrialists and government.

According to this governmental program, the industrialist was not only a private person intent on pursuing the satisfaction of his own interests; he was also identified as a public person. His function was not only economic; it was also political. Not only because the prosperity of a nation depended on the state of his industry, but because the nation depended on the *patrons* for future industrial society to remain harmonious. The new geopolitical order forced France to become an industrial nation. This conferred upon the captains of industry a public service mission where the government thinks its best option is in creating a space that guarantees the best development of industry's initiatives. It was nevertheless necessary that industrialists, through a kind of exchange, act according to their own properly political responsibilities. The objective of the government's dispositive was to make sure that the captain of industry integrated his political responsibilities into his economic strategy. It was organized around a sort of contract where, in light of the security that it guaranteed the industrialists, the government expected that, along with their workers' security, the industrialists would guarantee public order over their businesses' territory.

The politicosocial role assigned to the patron should not be practiced in addition to or outside of his function as entrepreneur; it was an integral part of the entrepreneurial function. If industrialists could be deputies or ministers, if they could aspire to positions of representation or notability, this was less the result of an excess of power or will to control the state than because it had been made their duty. In this governmental will to marry the economic and the political in the industrialist, one finds what is in a sense the official source of the *patron*'s "social duty." He had to govern his business not as a "master" (it is under this category that the law considers the *patron*) but, according to the expression of Le Play, as a "social authority."[26]

2. This governmental dispositive could well give industrialists their true place in society, guarantee their property, guarantee them the enjoyment of their future profits, and take care of the space of security necessary for the success of their businesses. Nevertheless, this dispositive was only an empty shape to be filled by the industrialist: it remained their job to *resolve the problem of production* in a context where it depended on the "creation" of a labor force that they must simultaneously "entice," shape, and discipline. Chaptal noted that if the success of a business depends on the industrialist's skills as a manufacturer and trader, it above all entails the proper policing of workshops: "Without a doubt, perfection would be reached, if one managed to join the merit of the administrator with the talent of the artist; but if I found myself unable to unite these two qualities, and if I was forced to choose between them, I would prefer the first."[27] This was to pose the problem of production not only in technical terms of manufacturing and preparation, but also, and fundamentally, in terms of power and government. To the degree that the problem of production was posed as governing a workforce that must be shaped and disciplined, the industrialist had to organize his business according to a type of calculation that could not just be economic. Techniques of production must inextricably be technologies of power. Thus, it is at the very heart of the business and the problems of production that one must look for the properly managerial source of industrial patronage and the responsibility-security dyad that defines it.

The example of mines will allow us to follow how the problems of the government of industry were posed and resolved by nineteenth-century *patrons*.[28] First of all, there were problems of "enticing" and "retaining" a scarce labor force. This was solved simultaneously by poaching workers employed in other industries and hiring the local peasantry. To achieve this, they offered salaries that were higher than those in other areas, created lodging, and allocated all sorts of bonuses, aid, and "charities."[29] There were as many practices inspired by local customs and tradition, always born of competition, that were replicated over the course of the long nineteenth century, as each new mining corporation was created. They obeyed an economics of necessity. They were as much a part of the mine's start-up costs as the site of production itself.

But if these practices first of all obeyed an economics of necessity, they were no less penetrated by a positive calculation. There are two main reasons for this: the first is that the *patrons* were dependent on this rare and necessary, undisciplined, mobile, and irregular labor force. The workers knew they were needed and shopped around for patrons. It was imperative for the captains of industry to turn this *relationship of dependence* to their benefit; to stabilize this labor force, immobilize it, connect it to the business, and "indenture" it. They did this by making sure that workers and their families depended on the industry for their existence, making sure that workers found the satisfaction of their needs in their affiliation with the business, whether those needs be for housing (provided by the company town), health (provided by relief funds and medical services), old age (provided by retirement pensions), the education of their children (provided by patrons' schools), and supplies (provided by company stores). To manage the insecurity and instability of workers' existence, to utilize their lack of foresight as the basis of their subjectification, such was the *patron*'s strategy.

Yet it did not suffice to immobilize workers, to indenture them. They also had to be shaped, disciplined, and made productive. In the mines, the workers' compensation accounted for 65 percent of the price of coal.[30] Productivity was not so much concerned with the workers' body and their abilities as the manner in which they exerted those abilities, with their diligence and will: "Even the slightest productive force of the worker depends more on his head than on his arms; will and attention are more important than physical strength. . . . Therefore one of the principal ends of a good and intelligent industrial economy is the application of methods that are the most apt to stimulate in all types of workers this ardor and relentless effort, this intensity and this continual attention."[31] Making workers productive would require, on the one hand, an apprenticeship designed to inculcate experiences and habits that would make workers use their abilities in a useful and efficacious manner.[32] But above all, it would, on the other hand, demand a long and continuous labor on their will. It is not enough to use workers; they must be given a body, habits, and above all a will, a soul.[33] Workers' labor must be "valorized," to appeal to their pride, to keep it in a state of perpetual emulation. Above all, the company must fashion the soul from the will so that the will "animates the soul." In order to do this, the company must take the worker from the moment of his birth and accompany him up to his death.[34] The company managers, describing the institutions they created for their personnel, said that the objective was to *moralize* the workers. To moralize—this is precisely it. This was an operation that, taking charge of the totality of the workers' existence, their needs, and their security, had as its function to incorporate into them this *being* that they lacked and that alone would truly make them productive.[35]

It was in keeping with this calculus, this strategy of moralization, that the practices and institutions of industrial patronage were born and organized at the level of the business. In the case of mining companies, the great steel businesses, they created factory towns and industrial cities with all of their social amenities (workers' lodgings, relief funds, retirement funds, community gardens, schools, churches, stores, musical and sports societies). These are instruments of production of the same kind as machinery, and the resources one devotes to them are a part of the directly productive investments. Their specific function is to integrate into a single technology imperatives for profit or production and power and government, to articulate one with the other, to interlock them, in such a way that they mutually enforce each other. Patrons' organizations have been the historic and distinctive manner through which the patron sought to resolve, at the business level, the problems of production, to the extent that they are posed as questions of human governance.

Their virtue was also to allow the captains of industry to exercise, concurrent with their industrial function, the political and social responsibility that was attributed to them in the general economy of industrial society. From the political point of view, the role of the *patrons'* organization was to *socialize* the worker through the medium of the business by connecting workers to their *patron*. In taking charge of workers, body and soul, in educating them, in moralizing them, in deciding on their behavior, in distinguishing good from evil, good and bad opinions, in sanctioning them through the multiple forms of largesse and gratuity that the *patrons* promise, *patrons'* organizations made the business itself an agent of order and public security. Using the business to socialize workers, *patrons'* organizations, integrated into the framework of production, were a response to the political problem posed by industrialization: the problem of the modes of organization, of an industrial society's political "constitution." From the social point of view, *patrons'* institutions were a response to the problems of workers' civil security, which (together with pauperism) were made the *patrons'* responsibility. And, as a consequence, with the problems posed by pauperism, like the analysis made of it, insisting on questions of workers' security would function simultaneously as accelerants for the development of *patrons'* institutions and the occasion for their rationalization.

Describing Le Creusot,[36] Louis Reybaud was astonished by the bizarre status of this "town of 24,000 backward souls administratively classified as a special case, subjected to peculiar treatment."[37] It was discussed along the same lines as factory towns and industrial cities, without a doubt in order to highlight the bond that connects them to the business on which they depend. We could perhaps call them "political towns,"[38] since they are not only institutions connected to industry, but complex machines of polyvalent dispositives whose function is to simultaneously guarantee the production of wealth, profit, and surplus value, as well as workers' security and socialization. By "political town," we must not only think of the industrial city, but the unified whole formed by the factory and its accompanying machinery, organized according to the principles of a single economy. From this point of view, a political town was an industrial venture in the sense that it tends to constitute itself under the unique direction of a *patron* as a *society*, which is to say not only as an instrument of production, but as a form of social organization. The economy of the political town was such that the workshop, the factory, the mine, the site of production are not in opposition to the worker's city and its social amenities. All of them are instruments of production, and, inversely, all of them are social amenities. The political town was constituted without an exterior. The life of those who lived there was conducted in such a way that work was not opposed to anything that could be defined as leisure or nonwork, that life could only be occupied by the business, which had become the unique destiny of each and every person. The political town organized the space and time of everyone who lived there.[39] It constituted them.

Each person had his or her assigned place and each had to find his or her identity in it. For each of its inhabitants, its operational guidelines served equally as rules of conduct. The political town had its own penal code; it defined its good and bad, what is required and what is forbidden, inadmissible, brought out by rules that are not necessarily written and sanctioned by those who manage the town and are "in charge of its soul."[40] The political town, at the same time it was the expression of the worker's soul and body, was the instrument through which the worker population found itself connected to political power. Such towns were political forms comparable and concurrent to other ways of organizing, representing, and leading workers, forms that were once represented by the corporate guilds and would soon be by the trade unions.

The political town had its own regime of obligations, its way of defining and deciding each person's respective responsibilities. It had its own justice and its way of pronouncing it, its own manner of analyzing behavior and resolving the conflicts it encountered. Political towns had their own framework of rationality resting on the objectification of individuals and the behavior prescribed to them. It is in political towns, in their economic principles, that one must look for a definition of the responsibility regime that *patrons* were able to claim as their own in the name of their workers' security.

The Empire of Benevolence

Regardless of the Civil Code's brevity on matters concerning labor, it did consecrate two principles that would go on to determine wage relations. The first was the *equality* of the worker and *patron*. Article 1780 drew out the second, that of the *freedom* of work: "One may only commit one's services for a specified time or undertaking." These two principles found expression in the idea that the only juridical obligation incurred by the contract for services involved the exchange of labor for a wage. The principles and practices of social economy radically contested this way of analyzing the wage relation. This is fundamentally because, according to the sociology on which the *patrons'* regime was based, *patron*-worker relations cannot be reduced to a contractual exchange. Not only did the contract's juridical framework not correspond to the practical reality of actual commitments, but the principles that the law sanctioned were incompatible with those that should preside over the government of businesses. Using the weapon of the law, the economy of patronage replaced the idea of a government based on liberty with a mode of government and a regime of obligations resolutely based on the problem of security.

Recognition, Respect, Affection, Love

The *patron* could not be his workers' equal. A fundamental dissymmetry inscribed in reality separated them and forever defined the nature of their relations. The *patron* is one who, while never required to do so, risked his fortune in an industrial venture whose success is always uncertain. It is the *patron* who sustains the workers and to whom, with the chance of work, workers owe their subsistence and living conditions. In the *patrons'* eyes, there lay a fundamental fact that made the wage relationship absolutely irreconcilable with the terms of contractual exchange. In effect, in this primitive act known as hiring, the *patron* provides everything (which is to say the worker's possibility of existence), while the worker provides nothing (except needs to be satisfied). The doctrine of patronage qualifies the act of hiring as its defining feature rather than the wage-labor relationship that follows. Workers are not the equal of their *patron*. They never will be. The inequality that relates the former to the latter is not destined to one day disappear. Sociologically based, inscribed in the nature of things, a wage relation will always be a relationship of hierarchy and subordination. This is the primary and irreducible reality that needs to be managed.

From the very start, *patron*-worker relations escaped law: the *patron* was the one who provides even though nothing required it of him; the worker was the one who receives without being able to demand anything. Coming from the *patron*, providing labor is an act of benevolence, and the worker should recognize it as such. The *patron* is obligated to the worker, this destitute being he takes in, to not take advantage of his weak situation by exploiting it and then discarding him. He must on the contrary accept the worker, shower him with a father's attention, and strive to make a man out him, because this business is primarily a school, a place of promotion, education, and reform, with the proviso that the *patron*'s pedagogy is not oriented toward a future enfranchisement. Rather, it envisions the worker's indefinite subjugation to the business.

Workers did not enter into a contract with their *patron*. In being hired, they adhered to the business and their position. They committed to respecting the regulations and matching their behavior to them. In committing themselves, workers did not lease their ability to work. They committed their selves. They recognized their subordination and that their existence depended on the *pa-*

tron's will. This is the condition under which they could become a member of the "great family" that is the business, that they might benefit from the labor the family offers as well as the services it promises. The demonstration of any reticence on the part of the workers, any ill will, any desire to invoke the law against their *patron*, any disrespect of rules will be interpreted as a breach of commitments and will incur dismissal or, according to Le Play's expression, "expulsion." The *patron*'s power may well appear, with regard to the law, arbitrary and despotic. It is so not because of excess but in principle.

The *patrons*' regime presupposed an understanding of the workforce very different from its juridical sense (as autonomous will capable of committing itself contractually) and from its economic sense (as a force of labor). Workers, in effect, simultaneously provided themselves to the *patron* as needy beings and as bodies that would become productive only after having been disciplined. Workers immediately manifested with two characteristics: as *burden* and as *impediment*, because they were costly and not directly productive. Engaged in the production process, workers first of all appeared with habits, traditions, desires, demands, a psychology—in a word, a *resistance* that revealed itself in its singularity and its human totality. If the economist might abstract from the person of the worker, the *patron* knows that the productivity of labor depends on "the complete man," on an entire psychology whose management constitutes the core work of the business.

This system of regulation is both total and individualizing and is not only addressed to the worker. The *patron* must be aware of himself and his authoritative power. The *patron* must not try to hide behind his profession, take shelter behind it. He should, on the contrary, resolve to turn his profession into a way of expressing his own *personality*. The *patron*, in particular, should satisfy a prime obligation that Le Play fixes upon as essential: the obligation of residency.[41]

It was on this condition that the *patron* might be at once the head and the heart, the person from whom everything proceeds and on whom everything converges, that he might be the "soul of this great body" that is his business.[42] The affective presence of the *patron* was the condition on which peace and harmony in the business depended, and the "absenteeism of the great proprietor" was the primary cause of disorganization and discord at the heart of a workshop.[43] Nothing was more opposed to the regime of patronage than anonymity.[44]

The regime of patronage defined a mode of governing men that should never take the form of an impersonal and bureaucratic administration. On the contrary, it involved direct contact between the *patron* and his workers. *Patrons*' practices involved the organization of a physical and moral proximity between the *patron* and his workers. This was the condition of their rapprochement, their mutual comprehension and thus their understanding. Individualization, personalization, proximity are so many necessary conditions that enabled a *patron*'s interventions—which are all on the order of a "sacrifice," "gratuity," or "liberality"—to appear in the eyes of their beneficiaries not as administrative interventions, but as so many proofs of the attention and always pointed interest that the *patron* directed to the physical and moral well-being of each of his workers. It is on this condition that the paternal, familial bonds uniting the patron and his workers might be established.

All of the practices of patronage were focused on the desire to turn the wage relation into a concrete, individualized relationship, one between two men—almost physical, between two bodies. *Patrons'* institutions were designed to organize this interaction. Two consequences follow from their organization: first of all these institutions were the observation posts that would allow the *patron* to be meticulously aware of each worker's life and lifestyle; they should be dealt with in a way that individualizes the workers, to distinguish each one from the others. The services they rendered, the relief they dispensed were not directed toward the worker as bearer of an abstract right, but to the individual, as a father or family member in need. If they were to be solely administered by the workers, they would lose the essence of their moral value: the establishment of a connection between the *patron* and his personnel. They almost necessarily presupposed the directorship of the *patron*, who should be present as the person from whom everything proceeds and who will, regardless of the rules, provide extraordinary relief or gratuities to each *patron*, reminding them all that he is the master and that his justice and good will do not obey abstract and administrative rules. Inversely, the *patron* should call upon certain workers to participate with him in the management of these institutions. Not because he recognized a right that might be, for example, correlative to the restraint he exercises on their wages, but because it was the very objective of the institution to connect the workers and the *patron*.

The practices of patronage sought to transform the risks entailed in the first encounter into a relation of reciprocal esteem, to change a relation based on necessity into a relationship of dependence and voluntary and reciprocal attachment. Workers respected their *patron*, in whose management, attention, and justice they believed. The *patron* respected the conduct of his workers, whom he has formed and who courageously devote themselves in his service. All of the practices of patronage entail substituting relationships of *sentiment* between *patron* and worker (recognition, respect, affection) for economic and juridical relationships. Émile Cheysson summarized these in a single word, which, for him, regulated all practices of patronage: *love*.[45]

The Permanence of Engagements

A "point of reference for patronage," the permanence of engagements placed the problem of security at the center of the government of business. The *patron* was "in charge of the body and soul" and must ensure the existence of his workers. This was a general responsibility that entailed the following components: the *patron* should ensure the civil security of the workers—guarantee them aid in the case of sickness or accidents and a pension in the case of disability and in anticipation of old age. It was up to the *patron* to have foresight for the both of them. The *patron* had responsibilities as a social authority. He had to protect his workers against themselves, against bad habits, and against influences. He had to guarantee his business is in good working order, ruling over it in constant preoccupation with its future by guaranteeing its long-term stability. To do this, he had to anticipate his own passing and train his successor to maintain the business' traditions and customs. He had to protect his workers against every cause of instability: in particular, to avoid unemployment, even in times of crisis, and maintain wages at a constant rate.[46] In sum, the *patron* could not abandon the conduct of his affairs to the fluctuations of the economy; he had to, on the contrary, aim to keep them independent of its fluctuations, avoid sudden changes, and maintain regular operation. He had to understand that the end of work is not wealth (which corrupts), but virtue. For the laws of the market he had to substitute moral law.

The permanence of engagements was also the principle that presided over the management of *patrons'* organizations, organizations whose rationale is not exhausted in the immediate services they render. Why house workers, in the event of sickness, accident, or disability? First of all, so workers could find the satisfaction of all their needs in their work environment. And secondly, inversely, to form the principle of the worker's own subjectification. Workers, in effect, would benefit from the advantages procured by *patrons'* organizations not because they are necessary for them, but because it rewards the workers' fidelity and is the duty of the business. Workers might contribute to their financing through a deduction from their wages; nevertheless, this will not grant them any right to relief that they could claim against the business. Workers may have paid into a *patron*'s pension fund for years, but if they come to leave the business or are dismissed they lose all their rights.

The politics of security inscribed in the economy of patronage expressed security through *immobility*. To fix workers in place, to socialize them and territorialize them at the foundation and site of the business, such is the objective. Hence the importance of two themes in the alliance between manufacturing and agricultural work—the tactic of workers' gardens and the family, which must be constituted as a "stem family," which is to say as a principle of stability and workers' heredity.[47]

Of course, this politics of immobilization recalls the police's need to combat nomadism and vagabondage. Of course, it came to reinforce this need for public order to which the worker's *livret* attests. It also reflected a more positive philosophy of industrial societies that had two essential elements: it was first of all, as we have sufficiently highlighted, a philosophy of distinction and social hierarchy. In the economy of patronage, workers had no future outside permanent patronage. The subordination that constitutes the wage relation was not intended to one day end. The *patron* of each business must ensure the reproduction of the workforce employed as a "race" that, from generation to generation, will faithfully reproduce the traits the *patron* sought to incorporate in them. Workers should find their fulfillment in the complete identification with the being the *patron* wished to give them; they would achieve this if they knew how to abolish everything separating them from their place in the business. We are far from the liberal program of enfranchisement through savings and smallholdings. It is also true that the philosophy of patronage was, second, a sociology: it refused the distinction between fact and law that allowed the liberal to imagine the equality of men despite their differences. Even if Le Play spoke neither of the working class nor the wage system, his *oeuvre* is a sociology of these necessary distinctions and of the social relationship as a relationship of power and dependence to be indefinitely stabilized.

Of course, this is not to say that certain noteworthy workers would not be elected to the position of masters. But this signifies less a liberation than a successful—because voluntarily assumed—subjectification. The economy of patronage left only two lines of resistance to the worker. The first line, frontal, was *evasion*, flight. Workers preferred liberty to security. The second or collective line would search for a small amount of liberty in the transformation of the wage relation into a legal relationship. It was from this legalist and parliamentary path that workers' rights would be born. It is not a given that this was the most radical option. In a certain sense, it was freedom through and in their subjectification: not the abolition of the wage system and the relationship of subordination that constitutes it, but its constitution as a juridically recognized status.

The patronage regime testifies to a truly ambivalent philosophy of business. On the one hand, there is no doubt that it expressed a constitutional project for industrial societies. This was its progressive side. But it was counterbalanced by a very reactionary manner of thinking about the effects of industrialization. The industrial future was impressive to the extent that it implied social transformation, moving populations, changing habits, the loss of "custom." Le Play was not far from thinking like Karl Marx: industry brings with it revolution. This was precisely what the patronage regime had to ward off. Its problem: How could industry be developed without its revolutionary consequences? The patronage regime was faced with this difficulty of having, in a certain way, to turn business against itself, to stabilize its mobility, to keep its continual disruptions unchanging: to inscribe this immense power of life and death, success and setbacks, creation and destruction, and history in a resolutely static time. The sociology of Le Play, which looked for unbroken custom in the history and geography of European peoples, is exemplary of this problematic. Everything in the social relationship that resists time, that maintains itself throughout history, was on this basis deemed good. If the *patrons'* practices sought to integrate the social into the economy, it is on the basis of a fundamental divorce. Where Marx looked to define the social relationship that would accomplish the economic revolution, Le Play, on the contrary, posited the social as that which would preserve society's identity in spite of the economy's uncontrollable movement.

Wage or Service

The patronage regime defined a specific economy of *patron*-worker relations, their obligations, their duties, and their responsibilities competing with and opposed to the juridical economy of wage relations. In particular, the regime of patronage constituted the practical critique of the two great principles of legal equality between the *patron* and worker and the freedom of work.[48] A fundamental inequality concerning the property of the means of labor distinguished *patrons* and workers from each other. This inequality was expressed through their respective capacities to independently satisfy their needs of existence and was reflected in the nature of their relationships. *Patrons* and workers had neither the same responsibilities nor the same duties: the *patron* was not only responsible for himself; he was also responsible for his workers, whose security he had to guarantee, whom he had to protect from themselves and to whom he had to provide moral instruction. Workers, in exchange for their security, owed to their *patron* recognition (for the labor he provided), respect (for the authority he represented), affection (for the attention he provided), and devotion. In place of the idea of a reciprocity of rights between *patrons* and workers was substituted a moral bond that consecrated their relationship as one based on dependence, subordination, and tutelage. And the general principle that would oversee the government of businesses and *patrons'* practices was to turn the relationship of material dependence that primitively connected the workers to the business that employs them and to the patron who manages into a voluntary and permanent relationship. Contesting the two principles that grounded the juridical economy of the wage system, *patrons'* practices naturally had to combat these principles in their material form: reducing their obligations to the sole exchange of labor for a wage.

The wage was first of all denounced as a bad way of remunerating labor: from the point of view of production, the rate of compensation had to be proportionate to the worker's labor. Yet, "the more the worker is paid, the less he will work." This was an economic critique that was supplemented by a social critique: you might think that the situation of the worker is connected to his rate of compensation, yet the growth in wages does not correspond to an improvement in his condition, and this is due to his lack of foresight. The more workers earned, the more they spent and the less they saved. The strategy of patronage would consist of modifying the terms of exchange: to substitute for the labor-wage dyad a relationship of services. The *patron*'s strategy would also consist of integrating the payment of the wage into the many tactics of remuneration: the wage would pay for the worker's labor; the *patron* would satisfy his moral and social obligations through subsidies, gratuities, and other acts of largesse: "The wage is the social instrument of production: the subsidy is the social instrument of patronage."[49] Wages and subsidies obeyed two different logics:

a. they were opposed to each other based on *how they were calculated.* The wage is proportionate to labor while the subsidy is proportionate to the needs of the worker. The latter also had to be guaranteed in the case where (due to sickness, accidents, disability) labor was impossible;
b. hence the second characteristic that distinguishes subsidies from wages: while the wage, which obeys economic principles, would vary (according to ability, the worker's age, the economic situation), as far as the subsidy is concerned, it had to remain stable. The subsidy was not a surplus wage. Rather, it corresponded to an "insurance wage" whose effectiveness depended on its fixed nature, its reliability, its permanence, whatever economic fluctuations or crises might exist;

c. wages and subsidies did not obey the same juridical regime ("the wage is a right"). By paying the agreed-upon wage the *patron* cleared a "debt." The subsidy, on the other hand, was "discretionary and benevolent."[50] Its allocation depended only on the *patron*'s good will, or, more precisely, on the way in which he envisioned the administration of his business. The wage corresponded to a commutative justice, to a justice of egalitarian exchange, to a *do ut des*.[51] Subsidies corresponded to a distributive justice. While wages equalized, the subsidy distinguished, individualized, opposed based on the hierarchies that defined the business' proper organization. The wage responded to the principle "to each according to his works"; the subsidy to the principle "to each according to his needs." The subsidy was adjusted to the hierarchical organization instituted by the *patron*; conversely, it was the means of instituting them;
d. as a consequence, wages and subsidies did not have the same social effects. First of all, this is because the wage had to be paid in currency, while subsidies were paid in kind. "Being almost always provided in kind, the subsidy goes straight to the need, by avoiding its monetary conversion; it does not fall prey either to variance in purchasing power or variance in price; it additionally escapes the danger of being diverted from its destination and sacrificed en route to inferior or condemnable needs."[52] The subsidy, because it was a means of remunerating workers that escaped their free disposition, avoided the consequences of their lack of foresight. It corrected the social misdeeds of payment in currency. The subsidy allowed the consequences of the worker's immorality to be avoided.[53] In the same stroke the subsidy moralized; workers would not benefit from it as a right, but would benefit due to their conduct, by virtue of their merits, of their affiliation with the business—fundamentally, through their fidelity. While "the wage is the indicator of the predominance of limited engagements,"[54] the subsidy on the contrary would allow for the establishment of permanent engagements.

Wages and subsidies were the two instruments through which *patrons* satisfied their obligations. The wage paid for the labor provided by workers. To what then did *patrons*' subsidies respond? What was being exchanged in the economy of patronage if it was not labor itself? The term that constantly appears in the literature concerning patronage is *service*. What distinguished labor from service was less the nature of the thing offered, which was the same in both cases, than the type of social relations implicated in both notions. While the idea of labor presupposed the independence and equality of the person who rented out work and the one who paid for it, the notion of service implied a relationship of dependence, of subordination, of master and servant. To go from a labor economy to a service economy was to establish a social economy of production where the labor provided was no longer taken into account but the manner in which it is executed was. We should understand it in these terms: the mental disposition, the attachment, devotion, the respect given to the person for whom you work. The subsidy was simultaneously what made labor a service and what compensated the service rendered. It was through the subsidy that the patron would look to reassure himself of his workers, of their fidelity and good will, and to reward their conduct. From this point of view, it could be said that the whole of the economy of patronage consisted of reinscribing the labor economy in a service economy, that the practices of patronage sought to substitute the exchange of subsidies-services for labor-wages. In this regime of patronage, a wage is not exchanged for labor, but one service is exchanged for another. The patron promised to guarantee the workers' existence, and, reciprocally, workers promised to serve the patron, to make the *patron*'s will their own, to devote themselves to the patron.

The practices of patronage involved a shift from the problematic of the wage (focused on the rate or value of wages) to a general problematic of remuneration: this meant setting up modes of remuneration that, from the point of view of the production economy, workers' wages would always be tied to and in proportion to their labor. From the social point of view, these practices avoided the workers squandering their income by predicting their lack of foresight and guaranteeing, with their security, the permanence of their engagements. The general principle of many of these practices of remuneration was that everything that connects the fate of the workers to their patron and everything that unites their interests is good.[55] The form of remuneration through wages would not be abandoned because it operated as a legal obligation and responded to the necessities of production. But its extension would be limited by supplementing it with other modes of remuneration—subsidies—that rewarded the workers' services and sought to satisfy their needs. On one side, modes of remunerating labor were instituted whose goal was to better respond to the necessities of production and the needs of an economic organization of labor. At the same time, what would be added to this is that the workers would not receive everything that was owed to them, or what they thought was owed to them, in the form of a wage. On the contrary, according to the principle of the economy of patronage, the desire would be to maintain wages at the lowest level to increase the amount of remunerations in kind as much as possible, of which the workers would not be able to freely dispose and which addressed their needs—such are subsidies. These were the modes of social remuneration, no longer based on wages, that served *patrons'* organizations. And the *patrons'* organizations were themselves nothing other than the specific practices of remuneration in the economy of patronage.

The regime of patronage contained its own rule and justice. Justice was not found in the contractual relationship: an exchange of services that imposed on each mutual devotion does not allow for a common measure that can appraise each party's offer. Or rather, the exchange would only be just if each person, despite his or her differences, fully gave his or her self over to the other. The patronage regime involved if not replacing then at least tempering the liberal rule of equality by the principle of the proportionality of needs. It would not be too much of a stretch to make the socialist maxim its own: "From each according to his ability, to each according to his needs." Thriving on the same refusal to distinguish between fact and law, is this affinity at all surprising given the basic consensus that the rule of justice must be respectful of true equality, which is to say respectful of factual inequalities?

Patrons' organizations were a type of benevolent aid. They were not legally enforceable. In the eyes of the *patrons*, this is what made them so worthwhile. Indeed, the *patrons* might hope that organizing their business affairs as much as possible according to the logic of patronage would allow them to escape the judge's gaze. This explains why the very *patrons* who were so opposed to the principles of liberal rights in practice would become its defenders when those principles were threatened at the end of the nineteenth century. Both their power and their liberty were at stake.

In fact, the categories of law and right only grasped the appearance of *patrons'* organizations, the mask they wished to don. One could, word for word, say about them what Michel Foucault wrote in *Discipline and Punish* about disciplines:

> They have the precise role of introducing insuperable asymmetries and excluding reciprocities. First, because discipline creates between individuals a "private" link, which is a relation of constraints entirely different from contractual obligation; the acceptance of a discipline may be underwritten by contract; the way in which it is imposed, the mechanisms it brings into play, the non-reversible subordination of one group of people by another, the "surplus" power that is always kept in place on the same side, the inequality

of position of the different "partners" in relation to the common regulation, distinguish the disciplinary link from the contractual link, and make it possible to distort the contractual link systematically from the moment it has as its content a mechanism of discipline. We know, for example, how many real procedures undermine the legal fiction of the work contract: workshop discipline is not the least important. Moreover, whereas the juridical systems define juridical subjects according to universal norms, the disciplines characterize, classify, specialize; they distribute along a scale, around a norm, hierarchize individuals in relation to one another and, if necessary, disqualify and invalidate. In any case, in the space and during the time in which they exercise their control and bring into play the asymmetries of their power, they effect a suspension of the law that is never total, but is never annulled either.[56]

This is the point: the practices of patronage do not fall within the jurisdiction of an *infra-law* but a *counter-law*. The regime of patronage, in effect, has two major characteristics. It first of all acts with an economy of *autonomous* power.

Autonomy does not mean that the regime of patronage could be constituted independent of the juridical, social, and political obligations that were defined as being the duty of *patrons*. But if the regime of patronage satisfied these obligations, they were not its effect. Rather, autonomy corresponds to the manner in which the *patronat* sought to integrate these obligations into the priorities of production. The second major characteristic of patronage is its claim to *totality*. Patronage practices were not a compensation, a workaround that would correct the misdeeds of a deficient economic order. In the same way that they integrated imperatives of production and political-social imperatives into the same dispositive, they can claim to provide the basis of a positive constitution of industrial societies.

So if *patrons'* practices might appear to follow the liberal distribution of obligations, there was at the very least rivalry between the social economy and the juridical economy. Le Play and his school incidentally did not hide their opposition to the doctrine of the "jurists." And there would be conflict between practices from the moment the primitive boundary of the liberal limit was no longer respected, as was the case in the legislative and jurisprudential realignments of 1841. Nothing could be worse for patronage than to see the principles of social economy implemented as a juridical doctrine. This was to reverse it, to turn it against itself. To legalize a relation of benevolence is in effect to destroy it, to neutralize its power relations. "The obligation is sterile: it removes, along with spontaneity, the organization's merit and social effectiveness. Once they become mandatory, savings, foresight, and patronage cease to be virtuous. They no longer unite the classes, mingle personalities. It's a tax you pay, not a necessary effort."[57] Even worse, to legislate a benevolent relationship is to make a condition of peace a cause for war. For the *patrons*, in effect, law is war. It divides instead of bringing together; it provokes disputes, protest, and disorder. This is the origin of the paradox: by casting the rule of juridical judgment over the economy of patronage, *patrons'* practices and juridical practices of responsibility came into conflict with one another.

This conflict of responsibilities would manifest in particular around the problem of workplace accidents. Specifically, that there had been jurisprudence surrounding workplace accidents, that a new economy of obligations would soon be formulated around the question of accidents, was made possible by this conflict of responsibilities. The history of workplace accidents is interesting and important precisely because it tells the tale of this conflict.

But it is still too soon to begin. We still lack, in effect, one of the actors in this philosophical theater: *insurance*, its type of rationality (probabilistic rationality) and its multiple institutional incarnations. Insurance practices would introduce another crack, another dividing principle, into the edifice of responsibility. At the beginning of the nineteenth century, insurance was practically a nonentity; some, however, are certain that it will soon be everything. They are not wrong. It is, in effect, at the heart of insurance practices, in their traditional framework as in their institutions, that we will find, at the end of the nineteenth century, the solution to the conflict of responsibilities.

PART II

Universal Insurance against Risk

The solution to this conflict of responsibilities (if indeed we can speak in terms of solutions at all), which questioned the hitherto dominant approach to the regulation of society, would be found neither in liberal rationality nor in an appeal to its socialist opposition. Where once everything was given over to the individual, it would make no sense to now give everything over to the state. Where once liberal philosophy posited the irreducibility and the necessity of evil as the guiding principle of behavior, it would make no sense to now accuse the poorly organized state of being the cause of evil and to charge the state with making it disappear.

The solution would no longer be sought in a sort of middle ground between the liberal and socialist positions, but elsewhere, in another world, so to speak, in another philosophy that allowed for the antagonism between the individual and the state to be surpassed: *probabilistic reason*. It is not widely known, in France at least, that the great political event of the last two centuries is without a doubt the application of probabilistic calculus to the administration of society. The problem of regulating modern societies would thereby be reformulated according to this specific type of rationality. On this basis, politicians, whether liberal or socialist, on the right or on the left, would now redefine their platforms.

"Probabilistic calculus owes its origin to the questions the Chevalier de Méré posed to Pascal about how to divide shares between two players who, after agreeing that victory would belong to the first one to win a set number of matches, decided to end the game before either of them had won."[1] This was in 1654. Pascal demonstrated that "at least in certain instances, it was possible to grasp the exact degree of plausibility of even the least likely future events."[2] He invented what was then called "analysis" or "geometry of chance."

Following this newly opened path, mathematicians like Christiaan Huygens or Pierre Raymonde de Montmort pursued the study of games of chance. Johan de Witt, grand pensionary of Holland, applied the new calculus to the formation of life annuities.[3] All of this happened without arousing great interest.

The situation would be upended with the 1713 publication of Jacob Bernoulli's *Ars Conjectandi*. This was the first work "to appreciate the connections between this branch of mathematics and nearly all quarters of philosophy."[4] In the unfinished fourth part of the work, Bernoulli explained how the new art of conjecture was not only an ingenious mathematical invention connected to games of chance, but that it also contained a new way of behaving (thus, a new *morality*), and of conducting the affairs of the state (an art of *governing*).

"A unanimous cry rose up in the world of science and announced to posterity that the analysis of chance was going to enter a new era and its good fortune had definitively begun."[5] The European eighteenth century thus saw a proliferation of the applications of the new calculus: in law and jurisprudence; in state loans; in political arithmetic; in the formation of the first "scientific" life insurance companies; in banking and financial practices; in the problem of voting and decisions arrived at through the plurality of voices—in a word, in the array of materials relevant to the "moral and political sciences."

In the transition from the eighteenth to the nineteenth century, Pierre-Simon Laplace would accomplish a twofold project of mathematical synthesis with the *Analytic Theory of Probabilities* and of politicosocial planning with his *Philosophical Essay on Probabilities*. And the nineteenth century would see probabilistic calculus colonize all of science's domains: the exact sciences, like physics, chemistry, or biology, but also the social sciences. The social sciences would constitute themselves precisely as sciences by applying the new calculus to their objects of study.

This brought with it a way of thinking about the relations between the whole and its parts that would allow political thought to escape from the impasse of the individual-state antagonism in which it had been caught. It was believed that socialization could only happen at the expense of individuals—that socialization went hand in hand with state control. It would be discovered that the development of business structures in no way implied the sacrifice of individual liberties, nor did the existence of social systems ruin the hypothesis of free will. Historically, it was Adolphe Quetelet who constructed this new logic of relations between the whole and the part that define what we might call the "sociological schema."

Probabilistic calculus, then, would allow for, if not the birth, at least the development of a new political technology, the *technology of risk*. It would be used as a general matrix for posing social problems and give them their modern institutional solution: *insurance*. Its considerable success has yet to be refuted.

Finally, by a sort of extension or projection, the preceding practices would serve as a point of departure for a new manner of envisaging political association. The philosophy of risk, the schema of insurance, would make it possible to rethink the formula of the social contract and to imagine a new diagram of regulation for industrial societies. Society would regain its harmony by realizing *universal insurance*, with guaranteed *social security* as its program.

CHAPTER 4

Average and Perfection

It is true that at the beginning of the nineteenth century there were two competing objectifications of society, both having the same pretensions to constitute the science of man, to impart scientific status to the knowledge of society, to found "social physics" or "sociology": that of Auguste Comte and that of Adolphe Quetelet. Comte thought that sociology could only be established on the basis of a history of social development. It was a question of rigorously thinking through the idea that human development obeys laws. Quetelet's position was of another nature: it stemmed from the application—repeatedly prohibited by Comte—of the mathematical theory of chance to the study of social phenomena. This is a statistico-probabilistic objectification of society. Comtean sociology is completely dominated by the political problem formulated by Saint-Simon: "to end the French Revolution." How? Through the positive organization of society. This program, which would dominate the whole century, endows Comte with great political importance. Quetelet was much more a scholar. His goal was to understand, even if his social physics is not without political consequence. Quetelet's importance was to have marked a crossroads, an intersection, or a point of precipitation. Thanks to him, things still isolated, dispersed, and separated would begin to mingle and take on a new form, initiate new developments, a new future. Quetelet is the man behind the universalization of probabilistic calculus—which is a universal exchanger—the person through whom astronomy communicates with the inclination toward crime, meteorology with mortality rates.

Comtean sociology, as interesting as it is, does not surprise us. It is inscribed in the categories through which we had already conceived of human history, the history of improvement, for instance, even if his sociology renewed these categories. Comte, without a doubt, teaches us things about ourselves, but it is always about us as we are. With Quetelet, things proceed differently: in one stroke his social physics makes us strangers to ourselves. It confers on us a new identity. If we wish to grasp the way in which the sociological objectification of society decenters the subject, it is Quetelet we must read.

Infinite Inventories and Perfect Tabulations

Quetelet did not elaborate his sociology as a response to the problem of understanding society. Society is not for him, as with Comte, an object that, having its place defined in the classification of the sciences, must now await the formation of its specific scientific knowledge. Quetelet's object of study was the "human" in a person's physical qualities (height, weight, strength) as well as in a person's intellectual and moral attributes (inclination toward crime, tendency to marry). Society, in Quetelet's work, results from the application of a method: the correlate of a certain type of understanding of the human.

From the outset, we encounter what we might call the astronomical postulate, Laplace's postulate, or that of the world system: "After having seen the journey that the sciences have followed with regard to worlds, should we not try to follow it with regard to humans; would it not be absurd to believe that while everything else is made according to such admirable laws, the human species alone remains abandoned to itself, and that it possesses no principle of conservation? We do not hesitate to say that such an assumption would be more injurious to divinity than the very research that we propose to conduct."[1] Quetelet would ceaselessly repeat this: the world, the great one, the world of the world system, like the small one, ours, is subservient to laws. Human affairs, whether they are physical or intellectual and moral, can be no exception.

Nonetheless, this knowledge, in a certain way inscribed in the nature and very idea of God as science reveals it, runs into subjective and objective obstacles. The subjective obstacle is within us. Deep down, we do not want a scientific understanding of man, because this would mean that we are subject to laws, because this knowledge threatens the way in which we self-identify: "What stands in the way of this type of scientific study is an exaggerated fear of detracting from human free will. It seems that we would reduce our species to operating like a mechanical ensemble."[2] We prefer even the illusory feeling of our freedom to the idea that it might be subject to laws.

But there is another obstacle that for its part is constitutive of the object we wish to understand: "When we place ourselves before nature and when we seek to investigate it, what strikes us right away is the infinite variety we notice in even the smallest phenomena."[3] Not only are the laws of man and his development not given to us, not only are we not disposed to discover them, but what is given to us (individuals in their individuality, the diversity of the diverse, the infinite variety of individual differences, the irregularity, incoherence, and inconstancy that the world displays), seems determined to prevent us from discovering their laws.

Hence the problem of a human science: to find the means that will allow us to approach the diversity of information as a whole, to discern the regularity of a law amongst this hodgepodge of individual particularities. The answer to this problem is a method: *the application of probabilistic calculus to statistics.*

All this presupposes a fundamental epistemological shift. We cannot directly have an adequate understanding of the individual itself. To get to individuals in their individuality, you have to take a detour through the masses, through the collectivity they belong to: "Before all else we must abandon the view of man taken in isolation and only consider him as a part of the species. By stripping him of his individuality, we will eliminate all that is accidental; and the individual particularities that have little or no effect on the masses will disappear of their own accord and allow us to grasp the general results."[4]

Society, according to Quetelet, is primarily the result of this method. It is objectified as the necessary correlate of a human science. It is not primarily a living reality, this density of material exchanges and social and affective relations that we call civil society. It is synonymous with the masses, multitudes, multiplicities, and majorities. Hence one of the greatest problems of Quetelet's sociology: how does one move from this "abstract" society that correlates to a calculus to "real" society? Doesn't such a method entail the temptation of the realist error, whereby we mistake for reality what is only part of an artificial construction? This is a problem inherent to the application of probabilistic calculus. Faced with such a problem, the calculus is not powerless, since it is created to resolve the problem. We know, in effect, that all probabilistic judgment is twofold: it consists of a statement, a judgment of reality that is only valuable insofar as it is indexed to the evaluation of its own probability. With probabilistic calculus, we enter a world of knowledge where the subjective and objective dimensions perpetually alternate to produce a sort of permanent flickering.

If the move from the individual to the masses constituted an epistemological problem, it also represented a gesture of great importance: in a way, individuals learn that they are only part of a collectivity, that their identity is fundamentally social, that it is not to be sought in the intimacy of a relationship to the self but in the group to which they belong. The human becomes a *social being*. Of course, this gesture had been in preparation for a long time, since William Petty's first population calculations, since the first mortality tables, since the population had become the basis of a state's wealth.[5] But if we had already learned to count the population, to calculate its median life expectancy, we perhaps still only considered it the product of a simple addition: the population was the sum of a country's inhabitants. As a population, it did not have its own properties or qualities. The number took the form of an assessment; it was a passive sum. Quetelet's gesture was to show that the number had acquired a power in its own right. The masses were no longer a simple collection; they became something that enables knowledge: the whole is more than the sum of its parts.

Statistics and probabilistic calculus are of two different orders: statistics consists of taking inventory, enumeration, tallying facts. But already, in this activity of taking stock, it must borrow its method from probabilistic calculus: "The statistical method is only the application of probabilistic calculus to the observation of facts."[6] Probabilistic calculus does not only have a guiding role at the level of statistical observation, one of regulating, evaluating, verifying if it is correct and sufficient—in a word, controlling observation. Above all its role is one of interpretation. The theory of probabilities elaborated by Quetelet, the theory of averages, is what allows a rigorous interpretation of statistics—an interpretation that, to be precise, constitutes science, explanation, and the formulation of human laws.

The definition of this method for the study of humans was not without consequence. First of all, it affected probabilistic calculus itself, the applicability of which was no longer limited to a specific domain of objects but became universal. However, it also affected statistics, which should evidently be numerical. This was a transformative moment in the production of a discourse of truth on society, the formation of a new template for political discourse that would mark the end of the publicist's eloquence. We must henceforth speak through charts, curves, graphics, maps, and diagrams—with the hope that the emergence of a definitively positive social discourse will put endless controversies to rest.

The second consequence: no more than probabilistic calculus, statistics has no specific object—knowledge of the state, its powers, its wealth, or its population—rather, it has a universal competence. Statistics is the science of observation concerning not only social phenomena, but all phenomena of any order, organic or inorganic. In Quetelet's work, this idea proceeds from the impression that the world is harmonious, from the existence of a law of uniform phenomena: social phenomena, those that relate to humans, are not of a different nature than those that are related to physical nature.

The third consequence: this universal statistics must take the form of an infinite inventory. This is a direct consequence of the application of probabilistic calculus: its results would be all the more reliable as they come to depend on more numerous, more detailed, and more minute observations. This is the utopia of the infinite inventory, of the perfect tally, of surveys without gaps. The best scenario would be one in which all people are perpetually, continuously observed, and their statistics are simultaneously recorded from the earliest age. But this form of truth-telling is less the task of individuals than state administration. In order for measurements so numerous and precise to be usable, a unit of measurement must be defined in order to guarantee that comparable things are being compared. It is up to the state to define this unit of measurement on its own territory and for its own population, just as it is incumbent upon the state to collect, centralize, and exploit the results. Finally, the statistical program could only be accomplished at the international level, under the direction of a coordinating and centralizing authority that would be responsible for standardizing questionnaires and inquiries: 1851, the birth of the first international statistics congress over which Quetelet would preside. This is also the reason liberal economists like Jean-Baptiste Say mistrusted statistics. "The quantity of information should be concise because it is of a limited usefulness for knowledge and because it irresistibly tends to proliferate, just like state bureaucracy. This is because the two phenomena are complementary and contemporaneous. To be more exact, the one reinforces the other, the accumulation of data justifies the growth of a civil service bureaucracy, publications, etc., that are expensive for the taxpayer and serve the growing influence of the state. 'When I see,' remarks Say, 'that there is no detestable procedure that has not been supported and shaped by mathematical calculation, I tend to believe that it is numbers that kill states.'"[7] The problem of "Information Technology and liberties" is decidedly not a new one.[8]

Norm and Average

Probabilistic calculus enjoys a very specific status in Quetelet's sociology. It very clearly functions as a cunning of reason. It is a means of mathematical investigation intended to compensate for the impossibility of physical experimentation. It is an instrument of experimentation through pure reason. Not only are we ignorant of the laws of the phenomena that appear to us in the infinite variety of their dispersion, fluctuation, and irregularity, but we also do not know their causes. Our ignorance is such that even if we managed to identify regularities, we would still not know if laws were really at work. Our posture in the face of phenomena is such that we appear reduced to being spectators (doubtless conscientious and meticulous ones) of facts about which we are powerless to comment.

The paradox of probabilistic calculus (and thus of Quetelet's method) lies in the fact that our fundamental ignorance is never going to be solved by knowledge on the order of a discovery, since we can never leave the field of observation. The whole art of calculation consists of playing this ignorance against itself, of getting around it, in a certain way, using it against itself. Quetelet's construction, the famous theory of averages, resides in the invention of ruses that force nature to reveal itself without it having to disclose its secrets. Hence this sociology's very specific usage of the concepts of cause and law. Law does not refer to a necessary relationship between real identified elements. It merges with the finding of statistical regularities that characterize certain phenomena once they are observed in large quantities. And the concept of cause does not designate the objective or efficient cause (Quetelet's sociology is of the order of observation and not explanation), but rather what we must assume to be the correlate of these regularities in the hypothesis of a minimal determinism.

Causes are nothing other than the *chances* that this or that phenomenon will take place. They are *tendencies, inclinations* like the "inclination toward crime, marriage, suicide," or, better still, *influences*. If we can no doubt measure the intensity of a cause, this in no way diminishes the circularity of these concepts with regard to the objects they describe. We will no longer be able to say why such a person is a criminal, as psychology would, nor even why crime exists in society. However, on the basis of an analysis of increased delinquency in urban areas, for example, we can say that urban life is a "cause" of criminality—which simply amounts to observing the consistency of a probability. We will be able to discern statistical correlations between such and such phenomena and the seasons, climate, region, without ever revealing their cause.

Quetelet distinguishes two main types of averages: the objective average and the mathematical average. The objective average corresponds to something real. Would we like to measure an object, a statue, a building? Ten, twenty successive measurements will be taken, none of which will match the others exactly. However, we will be able to say with a calculable probability, proportionate to the number of measurements, that the objective height of the statue or the building corresponds to the average of the different measurements. The differences in relation to the average, which in any case obey a specific distribution allowing us to verify after the fact if the measurements have been properly taken, reside in the act of measurement itself, without affecting the identity of the measured object. The mathematical average is quite different. It is what we obtain by taking the average of the measurements of houses on a street: it does not correspond to any house on that street. The concept of average life expectancy corresponds to this same type of average. It does not tell us the age of the average individual, nor does it say at what age the average individual is going to die, no more than we can deduce a person's age of death from mortality tables. We will note, nonetheless, that this average does not exactly correspond to "no thing": it is not irrelevant for a government to observe that the life expectancy increases or decreases over its territory. This purely mathematical average, which does not result from imprecise observations, gives birth to something of a very singular type. It could be said that Quetelet's entire sociology is defined by the manner in which it manipulates this type of average and interprets it from the standpoint of probabilistic calculus.

In brief, statistics provides a series of data and facts that will only be usable from the standpoint of probabilistic calculus. The problem is to decide which type of average these facts correspond to: an objective average, thus referring to an object, or a mathematical average? Probabilistic calculus indicates that in these two cases the distribution of observations does not take on the same form. In the case of the objective mean, the distribution obeys the famous binomial law (the Gauss curve), which Quetelet still calls the "law of possibilities."[9] It shows that variations are due to "accidental" causes that cancel each other out and that we can reasonably ignore, since they are unimportant for what they show. This does not happen in the case of a mathematical average. Or, rather, the decisive problem will be to interpret these cases where a mathematical average comes to match the objective average, as in the crucial experiment of the gladiator or the statue. What are we to make of the reality of such a coincidence?

Let us follow the experiment as Quetelet described it to the Duke of Saxe-Coburg:

> The gladiator is unquestionably one of the most beautiful works of ancient sculpture. This is why artists have rightly studied its noble and bare forms, and why they have often measured the principle dimensions of the head and body to understand their relationships and harmony.
>
> The measurement of a statue is not an operation as easy as one would first think, especially if one desires to take it with a high degree of precision.[10]

The experiment almost has the form of a syllogism. It unfolds in three parts: (a) The gladiator is measured. The measurements are regularly distributed according to the law of accidental causes that allows us to say that the average value properly corresponds to the effective dimensions of the gladiator. The average is objective; (b) Copies are made, reproducing the object; in place of having figures, one now has objects. These objects are distributed according to the same law as before. This makes sense: here, the original plays the role of the objective average value. Probabilistic calculus takes account of this regular distribution of copies in relation to the original; (c) The model is completely eliminated by moving on to real men: the observation that the distribution of dimensions of these men obeys the same law as before leads one to deduce, according to the same probabilistic inference, that the average of these dimensions corresponds to "some thing." The fact is that what appears to be only a mathematical average corresponds to an objective average: "It is as if the chests that have been measured have been modeled on the same type."

Based on this, Quetelet concludes:

> Amongst the admirable laws that nature attaches to the conservation of the species, I believe I can place in the first rank the conservation of the type. In my work on *social physics*, I had already sought to determine this type, through the knowledge of the average man. However, if I am not deluding myself, what experience and reason have made known to me here takes on the form of a true mathematics.
>
> The human type for men of a similar race and age is so well established that the differences between the results of observation and those of calculation, despite the numerous accidental causes that might provoke and exaggerate them, are hardly greater than those that clumsiness might produce over a series of measurements taken of one individual.[11]

From the theory of averages, from the interpretation of statistics through probabilistic calculus, directly stems the famous theory of the "average man," at once the object of sociological study and its most characteristic product. We find in Quetelet at least three formulations of the theory of the average man. In the first place, the idea of the average man proceeds directly from the concept of the average: "By gathering individuals of a similar age and sex, and in taking the average of their particular features, we obtain a set of constants attributable to a fictive being that I will call the average man among this group. If we had, for example, the height of all twenty-five-year-old Frenchmen and if we averaged them, the value that we would obtain would be the height of the average twenty-five-year-old man."[12] Defined in this way, the average man is a "fictive being": there is no twenty-five-year-old Frenchman who could be the average man. We could no more determine from a mortality table at which age X or Y will die.

The average man is also the type of man at a certain time for a certain place:

> Thus things occur here as if nature has a different type for the country and circumstances in which the type is found. The differences among this type are the product of purely accidental causes that act with more or less the same intensity. In considering things from this point of view and in supposing a sufficiently large number of observations, the average man of each age will find himself placed among two groups of equally numerous individuals, those larger and those smaller than him. Moreover, the groups would be distributed in the most regular manner according to the size of their dimensions. The most numerous groups would be those that diverge the least from the average: as the differences increase, the groups of men that present these differences are smaller; and toward the extreme limits, the giants and the dwarfs are very rare. Nonetheless this last group must not be considered anomalies as they are necessary to complete the ascending and descending series determined by the law of accidental causes. In effect, each group has its defined value. Thus, when men are mixed together in society and their sizes appear to vary in the most capricious manner, there exists between them a most mysterious bond that allows for each individual to be considered as the necessary part of a whole that physically escapes us and that can only be seen through the eyes of science.[13]

We will note that, in this second version, the average man is always a fiction. Everything happens "as if," as Quetelet rightly says, with this proviso, however, that the application of the law of accidental causes makes this fiction really correspond to something. It does not correspond to the average man of the society in question, but to the type of men in this society. Not the model, the original of which these real men would be the more or less accurate copies, but rather their common reference. This attests to the fact that they have a "natural" identity and that there are laws of man.

Finally, according to Quetelet, "The man that I am considering is, in society, the analog of a body's center of gravity; he is the average around which the social elements oscillate: this will be, if you like, a fictive being who experiences everything in accordance with society's average results," and in addition, "all phenomena of equilibrium and movement depend on its consideration."[14]

The average man is therefore not a man whose place in society is uncertain: he is society itself objectified by sociology. We find no trace in Quetelet's work of a realism of the average man. The average man is at once what makes a scientific judgment about man possible and its necessary correlate. Abolish the metaphysical reference to a human nature and you may only identify individuals, evaluate them scientifically according to a social judgment, precisely in reference to this average man. The average man is nothing other than what appears the moment we mourn the loss of an alleged state of nature and seek to establish a social judgment on man.

This theory of the average man provoked a surge of criticism, and all the more so because Quetelet did not hesitate to base his model of perfection and beauty on the average man. Cournot denounced it as being no more than a "deformed" man, Alphonse Bertillon as the "mediocre" type, and, a century after Quetelet had proposed the idea, Maurice Halbwachs dedicated a book to refuting it. Most of these critics denounced it from a realist point of view: this alleged man could not exist. And it is true that what Quetelet objectified under the name "average man" could only have a very specific mode of existence, a status perhaps comparable to the Stoics' incorporeals.[15] All of these critiques are reminiscent of those that would be leveled some decades later against Émile Durkheim's ambition "to treat social facts as things." They attest to the difficulties of thinking through the effects of sociological decentering, the displacements sociology introduced into the study of man.

Indeed, beyond the question of its mode of existence, what else is the theory of the average man, if not another mode—the modern mode—of individuating a population's individuals? This is nothing other than the definition of what we today ceaselessly cite as the norm and the normal.

With the theory of the average man, Quetelet does nothing other than propose a mode of individuating individuals that is no longer based on themselves (on what their nature might be or what their ideal being should be), but on the basis of the group to which they belong. The theory of the average man is nothing other than this instrument that would allow us to refer a population, a collectivity (and the individuals that compose it) to itself—no longer to something exterior to it, its lost origin, its blissful future, or some kind of finality. With the construction of the average man, Quetelet accomplished no less than this foundational act of sociology, allowing society and the individuals who compose it to be understood without reference to anything else.

In *Discipline and Punish*, Michel Foucault showed how disciplines "normalize."[16] He very carefully detailed their different processes of "normalization." We might say that disciplinary normalization remains a classical type of normalization: individuals are not identified and judged by reference to an average, but according to a norm, a rule or a scale exterior to them, proceeding from best to worst, from the perfect to the hideous. The normalization that attaches to the concept of the average man is of another type: it implies a completely different process of standardization. We no longer begin by taking individuals one by one to measure them according to a scale of capabilities. We begin with the masses, the collectivity itself, and classification occurs as a function of its own normality: no longer in a hierarchical order of zero to ten, but according to distances in relation to an average that does not mark the minimum standard but the group's type. The average size and the average weight do not designate the size that well-constituted individuals in a well-policed society should have; they are what allow for individuals to be distributed into groups in relation to each other. Quetelet's average does not operate according to an imperative—or at least not by initially stating an imperative. The politics of normalization do not have the form of disciplinary requirements. A test is not an exam, even if the two look alike.

Far from canceling each other out, in practice these two different modes of individualization would combine. In school, for example, sociological normalization would come to the aid of disciplinary normalization: IQ tests would come to supplement academic results. Psychosociological identification would allow for the definition of the appropriate procedures for special needs education and a specialization of disciplinary norms: we would define for each, in function of their social identification, the disciplinary norm they should meet. Each person has his or her own place. We can measure the distance that separates this mode of sociological individualization, this type of relationship between the whole and the parts, universal and singular, from the man of the Declaration of Rights. Man is no longer here a universal, a summary of properties that were found to be identical in each person. We are very far from the Kantian "every man an end in himself" or Descartes's "reason whole and complete in each person." With the average man, there is no longer a universal. At most, there is the general, and the general is always specified.

The theory of the average man represents the properly sociological manner of thinking about the relations between the whole and its parts, a way of thinking about the regime of identities and differences from the standpoint of the sole reality of inequalities; explaining how, despite the differences and inequalities that are the only true realities, there is nonetheless a social or collective identity. The average man is not exactly each of us, but we are all a part of him. He resembles us so closely it is hard to tell the difference, and yet we distinguish ourselves from him all of the time through the miniscule and accidental facets of our identity. With the theory of the average man, we shift from the regime of moral or metaphysical identities to a regime of sociological identities.

How is the average man made into the standard of beauty and the model of perfection? How does this strange reduction of the perfect to the average, which so shocks our habits of thinking, happen? Aren't the terms "perfection" and "average" mutually exclusive? Everything depends on the way we think. If we adopt the schema of history or the matrix of progress, the perfect can never be present or realized. It is always beyond, elsewhere, and at the end of an indefinite process of perfecting. Jean-Jacques Rousseau, Immanuel Kant, the Marquis de Condorcet reason within this schema of indefinite perfectibility. But as soon as we think of individuals, their relations, and their identity not in terms of a desirable future but in the strict confines of their present moment, the perfect itself becomes current. It is always realized to the extent that it provides the benchmark. In the same way, if the average man can be a model of beauty, this is explained by the fact that our own self-estimation, our senses of what we wish to be and what we like, is always a social judgment. What we depict as ideal is only ever a representation of the social. The theory of the average man announces the era when perfection will be identified with normality, when social morality's great imperative will be to normalize. Quetelet would say that what characterizes great men is less the distance that separates them from their peers than their conformity to this famous "average," a conformity that will allow the common man to identify with them. Some have searched for a model of the ideal society in the ancient Greek city or the Roman Republic. Others have looked to the utopia of communities for the happiness promised to humanity. Quetelet and the sociological tradition that he inaugurated bring us back to the reality of a world where the ideal is already here, always present, under the form of the norm and the average that defines it. Perfection, duty, the good, and well-being shall be found in the norm and the average. The ideal would no longer involve escaping from the norm, distinguishing oneself from others, setting oneself apart, but rather being the most well "socialized." However we wish to interpret this singular identity of the norm and morality, of the perfection and the average—this manner of envisioning no other norm for each person than an always current relation to others, this manner of ultimately reducing the being of each person to his or her social being—all of this is without a doubt characteristic of the era thus begun and that an English historian, Michael Bidiss, has aptly characterized as *the age of the masses*.[17]

The Whole and Its Parts

The second great series of critiques leveled against Quetelet concern the "materialism" that follows from his sociology. This implied, his critics argued, a fatalism destructive of our liberty—expressed in the now famous conclusions he would draw from his study of the first criminal statistics: "This consistency with which the same crimes recur annually in the same manner, and attracting the same punishments in the same proportions, is one of the most curious facts court statistics teach us!—Sad condition of the human species! We could list ahead of time how many individuals will soil their hands with the blood of their peers, how many will be forgers, how many will be poisoners, just as we could more or less list ahead of time the births and deaths that will take place. Society contains within itself the seeds of all of the crimes that will be committed. In a certain way, society prepares these crimes and the criminal is merely the instrument of their execution."[18]

Here again what are at stake are the objectification and decentering that are proper to sociology, the very idea of a sociology. The problem is that of the relationship between the whole and its parts, society and individuals: if the whole obeys laws, then how can those who comprise it still be free? Doesn't the very idea of a scientific sociology imply the loss of individual freedom?

What characterizes Quetelet's social physics—and sociology more generally—is the abandonment of all individual or psychological perspective. The laws that sociology identifies are applied to the whole without being applied to each of its parts. No isomorphism exists between the individual and society: "These laws, thanks to the very manner in which we have defined them, no longer reveal anything about the individual, and as a consequence we can only apply them to individuals within certain limits. Any application of these laws to a particular person will be essentially false, likewise if we claimed to determine with mortality tables the time at which a person will die."[19] Sociology objectifies society as a reality "independent" of its parts. A paradoxical theory: how, in effect, could the whole exist independently of its parts? This thesis is well-nigh foundational to sociology. We find it in the celebrated Durkheimian rule: "To treat social facts as things." Society becomes a subject susceptible to a certain type of predication that is not applicable to the individuals who compose it. Society can be susceptible to laws even as individuals keep their free will.

Be that as it may, how are we to understand the relationship between the whole and its parts within a sociological framework where the whole and its parts each have their own mode of existence? What influence can freedom have on social evolution, and, inversely, what place does this determinism—the existence of social causalities—leave to individual freedoms?

From the point of view of the influence of individual liberties over society, Quetelet's response can be summarized in three propositions:

a. The first is epistemological. The effects of individual free will, considered en masse, cancel each other out. "The possibility of establishing a moral statistics and to deduce from it useful consequences depends entirely on this fundamental fact: human free will effaces itself and remains without observable effect when observations extend over a large number of individuals."[20] Individuals therefore only *appear* to be causes of irregularity. Freedom has the epistemological status of an accidental cause: it is chance itself. In other words, the hypothesis of the free will is not an obstacle for sociology, and sociology in no way implies that freedom does not exist. The question of freedom is not relevant to sociology.
b. Does freedom have a disruptive influence over the workings of the whole? Quetelet's response is surprising. The existence of free will, far from being a source of disorder, is rather a source of order: "This type of paradox is explained by considering that each man, by virtue of his free will and the circumstances that surround him, has created a normal state to which he constantly tends to return." And Quetelet further specifies, "This is the state that works best for our constitution: accidental causes may alter it, but we always tend to return to it."[21] Not only is free will a factor of order rather than disorder, but it is thanks to free will that social laws are more regular than physical laws: "Social phenomena, influenced by human free will, proceed from one year to the next with more regularity than phenomena purely influenced by material and chance causes."[22] Decidedly, Quetelet could not have been more successful in reversing the objection leveled against him: not only is the question of freedom indifferent to the sociologist, but, if we adopt it as a hypothesis, we must thank freedom for making sociology possible.
c. What are the effects we can expect from the exercise of liberty? Do individual liberties have an effect on the working of the whole? And if so, what kind of effect? What is freedom's power? "I believe," Quetelet writes, "that man possesses a moral force capable of modifying the laws that concern him; but this force only acts in the slowest manner, in such a way that the causes that influence the social system cannot succumb to any brusque alteration; as they have acted over a series of

years, they will continue to act during the years that follow, unless we manage to modify them."[23] In sum, no possibility of revolution exists. More precisely, if it is possible to have political revolutions, it is not possible to have a social revolution. This results from sociological decentering. The idea of social revolution implies a sort of omnipotence of liberty, whereas sociology wishes we mourn it.

Quetelet goes even further. Men, left to themselves, would have lived in a stationary state: "Man deprived of the benefit of science would necessarily be stationary. . . . He would endure the fate of all animated beings and in his diverse elements would display fluctuations that have their phases and their determined limits. But, since the beginning of the world, these fluctuations would not have undergone any variations, because nothing indicates that nature has altered its laws since this time." Put another way, to the extent that freedom is natural, it does not bestow on humans a status different from other living species. If humans have a history, if humans are more varied than any other species, if they are freed from their bare biological existence, it is thanks to science: "The only causes that can tolerate alterations in natural laws come from man, who, by using science, changes culture and manages to alter the averages and limits."[24]

But this first approach to the relationship between the whole and parts, in the sense of individuals and society, does not exhaust the problem. We have to envision the relationship in its inverse sense: if the hypothesis of freedom does not prevent the identification of social laws and remains compatible with the constitution of sociology, is it true, conversely, that the affirmation of social causalities does not entail a determination of wills? Quetelet's thesis is the following: "It is here that on the contrary we find an admirable harmony that, completely leaving man his free faculty of acting, has limited it with such wisdom that it can in no way hinder the immutable laws that preside over the conservation of worlds and the simplest elements that compose them."[25] In no way then does the existence of social laws entail a refutation of the existence of a free will.

The relationship between society and the individual is a complex one. On the one hand, there is the influence or action of society over individual behavior. The observation of social laws obliged us to assume the existence of factors that translate them into reality, an intermediary zone, an in-the-middle between society and individuals: influences, circumstances, morals, habits, practices, customs that chart society's influence on behavior. "These influences are so strong that we have no trouble predicting their outcome, even when we hardly know or do not know the persons concerned. Why then do you every day let yourself be influenced by these prejudices, if you are not convinced ahead of time that it is extremely probable the empire of causes will triumph over free will?"[26] And Quetelet specifies, "Our clothing, our strolls, our discourse, our pleasures, our meal times, even our sleeping times, are established by others. Is it surprising then that the traces of this slavery remain in the ensemble of statistically collected facts? Wills are subject to certain habits to which they yield as if they were necessities and, as these necessities remain the same each year, we also see them reproduce the same effects."[27]

If we must assume so many determinations, what status does liberty then have? Does it have the status of a power or a reactive force, of resistance or opposition? At the same time that Quetelet affirms that "the human inclination toward evil depends on his particular constitution, on the education he has received, on the circumstances in which he is found," he further specifies that it also depends, on the other hand, "on his free will, to which I freely attribute the greatest ability to modify all of his inclinations. He can therefore, if he wishes, become something other than what he is." In sum, we must abandon the metaphysical vocabulary of freedom for a more positive vocabulary of relations of force and resistance. Freedom is not a power of absolute self-determination. Being free does not mean being independent or undetermined. Freedom is doubtless a real power, however limited, to resist and react to the influences we experience.

And Quetelet uses the metaphor of the fall[28] and the accident in order to think about the relationship between social action and individual reaction in the case of crime: "If I took it upon myself to pull up the paving stones in front of my door and if someone came the next day to tell me that several people fell and were injured over the course of the night, should I be surprised? On the contrary, aren't these accidents very natural, and won't they be reproduced over the following nights? Would I not be in the wrong to continue pretending that I am not the cause of evil, that each person was free to come and go as he or she pleased and that those who fell only had themselves to blame? Well, many moral downfalls that transpire in the social order have the same origin; and we cannot try hard enough to remove the occasions that give rise to them."[29] Crime, fall, accident, this singular combination of a religious mode of objectification with the utterly dispassionate one of the accident is far from arbitrary. The fall is now replaced by the accident, which is defined exactly as the point of articulation between statistical regularity and individual freedom.

The Politics of Sociology

The sociological objectification of society is at odds with that of political liberalism. It is as if we were in another world: the whole has gained an existence almost independent of its parts. It is as if the relationship between the whole and its parts were inverted. On the one side there is the whole and its laws, such as the famous inclination toward crime. On the other side are individual liberties, which, if they permanently hold the power to modify these laws, in practice contribute to their formation. This all implies the disqualification of the politics of moralization, whose logic was precisely that of social change by means of individual action.

The consequence of this position is neither resignation nor passivity. It only entails changing the site where reforms and political action are applied—that we no longer act this way over individuals, but rather over what influences individuals (the "milieu"), over the causes of social evils, which is to say society itself. Society was no longer the setting in which (nor the instrument with which) reforms could operate according to the moralization-penalization dyad. It became its own object of reform. It now had to act on itself. Its first effect: to the extent that politics had to now set itself the task of acting on social causalities, sociology, whose task it is to make these causalities apparent, became political sociology. Political success would depend on the progress of sociology. Sociology carried with it a transformation of governmental rationality. As Louis-René Villermé expressed:

> These conclusions, or the information they express, are the necessary result of inclinations and conditions in which we are now or have been. The most effective thing that a skillful government and the zeal of enlightened, powerful, and philanthropic men can do is to change, insofar as it is allowed to them, the conditions in question, by counterbalancing evil effects with their opposites. Claiming to correct and prevent legal infractions with punishments and torture alone is to ignore the human heart and spirit, it is to fail to realize that the morality of peoples completely resides in habits and circumstance, that if there are guilty individuals, there are also prejudices, customs, positions, institutions that spawn crimes, and that these are, before all else, the institutions, positions, customs, prejudices that must be attacked or changed in order to stop public moral corruption.[30]

This politics has a name, social hygiene, as well as a privileged form, prevention (of which repression must be only one method), and an instrument, no longer justice, but administration.

If social policies had to change their target, they also had to revise their ambitions in the struggle against social evil. Penal policies, for example, could no longer claim to eradicate crime, as Quetelet's oft-used metaphor of the "budget" so aptly expresses. For every society there is a rate of criminality that is simultaneously unavoidable, normal, and even necessary for the stability of the whole. This is itself one of the facts of social preservation—Durkheim will go so far as to say "of health." It is without a doubt possible to contain it, master it, perhaps even make it decrease, but certainly not to make it disappear. What is abnormal is not the fact of crime in itself but rather the excessive variation of its rate.

As a consequence, a proper penal policy had to be one of prevention—penalizing offenders, of course, but above all aiming for reparation. If a certain level of criminality is normal, necessary, it also becomes imperative that those who suffer from it should not be left alone to bear its burden. If certain individual pains are necessary, it should be no less necessary to redistribute the burden socially. The offender, his crime, and his responsibility are connected, preemptively, with the conditions that caused them to be committed and, after the fact, with the protection of his victims.

Quetelet's sociology comprises a more general political dimension: it proposes an art of governing. Referencing a model that could have been inspired by Machiavelli's *The Prince*, Quetelet proposes no other art of government than one of self-preservation. The laws of the social system, like those of every other system, obey a unique principle of preservation. Sociologically, society can thus strictly have no other project than to preserve itself. Preserving the social system depends on maintaining the equilibrium of forces that comprise it. The art of governing is that of maintaining the system in equilibrium. Equilibrium must be the guiding principle of politics: "If this equilibrium does not occur on its own, we can produce it by adding to the existing forces a new force that is equal and directly opposed to their result. The art of governing resides in estimating the nature and direction of this result. We must perfectly understand the forces and tendencies of the parts that ordinarily divide a state in order to ascertain the means most capable of combating and paralyzing them."[31]

Machiavelli is reputed to have liberated politics from morality. He is thus credited with establishing the conditions for a realist politics. Quetelet proposed another kind of politics, based on another kind of positivity. Who can forget chapter 25 of *The Prince*, where Machiavelli explains that, when all is said and done, the prince is himself mastered by "Fortune": "Restricting myself more to particulars, let me say that one sees a prince prospering today and coming to ruin tomorrow without having seen him change his nature or his qualities. I believe this happens first because of the causes that have been discussed at length earlier. That is, that the prince who relies completely upon Fortune will come to ruin as soon as she changes. I also believe that the man who adapts his method of procedure to the nature of the times will prosper, and likewise, that the man who establishes his procedures out of tune with the times will come to grief."[32] This text evokes a relationship between politics and circumstance, history and nature that is perhaps no longer our own. In any case, it is not the kind of relationship we have learned to dream of since Quetelet and other sociologists taught us that, given the possibility of a scientific understanding of society, it was now possible to produce positive political outcomes without resorting to Machiavellian expedients.

CHAPTER 5

An Art of Combinations

The term "insurance" is particularly equivocal. It first of all designates institutions—that is, insurance institutions with various specializations and social forms: private companies, nationalized insurance, social insurance, mutual insurances, premium companies,[1] life insurance, accident insurance, fire insurance, liability insurance. Each of these insurance institutions is different from the others. In this first sense, it is more accurate to speak of "insurances" in the plural.

The use of the plural itself poses a question: what makes us group such different institutions under the same title of "insurance"? What qualities do they share? The term "insurance" can designate not only institutions but also what unifies these institutions in their diversity. In this second sense, "insurance" does not designate a concept so much as an abstract technology. In the vocabulary common among actuaries, economists, or public law advocates, one would say that insurance as a technology is an art of *combinations*.[2] Insurance itself is not a combination, but a matrix that allows for the creation of various combinations of insurance, appropriate for the function assigned to them and the useful effects expected of them, using the principles of a unique technology, the *technology of risk*. Insurance as technology is the art of combining elements of economic and social reality according to an ensemble of specific rules. The different insurance institutions follow from these combinations.

But the term "insurance" should also be understood in a third sense. In effect, what is the relationship between the abstract technology of insurance and the multiple institutions with which we enter into contracts or to which we are affiliated? It might be said that these institutions are applications of the technology. This would mean that insurance institutions are fundamentally all the same, apart from their specific objects or management style. This is not the case. Insurance institutions do not reproduce the same form for different objects. The form of maritime insurance is not that of nonmaritime insurance, and social insurance systems are not the same as nationalized insurance systems. Insurance institutions are not *the* application of the technology of risk. They are only ever *one* of its possible applications. The term "combination" suggests as much. Insurance institutions only ever express one combination among other possibilities. In this way, between the abstract technology and insurance institutions, there is room for a third term that we will call the insurance "form." If the elaboration of the abstract technology is the work of the actuary, if the creation of institutions is the work of the entrepreneur, we could say that the object of the sociologist, the historian, or the politician would be to determine why insurance institutions have taken one form rather than another at a specific moment, or why they should take this form rather than that one. Why do they use the technology of risk in this way rather than another? All of this, which cannot be assigned to either the technology itself or the institutions, refers to economic, moral, juridical, and political conditions—in a word, the social conditions that provide the market, the security market, for insurance. These conditions are not simply constraining; they will rather serve as a reference point for a business or a politics. The deciding factor in determining how the technology of insurance will be institutionalized, in what form and at what time, is the *insurantial imaginary*—that is, what is imagined to be a profitable, necessary, and sensible use of insurance technology at a certain stage of social development. For example, the birth of social insurance at the end of the nineteenth century should be analyzed as the realization of a new form of insurance, as an insurance combination tied to the development of an insurance imaginary that is in this instance political.

There is one insurance technology that takes on a certain form in certain institutions, according to a certain imaginary. It is clear that the articulation of these categories—*technology, institutions, form, imaginary*—proposes a mode of logical description of insurance and does not correspond to the historical process by which insurance, whether maritime or nonmaritime, was formed. The technology of insurance—that is, actuarial science—did not fall from the mathematical heavens to be incarnated in these institutions. It slowly emerged from the multiple practices that it had served to represent and rationalize. It is more the effect than the cause of these practices. And we would be wrong to think of it as definitively constituted. The practice of insurance never ceases to reform its own technology in ever-changing economic, moral, and political circumstances.

Risk

Insurance can be defined as "technology of risk." The term "risk," which we today find employed everywhere, only acquires a precise meaning as a category of this technology. It is an insurance neologism. It comes from the Italian *risco*, "that which cuts," which leads us to "ocean reef" and then to "a risk of the sea trade."[3] Jean-Baptiste Say's *New Dictionary of Political Economy* indicates that "the whole theory of insurance rests on the fundamental concept of risk."[4] The concept of risk is also to be found at the center of the juridical definition of insurance. Maurice Picard and André Besson write, "Risk is the fundamental element of insurance," specifying, "The concept of risk is an original concept belonging to law and the science of insurance, very different from the concept of risk used in civil law or contemporary language."[5] What then is a risk?

In everyday language, the term "risk" is taken as a synonym of danger, peril, or an unfortunate event that could befall someone. It designates an objective threat. In insurance, "risk" designates neither an event nor a type of actual event—"unfortunate" events—but a specific way of treating certain events that might happen to a group of individuals or, more precisely, to the values or capital possessed or represented by a collectivity of individuals, which is to say a population. In itself, nothing is a risk. No risk exists in reality. Inversely, everything can be a risk. It all depends on the manner in which we analyze danger and consider the event. As a technology of risk, insurance is first of all a schema of rationality, a way of taking apart, putting back together, of arranging certain elements in reality. The expression "to take risks," which characterizes the spirit of business, derives from the application of this type of calculus to economic and financial affairs.

More so than with the concepts of danger and peril, the concept of risk must be paired with the concepts of luck, chance, probability, eventuality, or happenstance on the one hand and with loss or damage on the other. The concept of the accident is located in the encounter between these two series. We only ever insure against an accident, against the probability of a loss of a good. Insurance, through the category of risk, objectifies every event as accident. The general model of insurance is the game: risk and accident are like the number on a roulette wheel or the randomly drawn card. With insurance, the game becomes a symbol of the world.

Insurance is not primarily a practice of indemnity or reparation. It is the practice of a certain type of rationality, one that is formalized by probabilistic calculus. This explains why we only ever insure against risks and why these risks can be as varied as death, an accident, hail, a sickness, a birth, military service, bankruptcy, or a trial. It would be hard to imagine today the number of risks already invented by insurers, many of which have not been commercial successes. The insurer does not spend his time passively noting the existence of risks to be guaranteed against. According to accepted wisdom, "he produces risks," making risks appear where once people believed they must endure or give in to the blows of fate. The purview of insurance is to constitute a certain type of objectivity, to give to certain familiar events a reality that alters their nature. By objectifying certain events as risk, insurance inverts their meanings: it turns into a possibility what had to this point been an obstacle. Insurance gives a new mode of existence to events that had previously been dreaded. It is a creator of value: "Insurance is eminently creative, when, having finished the work interrupted by the death of the frail father, it immediately provides the capital that should have been the fruit of savings. It is eminently creative, when it provides the elderly person who only has insufficient resources the income necessary to support his final days."[6] Insurance is the practice of a type of rationality that has the power to change the lives of individuals and populations.

There is thus no exclusive insurance domain, no type of object that by its nature might be insured. Everything can be a risk, to the extent that the type of event in question is susceptible to being treated according to the principles of the technology of insurance. Of course, there are technical limits to insurance. Of course, we can only insure risks that are sufficiently divided and dispersed, whose value does not exceed the capacities of the insurance fund. But it is remarkable that what at one moment appeared uninsurable subsequently becomes insurable, thanks to the progress of insurance practices, to the work of coinsurance or reinsurance.[7] The practice of reinsurance, in particular, with its own type of alchemy, clearly demonstrates what a risk can be from an insurance point of view: an abstract quantity that we can freely divide, so that an insurer can give up a part of it to a reinsurer from Munich or Zurich who will balance it with similar risks that happen to be at the other end of the world. What is the common ground between this unique event that each person fears individually (danger) and this singular being (risk) that is manipulated by the chain of insurers?

Insurance is one of the practices connected to what Pascal called "geometry of chance" or "algebra of luck" and what we today call "probabilistic calculus." It is one of the sister sciences, along with demography, econometrics, and opinion polls, of Quetelet's "social physics." Like the latter, it involves the application of probabilistic calculus to statistics. If sociology identified very different factors of social regularity than those of the law, if it only gave the law a localized function in social regulation, it did not affect the law in its own domain. It did not follow from the sociological analysis of crime's regularity that the juridical treatment of criminality in terms of liability was inadequate.[8] Although in philosophical terms, sociological analysis certainly undermined the law's pretension to being the great social regulator, it did not affect it in practice.

The same cannot be said for the development of insurance: insurance is a practice on the same order as law, which, like liability law [*le droit de la responsabilité*], is focused on the reparation and compensation of damages. Insurance and law are two practices of responsibility that proceed from different categories, a different economy, and a different regime. As such, they are exclusive in their claims to totality. For nearly two centuries, the famous conflict between *risk* and *fault* has fed the debate over civil responsibility. Sociology and insurance are animated by another theory and another practice of law—hence their historical importance. Their specificity is not based on politics or arguments in favor of social equality but is inherent in their type of rationality as *technologies*. Liability law and insurance are two techniques that apply to the same object. As technologies, they are independent of the politics that make use of them. It would be false to say that in the nineteenth century liberals were partisans of juridical responsibility, whereas socialists were advocates of insurance. Each drew from both technologies in their policies.

For the purposes of insurance, risk has three major characteristics: it is calculable; it is collective; it is a form of capital.

1. *Risk is calculable.* This is essential and what radically distinguishes insurance from gambling or the lottery. For an event to be a risk, it has to be possible to calculate its probability. Insurance rests on two foundations: on the one hand, the table or statistical chart that demonstrates the regularity of certain events; on the other, the probabilistic calculus applied to statistics, which allows us to assess the chances of the same events occurring.

In the logic of judgment that pertains to responsibility, the judge begins with the reality of the accident or damage in order to infer the existence of its cause in a behavioral fault. He supposes that without fault, no accident would have occurred. The insurer bases his calculations on the objective probability of an accident, independent of all will. It matters little whether the accident is the fault of one person or another, or that it could have been avoided. The fact is that whatever the good or ill will of individuals, whatever they did or did not want to do, the accident appears with a certain regularity.

The individual accident that seems simultaneously random and (with a little care) avoidable appears as calculable and foreseeable in the context of a population. We can foresee that there will be a certain number of accidents within the next year. The only unknown is: Who will be the victim? Who will draw the short straw? This does not mean that accidents are unavoidable, that they are in any way destined, but that their juridical perception in terms of fault and liability is not the only way of seeing them and that this way is perhaps neither the most relevant nor the most effective.

2. *Risk is collective.* If the accident as damage, misfortune, and suffering is always individual, if it befalls one person to the exclusion of another, the risk of the accident itself concerns a population. Properly speaking, there is no individual risk, otherwise risk would transform into a wager or a bet. In effect, it is only on the scale of a population that risk becomes calculable. The work of the insurer is precisely to constitute this population by selecting and dividing risks. Insurance can only matter for groups. It operates through the socialization of risks. Insurance makes each individual a part of a whole. Risk itself only exists as a unity, as a certainty, in the whole. Each insured individual only represents a fraction of the whole. Insurance operates through the constitution of mutualities, consciously in the case of mutual funds, unconsciously in the case of premium companies.

In the schema of juridical responsibility, the accident isolates the victim and its author—it distinguishes, singularizes, and separates them from others—since, in this system, the accident can only ever be the exception, something that comes to trouble an order considered naturally harmonious. The accident is due to an individual fault, negligence, or lack of prudence. It cannot be the rule. Insurance implies a completely different type of individualization. The idea of risk supposes that each individual composing a population can be treated the same: we are all risk factors and all subject to risk. This does not mean that each individual contributes to and runs the same risks. If the risk defines the whole, each individual is distinguished by his or her own probability of risk. Insurance individualizes, it defines each person as risk, but based on an individuality that no longer refers to an abstract norm; it is an individuality relative to other members of the insured population, an average or sociological individuality.

Insurance mutualities have unique characteristics. They are abstract mutualities, compared to specialized mutualities, such as those for the family, the corporation, the workers' union, or the municipality. We "belong" to the latter, to the extent that we respect their obligations, hierarchies, and their own order. The family has its rules just as the union has its internal regulations. These mutualities situate you, moralize you, educate you, and give you your being and your conscience. Insurance mutualities are completely different. They leave you to your own devices. They only grasp individuals from the abstract point of view of their risks. Insurance manifests a form of association that combines a maximum of socialization with a maximum of individualization. Insurance allows each person to benefit from the advantages of the whole while leaving individual existence free. It seems to reconcile these two antagonistic terms, "society" and "individual liberty." This, as we will see, is what would ensure its political success.

3. *Risk, finally, is a form of capital.* What is insured is not the damage as it is experienced, suffered, and felt by the one afflicted, but a form of capital whose loss is covered by the insurer. The damage as it is experienced is irreparable: after this, things will never be as they once were. We don't replace a father, a mother, any more than our bodily integrity after it is attacked. All of this, like suffering, is priceless. However, the task of insurance is to propose a financial compensation. Insurance—that is, the translation of damage into the language of risk—works by separating what is experienced from what will be compensated. The same event acquires a double status as something that takes place with all the wholeness of the irreparable and as a risk that can be compensated. With this comes a major problem—how to decide what relationship to establish between this unique event and its financial compensation. If the relationship may be adequate when it comes to the insurance of things, to the extent that things have a price, how does one establish the price of the body, of a hand, an arm, or a leg? There is no possible common measure between the compensation the insurer will provide and the loss suffered. The compensation will necessarily be arbitrary in relation to the damage—this does not mean that it is unjust, or that it does not follow any rules. Unlike juridical reparation, which is meant to cover the totality of the damage, insurance-based reparation will involve a fixed sum. We can always tell ourselves that life, like health, has no price, but the practice of life, health, and accident insurance ceaselessly attests that everything has a price, that we all have a price and that this price is not the same for all.

This divergence between the damage experienced by the injured party and the standard compensation delivered by the insurer gave rise to pitiful speculations, discussions, claims, and misunderstandings between the insurer and the insured. Before workplace accidents were compensated through social insurance, workers had to take their *patrons* to court. This combat was certainly unequal and unjust for the worker, but it made the struggle for the reparation of damages suffered a struggle against patronal power and for the recognition of the worker's own dignity. The worker needed to establish that his patron had committed a "tort." With accident insurance, the nature of this combat changed: the worker would now try to obtain a maximum of money from his disability. The expert replaced the judge. The expert would give you your insurance identity, designate your place on the pay scale where, according to the selected criteria, you "objectively" had your place.

From these three characteristics of risk, which compose the "actual value of possible damage over a given period of time,"[9] followed the definition of insurance: "Insurance is the compensation of the effects of chance through organized mutuality following statistical laws. . . . It does not eliminate chance, as has been wrongly suggested, but rather assigns chance its place. It does not make loss disappear, but it prevents loss from being felt because the loss is shared. Insurance is the mechanism that makes this sharing possible. It modifies the incidence of loss that the individual passes on to the community. It replaces a relationship of intensity with a relationship of extent."[10]

One might reproach this definition for not emphasizing what is perhaps from the social and juridical point of view the essential element of insurance combinations: the element of *justice*. What characterizes insurance is not that it distributes the burden of individual damages over a group, but that it allows this allocation to occur according to a rule of justice and law rather than a principle of aid or charity. The liberal idea was that the natural awarding of goods and evils is, as such, just. The free play of chance should not be disturbed. It was up to each person to freely and voluntarily guard against chance. From this it followed that adjudications of justice should hinge on an inquiry into the cause of damages. It was a question of determining whether the damage suffered was due to nature or to another person who must take responsibility for it. Insurance proposes an entirely different idea of justice. The idea of cause is replaced by the distribution of a collective burden where we are able to decide the contribution of each person according to a set of rules. The idea of risk does not designate the cause of damage, but rather the rule according to which we will distribute its cost. Insurance proposes a rule of justice that no longer references nature but the group, a social rule of justice that the group is free to establish.

Thus, insurance is the practice of a certain type of rationality. It does not have a set limited scope. It provides a general principle for objectifying things, humans, and their relations. It is simultaneously:

a. an economic and financial technique. This is moreover how it was born: from the church's prohibition of usury, which specified that interest was not to be condemned if it remunerated risk. Nonmaritime insurance derived from techniques of state borrowing, whether this took the speculative form of tontines or the already rational form Johan de Witt gave to the calculation of life annuities;[11]
b. a moral technology. To calculate a risk is to master time and discipline the future. As of the eighteenth century, to lead one's life as a business became the guiding principle of a morality whose cardinal virtue was foresight. To exercise foresight is not just about ceasing to live day to day, to safeguard against fate; it is also about mathematizing one's engagements. Above all, it means no longer suffering providence's judgments or the blows of destiny, but transforming one's relationship to nature, the world, and God, in such a way that if misfortune affects you, you will always be responsible because you have the means of dealing with its effects;
c. a technology for the reparation and compensation of damages. Insurance is a way of administering justice that competes with the law. It establishes a type of justice where the damage suffered by one person is borne by all, where individual responsibility becomes collective and social.

Taken together, these elements make insurance a *political technology*. It is a technology of social forces that mobilizes and uses such forces in remarkable ways: "Men are not simply juxtaposed against one another in society; the reciprocal penetration of souls and interests establishes a strict solidarity between them. Insurance contributes for a large part to the sense of a solidarity of interests."[12] It constitutes a mode of association that allows those involved to establish a consensus on the rules of justice governing over them. Insurance allows one to dream of a contractual justice where the order of conventions replaces the natural order; the ideal of a society where the logic of a social contract, which is no longer mythical but truly real, allocates each person's share of social advantages and burdens. Insurance gives us a glimpse of a solution to the problem of workers' misery and insecurity. Thanks to insurance and the minimal contribution it required of them, workers could protect themselves against the evils that constantly threatened them.

Insurance, finally, frees from fear: "Delivered from fear, man is king of creation: he dares to explore; the ocean itself obeys him, it hands its fortune over to him."[13] Insurance allows us to be entrepreneurial; as such, it multiplies wealth. From this point of view, insurance should be compared to religion: "The emancipation of action through insurance can only be compared to what religion achieves in another domain. . . . The feeling of comprehensive security that is already provoked by piecemeal insurance and that will be much more fully provoked by complete insurance seems to transpose the religious faith of the believer onto an exclusively earthly plane."[14]

The Most Precious Capital; or, How Yukong Moved Mountains

While it is true that there is an abstract technology of insurance and an art of insurance combinations, it does not follow that insurance institutions represent their straightforward application.[15] The history of insurance does not recount the successive applications of a technology that was invented once upon a time in the eighteenth century by Richard Price and William Morgan, cofounders of the first "scientific" life insurance company, the Equitable Life Assurance Society (1762). Actuarial science did not precede the practice of insurance; rather, it followed it. This is evident for maritime insurance, born at the end of the Middle Ages in Genoa or Florence, well before the Chevalier de Méré asked Pascal for the solution to his problems. It is also true of non-maritime insurance. The fire insurance that historians date to the Great Fire of London (1666) preceded the birth of actuarial techniques by a century. The history of insurance is as political as it is technical or scientific. Insurance slowly emerged from neighboring practices that had long rivaled it, from speculative practices that were both closely aligned and very different: mutual aid societies and fraternities, gambling and lotteries, and finally the formation of life annuities and other forms of state borrowing. The history of insurance should be written in terms of the rationalization of institutions and existing practices and the successive rationalization of the first forms of insurance.

Probabilistic calculus was one of the essential instruments of this process. What is noteworthy here is that this work of rationalization did not only make existing institutions more effective, it also changed their nature by making them instruments of a new morality. The history of insurance recounts the history of modern struggles in the field of morality: however much we boast of the morality of insurance strategies, opposing them to the immorality of wagers or bets, this does not mean that these new institutions immediately replaced the old. The form taken by the first types of nonmaritime insurance was connected to this political-moral struggle. The victory and current dominance of insurance also represent the victory of a certain type of rationality in morality and politics, a certain alliance between calculation and morality.

It would be entirely insufficient to explain insurance as a function of some hypothetical need for security. As the works of Jean Halpérin have sufficiently shown, in order for insurance to be possible, the conditions of a completely new need for security had to appear. Insurance is the daughter of capital. It is a form of security that had no place in feudal society, insofar as property was tied to land and the individual was inserted into familial, religious, or corporative solidarities. By contrast, it becomes necessary as soon as fortune becomes mobile, as soon as capital is set in circulation and finds itself exposed to the dangers of circulation. It is not by chance that the first form of insurance was maritime insurance: "The only domain that allowed one to escape the rigid feudal framework is the sea. The foundation of the feudal world is essentially landed property; the sea escapes social and political hierarchy."[16] As security of capital, insurance was also born as a means of bypassing the church's prohibition against usury. Thus, for Halpérin, the origin of insurance is not to be found in the old forms of "interdependent security": "It is not in the feeling of solidarity but in the spirit of profit and gain that insurance appeared for the first time as an autonomous social institution."[17] Insurance goes hand in hand with the dislocation of feudal solidarities, the liberation and self-determination of the individual. It is a security practice tied to individualism. Insurance is the daughter of the capitalist ethics that authors like Werner Sombart and Max Weber so well described. When Weber describes capitalist rationality, when he demonstrates that the spirit of capitalism is defined by the fact that its rationality became a morality, what better example could be found than insurance? The birth of life insurance in the eighteenth century latched onto the moral reform movement that made foresight the cardinal virtue of social man. Life insurance would be its essential and model institution. And if the first insurance institutions made the proportionality between premium and risk the golden rule of insurance (thus excluding the idea of social transfers), this was less indicative of a technical actuarial imperative than the political-moral imaginary in which insurance was born, an imaginary that would direct the first forms of insurance institution.

Insurance not only involves the introduction of calculation into the conduct of life—its "economization"—but also brings with it an appropriate manner for individuals to objectify themselves individually and in their relation to others. Individually, it makes humans appear as capital. In the 1860s, a whole campaign in favor of life insurance was based on this theme. "Man is a form of capital," announced Louis Richard, for example, explaining, "There is no form of capital more precious than the human, source of all wealth."[18] The source of all value is itself a potential value that becomes current value thanks to insurance. If insuring oneself can be a duty, it is first of all thanks to the elementary desire for frugality that directs us to not destroy wealth.

"Man is a form of capital," repeated Edmond About in a best-selling book on insurance, where he specified that the value of this capital depends on its association with others:

> You know that the wheels on cars, by being driven over paving stones, each day leave more than twenty kilos of iron in the streets of Paris. These twenty kilos of exceedingly precious metal are not annihilated but rather lost. Their so-to-speak infinitesimal division puts them out of use and makes them intangible. Suppose a patient and ingenious worker managed to collect these bits of iron, to restore their cohesion, their resistance and all their other useful qualities. He forges them into a lever. Hasn't he created capital for human use? A centime coin is no more a form of capital than a sliver of iron is a lever. It is hardly valuable. You will find very few individuals who would be sensitive to the loss or gain of a centime, because a single centime gets you nothing. But he who managed by an honest procedure to collect this useless little centime from his fellow earthly citizens would create 10 million in capital, which is to say an attractive lever for moving mountains.[19]

Where individually we are nothing, united we become everything. Insuring oneself is thus not only an individual duty, in the sense that not insuring oneself "is to commit an act of egoism and culpable frivolity against one's family . . . to take responsibility for one's future misery."[20] It is even a social duty. The uninsured weigh doubly on society through the assistance that must be given to them if they become victims of an accident, through the "centime" that has not been given and that, reunited with the others, would have created a form of capital useful for all.

The idea of solidarity belongs to the economy of insurance ahead of all other social concerns. All by itself, insurance induces a certain objectification of the relationship between the whole and its parts, between society and its individuals, one that we also find in future doctrines of solidarity—a solidarity in space and time, from which the objectification of individual duty as a social duty is derived. When the individual only takes his or her own limited point of view into account, he or she is guilty not only of egoism but also of causing an enormous social shortfall. Insurance, through the alchemy of its calculations, brings out the wastefulness of individualism. It moves us to derive individual obligations from the whole. Edmond About imagines the consequences of a million-dollar home burning down:

> From the sum total accumulated to our present day by man and for man, we must deduct one million francs. The great association of humanity is today less rich than it was yesterday. That does not sound significant, because you do not know how tight the solidarity is that unites us all. But reflect for a brief moment and you will understand that the poor, like the wealthy, are interested in the accumulation of social capital. . . . The destruction of one million francs already accumulated is more harmful to you than the destruction of 100 million centimes in the hands of 100 million individuals. You will tell me that the damage is fundamentally identical, since in both cases the total of public wealth will decrease by the same amount. But recall that capital is a lever, an instrument destined to make work less arduous and more useful, and tell me if the destruction of a lever weighing five kilos would not be a greater evil than the removal of one-hundredth of a gram of iron from 500,000 levers.[21]

One plus one equals more than two. The whole is greater than the sum of its parts. What then has the ability to foil the most obvious laws of arithmetic, to transform addition into multiplication? The "unconscious solidarity that unites men" and to which "insurance simultaneously gives a precise, scientific, and practical form."[22] Insurance is thus nothing other than the mechanism that practically reveals society to itself, manifesting it and explaining it as it truly is: "Life insurance is not only an imperious duty, it is the expression of a universal law. This law is one of the most salient, one of the most strongly ingrained in all of nature: we call it the law of the conservation of species; it dictates that the burdens of past generations will not fall upon their descendants and that future generations will be prepared, safeguarded, insured by the generation that preceded them."[23] The idea of solidarity, which represents one of the great social doctrines of the end of the nineteenth century, doubtless has multiple origins. One of them is to be found in the type of objectification that is implied in the very technology of insurance. It is not uninteresting to note that, before being an antiliberal social doctrine supported by the socialists, solidarity provided the theme for a great publicity campaign in favor of life insurance and was leveraged to promote the idea that insurance was a social duty. Here we find the properly capitalist source of the doctrine of solidarity.

Two Moralities in Conflict

This struggle for morality was also a tactical one on the part of the insurers, a way of winning recognition and legitimacy. It is difficult to imagine today, where insurance is one of the pillars of our economic and social order, and where Parliament constantly multiplies insurance obligations: at the beginning of the nineteenth century, insurance operations (aside from maritime ones) were completely suspect and, as far as life insurance and liability insurance were concerned, prohibited as being contrary to public order and proper morality. And if one allowed for fire insurance, it was exclusively in the form of mutualities, with the understanding that the reciprocal surveillance of the insured would prevent the abuses to which the institution was subject.[24]

Insurance was, first, accused of allowing the insured to relax the attention they should give to their own affairs when it did not open the door to delinquency. *Insurance leads to crime*: it seems that this adage dates back to these first forms of life insurance, which consisted in bets and wagers made on other people's lives, and which were, in effect, true invitations to make the "insured" disappear. Bets could be placed on everything: on King George III's return to good health, on the life of Robert Walpole, on the acquittal or the condemnation of the Duchess of Kingstown accused of bigamy, just as in France one bet on the life of the Duke of Orléans, the Regent of France, and on the lifespan or favor of Louis XV's mistresses.[25] These practices, which accompanied the first maritime insurance contracts, had been outlawed across all of Europe and particularly by Colbert in his 1681 ordinance on maritime trade.[26] They nonetheless persisted, as demonstrated by an insurance policy dating from May 21, 1813, and preserved in the archives of Lloyd's of London. In this contract, four insurers, at a premium of 3 guineas for every 100 pounds, agreed to pay William Barrington 500 pounds if Napoleon Bonaparte died or was taken prisoner before June 21, 1813.[27] For a long time after, life insurance contracted through a third party would be suspected of courting the disappearance of the insured. In 1864, during the trial of La Pommeraye (a doctor who assassinated a patient whom he had personally insured), the attorney general of the appellate court, Dupin, again reminded the court that no subsequent laws had overturned Colbert's ban.

The juridical hostility toward insurance was also motivated by the principled position that "it is against propriety and public integrity to insure human lives."[28] The same opinion was expressed by a number of authors, including Jean-Étienne-Marie Portalis: "Man exists beyond price: his life cannot be considered an object of commerce; his death cannot become the material for speculation. These types of pacts over the life and death of a man are odious, and they cannot be without danger. The greed involved in speculating on a citizen's remaining days is often a neighbor to the crime that would cut them short."[29]

It was conceded, however, that "good mores are decided by social mores," that yesterday's mores are not those of today, and are therefore relative. There was a legal morality and there were judges who were concerned, in a somewhat abstract fashion, solely with respect for life. There were also economic and political advantages that could be drawn from insurance strategies. On two occasions, in 1787 and 1818, the Conseil d'État,[30] which authorized the activities of the first life insurance companies despite Colbert's prohibition, had occasion to drive home the point: what the companies were offering above all was a means of escaping usury and moralizing financial investments; they would "also reanimate the feelings of affection and reciprocal interest that form the good will of society and increase its strength." The life insurance contract acquired its marks of nobility from the fact that it embraced the most tender family sentiments, that it gave expression to the most respectable virtues of sociability, and that by insuring life it became "the most powerful antidote against egoism."[31] In a sense, morality changed registers. It was no longer a question of deciding if there was some fundamental argument against life insurance, if life could or could not have a price, but only a question of evaluating the economic and social advantages of these calculations. Portalis had declared, "Such actions are in themselves vicious and have nothing of real use to offer that could compensate for the vices and abuses to which they are susceptible." He was wrong. Insurance was swept forward by this new morality of economy, time, and solidarity that became dominant at the very moment Portalis reproduced Colbert's old condemnation.

Moreover, the prohibition against life insurance rested on an analytic error, a confusion over the object of insurance. It was not life that was insured. The great jurist Jean Marie Pardessus, rightly distinguishing the insured risk from the thing insured, offered the following definitive explanation: "It is true that the life of a man cannot be sold for any sum; but we must not conclude, based on the impossibility of this particular calculation, that we cannot assess the harm caused by the death of a person. This, in fact, is the goal of insurance. An insurer does not purchase the things he insures; he undertakes to compensate the harm caused by their loss."[32]

The second great obstacle to the development of insurance concerned *malpractice insurance*.[33] If "good morals" were opposed to life insurance, in this case it was "public order" that made malpractice insurance difficult. If one can insure faults, thus shifting their weight onto others and onto the insured collective, then what will become of responsibility? How can malpractice insurance be tolerated in a political economy based on the idea that "responsibility is the perfect regulator of human action"? Is the idea that one might "cover" one's responsibility for a modest price morally, and thus socially, tolerable?

Furthermore, aren't such forms of insurance comparable to the kinds of limitations of liability that are naturally prohibited by the law? Eighteenth-century juridical doctrine was very firm on this point. Robert Joseph Pothier specified that "I may not reasonably contract with someone that he will be responsible for the faults I commit. Such a clause would be absurd, illusory, and fraudulent." And Balthazard-Marie Émérigon wrote, "It would be, in effect, intolerable for the insured to be compensated by another for a loss he himself caused."[34] Here, the conflict between law and insurance touches on something essential to the political economy of modern societies, something essential to the principle of their regulation.

At first we might have thought that there were technical obstacles to malpractice insurance. Aren't the unknowns that characterize insurable risk mixed up with what the jurists classify as unforeseen circumstances and that exclude all assignation of fault? The jurists would really have preferred this to be the case—that we could assimilate risk and unforeseen circumstances and fold insurance categories into legal categories. But the concept of risk, which expresses the statistical probability of certain events independent of their cause, is not the same thing as the unforeseen circumstance, which designates, on the contrary, a cause of damage independent of humans, their will, what they can foresee and should avoid. It matters little that the accident might be due to someone's imprudence or negligence. This doesn't imply that there are no risks, but only that agency is one risk factor among others. Insurance implies a specific objectification of liberty.

Evidently, this does not mean that insurers are not in practice interested in the conduct of those they insure. Insurance takes interest in the loss of the insured thing. Any behavior that could be attributed to chance, when considered abstractly, can become the object of speculation from the moment there is insurance. The problem of "subjective risk" is very different from the previous one: previously, the issue was knowing if a so-called criminal fault was insurable; now, it falls upon insurers to prevent frauds and scams, to prevent willful misrepresentation on the part of the insured. Why, in the nineteenth century, did insurers refuse to insure gross misconduct? The obstacle is not public order and its preventative measures, but rather insurers' fears regarding insurance speculation: "The insured is liable for the damage caused by his fault when the fault is of such a kind that he would obviously not have abandoned himself to such an excess of negligence if he had not been insured."[35] Moreover, several practical considerations militated in favor of malpractice insurance. The first concerned the insurance contract itself: "Insurance whose guarantee does not extend to faults would be illusory. The majority of accidents are caused by faults."[36] And the jurist Charles Bonaventure Marie Toullier wrote, "It seems to us that this proposition, that the insurer is not under any obligation with regard to the accident caused by the recognized fault of the insured, should be modified and restricted to the case of gross misconduct on the level of fraud: because, when I insure my house against fire, my intention is properly to safeguard against any accident, even one that involuntarily comes from my own action."[37]

The position of these authors testifies to a remarkable slippage. It consists of making the contractual logic of insurance prevail over the criminal logic of responsibility. The behavior of the author of damage, when insured, is not considered in itself, in relation to the needs of public order, but only to the extent that it might affect the good-faith terms of the contract, as if the insurance contract had become the reference for a new definition of public order—hence the recourse to a neutral concept of the accident and the marginalization of the question of fault.

This tolerant position can be understood in the context, which is fundamentally entirely private, of damage insurance: only the insured and their insurer were concerned by the matter. The insured was the first victim of their fault, and to fail to cover this fault would have resulted in the prohibition of a contract that had become too unequal. But the problem of malpractice insurance was posed in the form of liability insurance in those specific instances where, this time, the fault of the insured caused harm to another. In principle, liability insurance covers the crimes and misdemeanors of the insured. How can we admit, though, that we must use the contribution of another to pay for the insured's carelessness? Isn't it a flagrant contradiction of the principles of public order and its preventative measures to allow someone to escape punishment for their faults? With regard to the principle of responsibility, we cannot see how it would be possible to tolerate such a guarantee.

Absolutely. But this is to forget that if liability insurance contradicts the juridical administration of responsibility, it protects the same interests as the law, and, in particular, the victim's interests. The victim no longer has to fear that the author of the damages might become insolvent. This formidable conflict over the best way of protecting the same interests was decided in 1844–45 in a case concerning the legality of the actions of the first accident insurance company, L'Automédon. On August 21, 1844, the Paris Court of Commerce declared that "while it was allowable to insure accidents that could befall the insured, it is contrary to public order to admit insurance for misdemeanors that may be committed by the insured or those they employ. It would result in an incitation to negligence." As a consequence, without the question even being asked, the court declared, "the agreements between the parties to be void, since contrary to good morals and public order."[38] Thus the principles of public order were reasserted: we cannot contract our way out of responsibility.

This judgment condemned the very principle of liability insurance. In order to respond, L'Automédon had to appeal to the greatest jurists of the era, including Pardessus. Why ban this contract, he began, when other insurance contracts (relating to fire, leases) are authorized? And why do this when liability insurance, in contrast to damage insurance, profits the victim, not the insured? In liability insurance, the insured has no interest in causing damage when he or she will never profit from it. In sum, liability insurance safeguards the victim rather than the author of the damage.

Even better, this type of insurance, which protects the victims of carelessness, responds to the spirit of the law by refusing "to evenly weigh the author of a fault and careless harm of another with the person who suffers from this carelessness." Finally, the guarantee offered by L'Automédon was limited by its insurance rate and only covered the misdemeanor of the insured, which is to say, according to Pardessus, "deeds that doubtlessly have harmed someone, but that were committed without malice, without intent to harm, and only through simple carelessness." Nothing, then, is more useful and more moral than this institution. Through a ruling of July 1, 1845, the Paris court decided in favor of L'Automédon's defense.

Guiding the 1804 parliament was the idea that social interests falling under a dispositive of responsibility would be best protected once all carelessness, all error was designated as fault and all fault was punished. The victim would always be compensated, and, with no leniency in place, each was called upon to act with the greatest prudence. The idea of fault allowed for compensation, penalization, and prevention to be defined in relation to each other, for the good of the public order. Insurance introduced a new manner of protecting the same social interests: on the one hand, the interest of the insured who is saved from destitution thanks to insurance, and on the other, the interests of the victims who are simultaneously protected against the uncertainty of a trial and the eventual insolvency of those responsible. Insurance ended up compensating for the shortcomings of the juridical dispositive of responsibility more than it contravened it. It would not be long before the protection of public order through the punishment of faults would appear as a very theoretical, complex, inept, and somewhat incomprehensible objective with regard to the practical needs to be satisfied—when the juridical technique of responsibility would appear as truly rudimentary with regard to what insurance was capable of, since insurance had an advantage over the juridical dispositive of responsibility. The juridical dispositive only offers compensation by condemning the activity causing damage or, at least, the manner in which the activity occurs. Insurance, on the contrary, simultaneously enables the continuation of the activity and the protection of its eventual victims. Now the development of industrial societies would multiply the situations where a profitable and useful activity causes damages that cannot be attributed to a fault, situations where the legal distinction between the activity and the manner in which it is conducted are shown to be artificial—so much so that when forced to choose between forbidding the activity and forcing it to compensate for any damages as if they were intrinsic risks, the second solution is chosen. Thus we arrive at insurance.

In practice, it was the courts that would end up managing this conflict between morality and responsibility. They would do so with the dual intention of according total value to the insurance contract and ensuring that victims received always greater protection. So they multiplied the number of faults, thus creating the very market for responsibility exploited by insurers. In return, insurance allowed judges to extend both the domain and the rate of compensation, and with it the domain of responsibilities that were themselves inconceivable without insurance, according to a spiraling process that could only effectively lead to the disqualification of liability law from the task of managing the reparation of damages.

CHAPTER 6

Universal Politics

Our vision of insurance assumes a rift between social insurance and its other institutional forms, such as premium companies and mutual funds. It is assumed that the former, eminent instruments of the welfare state, were created without a lucrative end in order to come to the aid of the most destitute and provide them with necessary security. The latter, on the contrary, covering civil risks, are assumed to obey (at least in the case of premium companies) the capitalist logic of the market and profit. We make such a distinction between these two institutions that it is difficult to imagine that they might be branches of the same tree, that they could have a common history and could proceed from a similar political preoccupation. Initially, insurance was social. It was as social institutions that the first companies sought and gained recognition beginning in the eighteenth century. And it was only through subsequent splits, as part of the same project of security, that different insurance institutions became progressively distinct from each other and finally became opposed to each other, as they are today.

Since its birth, insurance has maintained a special relationship with the political.[1] Initially, insurance was presented as the most adept instrument for carrying out the new politics of assistance that formed at the end of the eighteenth century. It would be a genuine prudential institution. At least that is how its first entrepreneurs sold its merits in the difficult battle they had to wage to gain recognition. The state, in making this misunderstood institution (long mistaken for the speculative practices of financial pursuits) an element of its policy, gave it an official status. The state, at least in France, contributed more than a little to the creation and development of the insurance market. It was, and still is, one of insurance's biggest advocates. And by endowing themselves with a public service mission, private insurers found that public policies gave them a strong foundation for developing the security market. The relationship between insurance and the state, between popular or social insurance and private insurance, is as much a relationship of encouragement as it is one of competition. In any case, the history of insurance institutions in France since the eighteenth century is not one of private companies continuously threatened by ever-expanding projects of nationalization. It is a history in which political programs and the private companies that made use of them worked hand in hand.

Insurance is also a technique of association that immediately presents itself as symbolic of the social relationship. Already, Gottfried Wilhelm Leibniz, in a minor work titled *Insurances*, compared political association to a ship and suggested that it could not fulfill its proper role if the risks of sailing only affected some, while others suffered no losses.[2] In this perspective, the relations between insurance and the state could come to fruition under three broad forms. The first was that of the institution of *popular insurance*. The state used insurance to directly satisfy its constitutional obligations for assistance and security. This created, in contradiction with liberal principles, the problem of state intervention in the sphere of the economy. It was justified by the fact that in creating such institutions the state did not compete with private initiative, but rather filled in its gaps. The state could also become an insurer and nationalize certain branches of insurance in areas that had been previously exploited by private companies, like fire insurance or agricultural insurance. This hypothesis assumed a greater proximity between the state and insurance. Insurance was no longer leveraged only as a political instrument, but as a form of social relation. It was simultaneously maintained that insurance could only truly fulfill its role when organized by the state and that the state could only fulfill its vision by embracing the networks of insurance-based solidarity.

However, these initial ways of discussing the relationship between the state and insurance could be interpreted as being inscribed in a program where insurance was no longer solely an applied technique, but the defining principle of an autonomous politics. A more general philosophy could be drawn from the technique of insurance, a political philosophy from which we would derive the necessity of reforming the state and governmental practices. Here we discern a horizon of insurance utopias where insurance, as if internally divided between rational framework and institution, is well positioned to propose itself as a politics. Insurance thus becomes a principle of social reform. It allows one to conceive of an ideal society governed by its own internal principles of regulation. What begins to take shape here is a concept that no prior relationship between the state and insurance had provided: a politics of *social security*, which, strictly speaking, means a program for the autoinstitution or autoregulation of society.

These different modes of organizing the relationship between the state and insurance were either invented or institutionalized in the first half of the nineteenth century. The first institutions of social insurance date back to at least 1850; the program of social security as a political program was definitively formulated by Émile de Giraudin in 1852. Therefore, from the Second Empire onward (the era, we note, in which insurance operations truly began), all of the elements for a politics of insurance that could serve as an alternative to the liberal politics of law and responsibility were available.

Insurance and Foresight

The institution of popular insurance recounts the history of relations between a politics—the politics of foresight—and actuarial techniques. Initially, the project of a unique institution was formed, one that, addressing itself to all individuals of all classes, would offer to each individual a form of security adapted to his or her needs. But the technique of insurance is resistant to such vast projects: its institutions must obey the fundamental principle of the division of risks. Therefore, somewhat paradoxically, as insurance progressively penetrated society and integrated itself into the politics of security, it multiplied into separate institutions. Social insurance presupposed a plan, a program, and a politics: it materialized in the act of distinguishing between risks and coordinating institutions so that they would complement each other.

The Great Art

The first French life insurance company, the Royal Insurance Company, dates back to 1787.[3] Its founding is linked to financial speculations that took place at the end of the Old Regime. It bears witness to the fact that, in a context where a new politics of foresight was emerging, the market for security and popular savings accounts now appeared lucrative.

The Royal Company proposed an initial form of insurance characterized by the idea that a unique institution, in place as a monopoly, could support the needs of all categories of the population. Insurance was presented as a vast public service, the best auxiliary of the state with regard to civil security. But let's follow in a little detail the remarkable *Prospectus* in which Étienne Clavière, one of the company's founders, set forth his program.[4] In effect, in this text, Clavière sets out the framework that will guide the various insurance institutions for a long time to come.

The Royal Company, first, did not exactly propose to develop the particular branch of insurance that would be life insurance, but rather to use actuarial techniques for all circumstances. It offered each person a security that is always necessary, and even more so for the less fortunate.

The Royal Company presented itself as the kind of workers' prudential institution that had been hitherto missing, preventing workers from successful saving. Saving was now their sole salvation: "The impoverished worker is persuaded that it is impossible to make small savings bear any fruit. This prejudice removes from him the mindset of foresight and the habit of only seeing his earnings as a more or less abundant subsistence." Life insurance would allow workers to break free from the inevitability of poverty and despondency. Here they would find an opportunity to safeguard the meager savings that their modest earnings allowed them to make. These payments would become profitable, and workers would thus be able to escape from the abusive temptations of unscrupulous speculators.

Hear the polemical thrust throughout this discourse. If workers do not save, it is because they prefer to gamble and because the suffering of their condition means that only the outlandish profits of wagers are attractive to them. Insurance, through the wisdom of its combinations, offers the public authorities the chance to put an end to behaviors so detrimental to good social order. But insurance will only achieve this if it can take the place of these other forms of investment, adventurous but popular, such as the lottery or tontines. Behind Clavière's discourse, there is an offer and an appeal addressed to the powers that be: to use the world of savings to moralize the worker's behavior in exchange for monopoly rights.

But the Royal Company also targets the "owner of a modest sum of capital, necessary to his needs, who dares not lend a portion of it to a friend who is worthy of all confidence, but whose premature death might render the lender insolvent." Life insurance contracted by the borrower would allow the lender "to give in to feelings of friendship." It is also aimed "at the individual who, thwarted by unfortunate circumstances, has trouble finding the means of surviving along with his family." The individual glimpses a sure fortune in a faraway voyage, but dares not depart for fear of leaving his or her family in distress if he or she happens to die before returning. The Royal Company's operations are addressed to all situations because there is no economic action or initiative that does not carry its own risk and uncertainty, because there is no gain that could not also be associated with a loss. Insurance, by providing security, has the power to transform the negative into a positive. It has the power to liberate all the economic capacities that were hitherto constrained by justifiable fear, to the great detriment of the nation's prosperity.

Insurance is not only useful to each person individually. In Clavière's program, each particular usage of insurance supports the others so that the one is multiplied by the other. The Royal Company would unite these services and bend them toward the public good. Each person's rational pursuit of the good would lead to general utility. Life insurance, Clavière continues, comes "to the aid *of the precious sentiment that attaches the individual to the others who must survive him*." Indeed, insurance unites not only activities but also generations. The indefinite time of collective life replaces each person's limited lifetime. Precisely, by giving to each the guarantee of all, insurance offers the state the guarantee of its own eternity. It offers itself up as the best precaution against the danger of revolution.

The Royal Company of Clavière's design was thus not a combination meant for the rich, which might also happen to be of service to the poor. It was a combination that, by encouraging industry and allowing the "laboring class to use their savings to acquire resources against poverty," would multiply public wealth at the same time as it reduced begging. The main problem with the politics of assistance was that the money used was unproductive in several ways: charitable money, subtracted from production, impoverished the state at the very moment it needed money to create businesses and employment. Charitable money engendered poverty that charity had in turn to support indefinitely. Additionally, this was a mode of aid that embittered those it helped, demoralizing them, making them hostile to society. Insurance was this marvelous institution that could in a single gesture invert these signs: the poor would help themselves, the money pocketed would be invested in industry, and the assistance offered would no longer offend the assisted: "THE GREAT ART," if we can allow the Royal Company to express itself, "THE GREAT MEANS OF MAKING A SOCIETY PROSPER WITH GLORY, IS TO CREATE SECURITY WITHOUT DEPRESSING OR DEBASING THOSE WHO NEED IT." Insurance made a practical politics out of foresight. It could even claim to be the *institution* of foresight.

But insurance, if it is possible, brings with it even more benefits: "Insurance," Clavière pursues, "secures against misfortune, without harming either the industry or the activity. Insurance encourages, on the contrary, work or thrift. It gives reason to be confident on each occasion that confidence is necessary to support the exercise of talent and the love of work. Finally, the amenities insurance offers to the benevolent acts of friendship, filial piety, paternal affection, the conjugal union, in a word, to the generous sentiments, can only serve to multiply the practice of all virtues and reanimate this attractive sensitivity that tends toward the happiness of society." Insurance presents itself as the best instrument of social regulation. It is only ever the art of rationally associating the people with themselves. In this way government would only ever be serving its own interests when it recognizes the strategic interests of insurance.

Setting aside the ban imposed by Colbert a century earlier, the royal power did not remain indifferent to such attractive arguments. The Conseil d'État's declaration of November 3, 1787, which authorized the Royal Company and accorded it a fifteen-year monopoly, seemed, in effect, to be directly inspired by Clavière's *Prospectus*.

> The King being made aware of the nature and principles of various establishments founded in Europe under the name Insurance over Life, has recognized that they contain precious advantages; that, when naturalized in France, they would be of a great utility; that a considerable number of individuals of every sex and age would find in it the ease of insuring their life, or the terms of their life, their income, or their capital, either for themselves in their old age or for their survivors for whom they wish to leave resources or benefits, that these types of moderate and equitably managed Insurances would emancipate the sale of every type of capital and life annuities from all-too-common usury, or would extend their enjoyment to the surviving; that, finally, these varied strategies, usefully connecting the present to the future, will reanimate these feelings of affection and reciprocal interest that form the happiness of society and increase its power.

The Savings Bank

The Royal Company would not survive the French Revolution. The Revolution, indeed, would suppress every insurance business under the pretext that "insurance substitutes the service of calculation for the service of humanity and banishes the general sentimentality that forms the basis of society."[5] Thus began a long purgatory for life insurance companies that would not end until the Second Empire, which is to say at a moment when insurance was elevated to the rank of public policy.

This is not to say that the revolutionaries were hostile to insurance techniques.[6] Quite the contrary, the Revolution, by making foresight the guiding principle of the new politics of poverty, would definitively seal the marriage between social policy and insurance. But whereas the *Prospectus* of the Royal Company described the project of a unique institution that would unite the poor and the wealthy, the Revolution would introduce a fundamental division between popular insurance, which it tried to institute in the form of the *savings bank*, and the activity of insurance companies, financial institutions technically reserved for the ultra-rich, which remained banned until 1818.[7]

Driven by the philanthropic movement and the numerous projects for reforming public assistance, plans to create *savings banks* or *prudential funds*—the vocabulary is not yet set—would flourish at the time of the Revolution.[8] The same year, 1787, when the Royal Company gained its privilege, Antoine Lavoisier pleaded the case for a *project of insurance funds in favor of the people against the attacks of misery and old age* before the Orléans Provincial Assembly. "The poor have no resources for investing their earnings. The amounts they earn on a day-to-day basis are too small to form an interest-bearing capital. If they have neither the time nor the means to calculate, to watch over the use of their savings, to follow their investment, it falls upon public authorities to watch over and calculate it for them."[9]

The Revolution would see the birth of numerous other projects. In 1790, a geographical engineer proposed the establishment of a national insurance fund that would have been the first credit insurance company, since it planned to guarantee financial instruments using the assets of subscribers as collateral. On March 19, 1793, the Convention decreed that in order to "assist the foresight of citizens who would like to build up their resources, at whatever time, an establishment under the name of the *National Prudential Fund* would be formed, in accordance with a yet to be determined plan and organization." The plan was drafted by Laplace but remained in the initial stages.[10] And Condorcet, in the tenth stage of the *Sketch of the Future Progress of the Human Mind*, after noting that the population that lives off of industry confronts in its lifetime "a sort of life's savings dependent upon chance" and that this was "a necessary cause of inequality, dependence, and poverty," explained that we might

> in large part abolish this situation, by setting chance against itself, by ensuring a form of support for the person who attains old age, a support arising from their savings, but augmented by those of other persons, who, making a similar contribution, die before they have any need of using it; by procuring, through similar means, an equal resource for both women who lose their husbands and children who lose their father, or for those families whose patriarch lives longer than usual; lastly, in preparing for those children, who arrive at an age where they are capable of working for themselves and of creating a new family, the benefit of a capital sufficient

to employ their industry, and increased at the expense of those whose premature death prevents them from arriving at this point.[11]

And Condorcet explained that insurance should be employed in the name of social power or by associations of individuals for the benefit of the "entirety of society."

From all of these plans, it appears that the savings bank is more a form of insurance than it is an institution. It is first of all characterized by the fact that it is addressed to the poor. Only limited deposits are allowed. All speculation is to be avoided. The institution must offer all assurances of security. This is the great imperative that all public insurance institutions must obey: avoid any disappointment on the part of the account holder or the insured, offer an individual the greatest certainty regarding the results that have been promised. Fundamentally, it is a question of turning savings into a "right." The practical result was to connect the institution to the state through the appointment of state personnel.

The savings bank is an institution that, in a somewhat indistinct manner, puts actuarial techniques at the service of the less fortunate. It safeguards against all accidents, all misfortune, all needs. It is a liberal institution, structured around the two categories of liberty (the freedom to deposit and withdraw) and property: its true objective is not so much to ensure that workers find the necessary aid in their own savings as it is to allow them to attain property and to escape their wage-based condition, the true cause of insecurity.

The savings bank is, if we can use the term, a symbolic institution: its value is tied less to its results than to the gesture of thrift that it facilitates. Its justification resides in the very fact of its existence. The gesture of saving is such that once it is practiced it is sufficient to produce a true spiritual conversion in its practitioners, a change in their relationship to themselves, when they discover in themselves a great contentment, as if they were another person. Moreover, the new ethical relationship facilitated by the savings bank assumes an immediately political value: "The worker, the artisan, and the domestic servant who develop the habit of depositing what they can from their wages, devote themselves to conserving even the smallest amounts . . . he makes a future for himself, a sense of ownership is established . . . the word property has reverberated in his heart, he is now enveloped in this magic and powerful bond that so strongly attaches man to the country in which he is born, which guarantees his devotion to the laws, his attachment to his country's institutions, to its rights, to the freedoms they promise, and the framework that protects them," says La

Rouchefoucauld-Liancourt, the first president of the Paris Savings Bank.[12] The savings bank, then, is an essentially moral economic institution that, modifying the subject's ethics, ties together morality, economics, and politics.

Paradoxically, while, at the end of the eighteenth century, savings banks would arise almost everywhere throughout Europe, the first savings bank in France, the Paris Savings Bank, would only emerge in 1818. There are doubtless several reasons for this late date. First of all, political ones: the instability, confusion, and difficulties of the Revolution did not provide the proper conditions for its emergence. But this late date also attests to the fact that insurance, despite the quality of its champions, remained a technique that was too new, little known, and suspect. Why would one put more faith in Clavière's or Condorcet's speculations than in practices (certainly less rigorous, but nonetheless familiar and proven) like tontines? The fact that the Revolution witnessed a highly popular revival of tontines—these forms of wagers on life that were suppressed as official loans in 1770 and that insurance advocates ceaselessly denounced as irrational and (thus) immoral—attests to this.[13] The benevolent administration of the savings bank testified to its morality in the eyes of the powerful. This served almost as a way of whitewashing a financial strategy whose legality, at the time, was far from established.

Setting aside the brief experience of the Royal Company, the savings bank is the first form of public insurance. It would remain the very model of the prudential institution for the working classes up until 1840. In keeping with the moralizing view of saving that we have already seen formulated by Clavière, the savings bank was designed to do battle against the speculative practices of gaming, betting, and the always-popular lotteries. The same Benjamin Delessert, who in 1818 founded the first savings bank, banned the lottery in 1835. And when, in the wake of the Revolution of 1848, Adolphe Thiers, responsible for a report on prudence and public assistance, compared the different prudential institutions for workers, he concluded in favor of the savings bank: "There," he said, "everything is moral, fertile, because man raises himself, raises his children, and is ensured bread in his old age, not from the hands of a public institution, mathematically paying out what he had invested, but from the appreciative hands of his children, whose fate he has provided for."[14]

Mutual Aid Societies

The discovery of pauperism, the new objectification of the poor, and the marked modification of the politics of foresight that characterized the 1830s would highlight the deficiencies of savings banks. The savings bank was tied to the idea that a politics of workers' foresight was possible; it rested on the idea of a worker's good nature, only awaiting the right occasion to manifest itself. The discovery of pauperism led to the abandonment of this philosophy. It was not because workers were bad, but because their nature was discovered to be different from the one previously attributed to them. This is an important change of direction: as the movement in favor of patronage and patronal institutions attests, from now on the policy was no longer to turn workers into property owners but to turn the condition of wage labor (to this point synonymous with insecurity, uncertainty, and dependence) into something insured and stable and to offer workers a minimal guarantee for their needs and those of their family.

It had been assumed that savings banks were sufficient for everything. Now its limitations were denounced: the capital saved by workers would only really be helpful over the long term; yet their needs were pressing and immediate. Indeed, given the modesty of the savings, their needs would never be met. Deposits are voluntary, but workers are not bound by any regularity, and at any moment they can withdraw what they have just deposited; their savings are dependent on their slightest whims, liable to be squandered at every opportunity. The savings bank, finally, leaves workers to their own devices; it obliges them to muster the courage to save from within. Jean-Baptiste Ferrouillat summarized this series of now-common critiques in his report to the 1848 Constituent Assembly's Committee on Labor: "The factors that render this institution powerless to protect the worker against disease, disability, or old age are firstly that they do not sufficiently bind the worker to saving and secondly that saving thus constituted is only the result of an isolated effort, an individual power."[15]

"What is to be concluded from this?" asked Ferrouillat. "That the savings bank is not an admirable institution? No, it doubtless is, but it must be supplemented." The focus will now be placed on a particular kind of workers' institution whose origins often date back a very long time, institutions that were tolerated even when they were not encouraged by those in power, despite the Le Chapelier law: *mutual aid societies*. These institutions were credited with all possible virtues: first of all, the virtue of voluntary association; the virtue of a contractual obligation that connected workers to foresight, protecting them against their own inconstancy; the virtue of a protection that was rendered sufficient by the combination of resources and that was in practice established upon the first payment of members' dues; finally, the virtue of a mutual surveillance, ensured by each member's desire not to have to bear the burden of another member's misbehavior.[16] The investment in mutual aid societies marked the passage from a problematic of being free to save to the problematic of *being obliged* to exercise foresight, a concern that would remain central to security politics until the beginning of the twentieth century. The mutual aid society presented the advantage of creating a worker's right without recourse to a statist constraint, which is to say in a manner that remained compatible with liberal principles. This was an institution that presented the dual advantage of linking together liberty and obligation and presenting the very form of mutual aid as consistent with morality.

Nonetheless, mutual aid could only become the pivot of workers' security on two conditions: by ensuring that mutual aid societies did not serve to foment troubles and political alliances and by making sure that they offered the worker the true guarantee of a right. Thus, workers had to reform themselves: no longer living day-to-day, spending the money left over at the end of the year or on the useless banquet celebrations of patron saints. Mutual aid societies would have to learn to divide risks: to distinguish between aid in the case of illness or injury and the much more complex problem of retirements; to set contributions in proportion to the risk represented by each member covered; to know how to adapt the number of their members to the technical imperatives of the risks they planned to cover, but without ever extending coverage and thus jeopardizing the principle of mutual surveillance and the prevention of inevitable abuses. Put simply, they would have to become true mutual insurance societies.[17]

Thus, in the 1830s, under the impetus of a new politics of workers' foresight, insurance and its technologies would inspire a general reform of mutual aid societies. Gérando recommended that parliament protect and encourage them: "Does it not fall to the public authority to prompt them, to favor them through properly formulated exceptions, to simplify formalities and procedures in their favor, to make sure they offer indispensable safeguards, whether to their members, or third parties, or the general community? Is it not obliged to establish a system of control, or demand a reporting process, to protect them against their own shortcomings? The law, in this regard, will pose several fundamental rules, and the administration will execute them. This tutelage, trained in liberal views, will be the most effective way to guard against abuses."[18] Mutual aid societies that had hitherto been administered by and for workers would now have actuaries as honorary members who would watch over their proper administration in the guise of *patrons*, contributing to the institution's services without benefiting from them. Above all, mutual aid societies were expected to rigorously separate risk involving sickness (and injury) from the risk of old age, their confusion being the source of inevitable failures. Even better, they would have to exclude the coverage of old-age risk (even though this was one of their principal attractions) and limit themselves to the risks of sickness, the only risks they could reasonably insure. Mutual aid societies that had once been traditional instruments of fraternal aid, offering their aid according to needs, were now transformed into institutions specializing in the coverage of a defined risk.

The use of insurance techniques in the politics of foresight thus led to a new institutional division. This time, in the very heart of popular insurance institutions, there would be savings banks offering a generic protection, structured over the long term and for setting up a first home, and mutual aid societies, schools of sociability for covering the risks of illness, while old-age insurance, for its part, would be organized at the national level.[19] This institutional framework describes the dispositive of social insurance that was formalized under the Second Republic. From this point on, the merits of mutual aid societies would be incessantly rehearsed. To the extent that they observed the principles of insurance, they would have to be developed and multiplied. This politics would garner the largest possible consensus: liberals, whether they be monarchists, Bonapartists, or republicans, would come together with a nonnegligible portion of the working class. The alliance was consecrated by the law of April 1, 1898, known as the "Mutual Aid Charter," which turned mutual aid societies into health insurance institutions.[20]

The First Social Insurance

With the Revolution of 1848, the question of aid became the focus of two debates: the first, begun as a discussion of article 8 of the Constitutional Project, concerned the principle of a *right* to aid in favor of the poor and destitute. This famous debate, more theoretical than practical, concerned the recognition of a *right to work*. The second debate, taking place in the more restrained setting of the labor committee, sought to practically organize the new policy of workers' foresight. The Legislative Assembly returned to the reports of the Constituent Assembly committee and adopted two laws on June 18 and July 15, 1850, the first relating to the creation of a *National Retirement Bank* and the second to the creation of *mutual aid societies*. Without being too anachronistic, they can be seen as the first French social insurance laws.

Two members of the Constituent Assembly, René Waldeck-Rousseau (the father of the future minister of the Third Republic) and Pierre Marcellin Rouveure, had submitted, on June 8 and December 9, 1848, two legislative proposals concerning the creation of *national prudential funds*.[21] Organized on a communal basis, nationally federated, these funds would guarantee workers against the risks of unemployment, sickness, accidents, and old age. Sustained by the workers, they would also benefit from the contribution of the state and local collectivities.[22] They would admit honorary members. These projects turned the problem of workers' aid into an occasion for the creation of a vast system of association and cooperation between the poor and the wealthy, the workers with the patrons, and everyone with the state. These were communal utopias inspired by the model of mutual aid societies, simultaneously seeing themselves as their extension and universalization. Their defect was to go against the now dominant principle of the division of risks, to fail to distinguish between the idea of solidarity and its technical organization, between social insurance as a program of associating society with itself and the institutions capable of practically setting it in motion.

This is at least how the rapporteur Ferrouillat responded to them, in the name of the Labor Committee, in an important text synthesizing the new program of social prudentialism. "It is not enough for the Republic to proclaim liberty as an absolute right; it must strive to give freedom to each person as a real faculty. *It must follow the worker in all the phases of his existence, from the cradle to the grave, constantly covering him with its ceaseless protection and guiding him by the hand, incrementally, to the possession of capital, property, the real protector of his liberty*, the material sign of his emancipation."[23] What we find here is a principle of state intervention that states that such intervention should obey the principle of the division of risks. Unemployment is not insurable, for reasons that are both objective—inherent in its nature—and subjective: "How is forced unemployment distinguished from voluntary unemployment, the cessation of work inflicted by necessity from unemployment that is only the fruit of laziness, ill will, or lack of foresight?"[24] As for the risks of illness and old age, they cannot be covered by the same institutions and do not call for the same type of state intervention. The risk of illness (and accidents) is the purview of mutual aid societies. The most important thing is to leave them the greatest creative and organizational freedom. Yet it still falls to the government to "establish societies where they are missing" and to "improve those that exist."[25] The government should "clarify" things for institutions by providing them with statistics that "will give them the appropriate model of illness, accidents, occurring in each locality, each industry, each profession" and will allow them to determine their best operating conditions.[26] A cantonal commission would be charged with gathering and redistributing this indispensable knowledge and encouraging the formation of new societies. Finally, it is up to the government to favor, in particular by acknowledging their public utility, those institutions that conform to the requirements deemed necessary.[27] The conclusion of Ferrouillat's first chapter: "We have attempted to reconcile the legitimate needs of liberty with the workers' best interest. We have made the state the representative, the protector, and not the general regulator of these mutual aid societies. It does not command, it invites; it does not oppress, it directs; it does not constrain, it encourages."

The problem of retirement was posed in a completely different manner. "Here, everything is yet to be done. The mutual aid societies were not adequate to the size of the task they undertook. The state, through the power of its means of action, through the reach of the resources at its disposal, is perfectly capable of filling this gap. It alone is placed high enough to be accepted as *general insurer* by workers of all professions."[28] Thus, the new politics of foresight, built on insurance techniques, by breaking with liberal principles, led to the state being given the role of insurer. But it was no longer so much the principle of state intervention that caused a problem as it was the conditions of this intervention: in particular the problem that would now infuse the politics of security was that of *obligation*. Ferrouillat opposed it, recalling the principle that "foresight, as useful as it is, should never be imposed." The state would create a pension fund; the worker would be free to benefit from it.

The Legislative Assembly was to reconsider these two legislative projects in the terms posed by Ferrouillat. Nonetheless, their draftsman, Denys Benoist d'Azy, would seek to imbue them with a greater respect for liberal principles. While Ferrouillat had not even mentioned the term, Benoist d'Azy from the very start recalled the role ascribed to "benevolent aid" in the alleviation of misery: "What is needed for real progress *is for foresight and benevolence to develop in equal proportion*."[29] Concerning mutual aid societies, he proposed the guiding principle that "the law can do very little, because the first foundation, indispensable to these institutions, is complete liberty."[30] Of course, mutual aid societies should be designed according to insurance techniques, but without ever becoming, as Ferrouillat intended, true "mutual aid societies," regulated by a law that would allow them to escape the economy of benevolence. The use of insurance should satisfy the traditional imperatives of the politics of security: to make the administration of aid the occasion for an exchange of commitments that reinforces the social bond.

The major problem was how to organize a retirement fund, given the decisive problem of obligation. One might be afraid, in effect, that if workers were not forced to contribute, then the fund, which was nonetheless created for workers, would remain unused. Firstly, because the workers' wages were so low that they would not allow them to make the necessary deposits; secondly, and above all, because the lack of foresight that was now presumed to be innate in workers would never allow them to make the effort required. Liberals were in a truly difficult position. They would not and could not rely on an obligation that meant for them the end of the politics of foresight, which is to say their own undoing, all the while knowing well that the partisans of obligation, already numerous, were in practice right: the success of the institution required obligation. Hence their arguments oscillated between an appeal to rather abstract first principles such as respect for freedom of commerce and industry and an invocation of the insurmountable practical difficulties that would result from an obligation to pay into the system.

Napoleon III and his minister Jean-Baptiste Dumas, deeming these reasons insufficient, sought to reinforce the role of the state. Concerning retirements, they proposed a system of subsidized liberty: the state was committed to helping those who helped themselves. It was no longer only about providing workers with institutions they would be encouraged to use (as had been the logic of the savings banks) but to turn these institutions into true instruments of the state, means of penetrating civil society, ways of organically connecting the citizen to the state.

Napoleon III understood the political benefits he could draw from state-organized insurance. Insurance was a mode of socialization that promised to resolve the problem whose importance Napoleon III had highlighted in his political works: that of the organization of the masses and the role of the intermediary classes. The presidents of the mutual aid societies would have to play the role of "intermediaries."[31] In insurance there was the idea of a direct contractual connection between the citizen and the state, one that Ferrouillat, at the end of his report, had expressed remarkably well: "Seen from the political point of view, this institution does not have a lesser importance. *It is a guarantee of the country's order and security. It creates a solidarity, a community of interests between the state and the worker that can only benefit the public interest.* . . . Having entered into this vast association, the worker remains interested in the strengthening of society and the development of public prosperity throughout his entire life. *His fortune is connected to that of the state.* Now the day when a man, who in the past had been embattled against society by poverty and suffering, exploited by criminal passions, can genuinely say to himself, '*I am the state*,' *will be the day when the era of revolutions will be over (of this, citizens, you can be sure).*"[32]

The savings bank was praised for its moralizing value. The act of saving supposed on the part of the saver a relationship of the self toward the self that immediately created a citizen connected to the public good. By giving it a sort of contractual materiality, insurance made this relationship both stronger and more limiting. Benoist d'Azy and Dumas repeatedly stressed this point over the course of the debate: "This is a contract that is established between a paying worker and the state."[33] Social insurance no longer made the law an instrument of constraint, but a contract. It transformed the nature of the law and the relationship between society and the state. Insurance introduced the original idea of a body of law that would be neither public nor private and that would soon be defined as "social." Well before Otto von Bismarck, Napoleon III understood social insurance. And if he could only bring it about under the still imperfect form of the laws of 1850 and, as we will see, of 1868, it is because the political circumstances, still mostly dominated by liberal arguments, did not allow for anything else.

Insurance and Universality

From the first savings banks to Napoleon III's social insurance program, the relationship between insurance and politics remained an instrumental one. Once the politics of security was defined as a politics of foresight, the technique of insurance presented itself as that which should inform the institutions to be created. At the same time that benevolence and foresight took the place of charity in the politics of assistance, insurance took the place of the general hospital and the poorhouse. Each new inflection in the politics of foresight was the occasion for a more insistent demand on the techniques of insurance. These latter, in turn, impose on aid programs their own categories and their own type of rationality. Savings banks, mutual aid societies, the National Retirement Fund, eventually the National Accident Insurance Fund, these are the institutions that trace the growth of insurance in social policies.

In the same stroke, another relationship between insurance and politics became possible, conceivable, even necessary. Since the birth of insurance, the singular homology between insurance and the idea of society had been noted: insurance offered one of the most eminent expressions of the idea of association. Inversely, society, in order to be conceptually consistent, would have to organize itself as a vast form of insurance. Thus emerged a new proximity between insurance and the political that forms the basis of projects to nationalize insurance and bring it under the control of the state. The term "nationalization" should be understood in two senses:

- Either we think that insurance needs to be national, because, given the statistical laws that govern it, it is only on the national level that it will produce all of the useful effects we expect from it;
- Or, in a slightly different sense, insurance should be nationalized, because it is only when it is nationalized that it will be conceptually consistent. This is what the phalangist Raoul Boudon advocated in 1840 while formulating the project for a Unitary and National Insurance Organization.[34] It would be natural for insurance to take the form of mutual aid and be organized by the state. Uniting "all contributors across all national departments, it would allow for all types of risks to be covered at the fairest price." Better, "with large and small lending mutual support to each other," premiums should not only be calculated proportionally "according to the chances of ruin courted by each," but also according to the resources each person disposes of, which is to say according to a mechanism of social transfer so that "the economy and humanity are found in perfect agreement." Napoleon III sought to place the form of the private contract in the service of the political; Boudon's project, on the other hand, was inspired by an inverse dream: to give the insurance contract the same form as the social contract, as if society and insurance could only definitively become themselves by overlapping each other.

Of course, these were only utopias. They were self-justifying. The Revolution of 1848 would see numerous projects for nationalizing insurance, some of which carried official weight, like the one defended by Charles Duclerc, the finance minister, concerning fire insurance: "What greater mission is there for a government than to generalize the application of a principle, which, until now, in France, has only imperfectly penetrated the habits and spirit of populations?"[35]

Insurance therefore has a much more general political purview than social matters alone. It is not only a function within the state, a principle of socialization, a way of instrumentalizing the contract that connects the state to the citizen. Insurance will only fulfill its social function when the state itself becomes the insurer. This osmosis contained an implicit reversal of the relationship between insurance and politics: if the state alone can give its full power to insurance, this is because it is itself nothing but a vast form of insurance and should itself be organized in a manner that is conceptually consistent with this fact. Insurance is not just a technology that politics should know how to put to work. It is a defining principle of politics, a principle of social reform.

Émile de Girardin would implement this change of perspective in *The Universal Politics*, which he published in 1852 while in exile in Brussels.[36] De Girardin made insurance appear as a pure political technology, as if abstracted from the institutions that had hitherto embodied it.

The first move made in *The Universal Politics* consisted of elevating the category of risk (which had to this point been considered technical) to the status of a philosophical category. The philosophy of risk is characterized by the suspension, the abstraction, of every moral or religious interpretation of the world:

> Universal politics, such as I have conceived it, is universal insurance. Each has his role. For Catholic priests it is to teach and demonstrate the existence of the Holy Trinity, original sin, eternal damnation, purgatory, transubstantiation, etc. For Protestant ministers, it is to teach and prove the opposite of everything that ministers of every other denomination teach and show. More limited is the role I have given myself. I suppose, I would like to suppose: that God does not exist, or, if he does exist, it is impossible for man to prove his existence; that the world exists by itself and by itself alone; that man has no original sin to redeem; that man possesses memory and reason the way a flame possesses warmth and light; that man can only be corporeally reincarnated in the child he produces; that man's intellect only survives in the ideas for which he is known; that man should not wait to receive in a future life reward or punishment for his current behavior.[37]

Theology and morality are modes of evaluation necessarily characterized by disputes and divisions because they do not keep to the strict materiality of facts. The philosophy of risk, on the other hand, can claim universality because it reduces each event to its pure facticity. "Morally, there exists neither good nor evil; materially, there are only risks." This is a universalization of risk, then, that produces a general secularization of values. Crime, theft, war, earthquakes, death, misery—these are nothing more than nearly identical risks.

The philosophy of risk proposes a particularly unique type of analysis: a sort of zero degree of analysis, a way of neutralizing values from the moment they are affirmed, which, however, is not a skepticism. It recognizes no other principle of evaluation than the pure relationship of attack and defense, the pure relationship of forces with no other qualification:

> Effectively, only risks exist, risks against which man, obeying his inherent law of self-preservation, which is also the law of the conservation of matter, seeks to insure himself through his available means. . . . The necessity of

defense is born of the risk of attack. The idea of associating with others is born of the necessity for defense. From the idea of association are born, under diverse names, the town and the nation. Each risk gave rise to a corresponding means of weakening or averting the risk. Religion itself was a means primitively and universally conjured up by the weak to rein in the strong, used by the oppressed to bend the oppressors to their will, and by the poor to gain the pity of the rich.[38]

The philosophy of risk is a philosophy of social defense that introduces the essential idea that society cannot locate the principle of its own governance outside of itself. It abolishes all reference to a nature and posits that truth does not exist anywhere else than in the current status of the social relation. Émile de Girardin would derive a complete political philosophy from this premise of a radical socialization of judgment. Political association should be defined in relation to the risk that it has to combat: it should take the form of a "universal insurance," and the social contract should be a contract based on mutual insurance. Furthermore, since the risks are calculable, the new politics could conceivably take a scientific form: "Probabilistic calculus, applied to the life of nations, to the events of war and revolution, is the foundation of all high politics. According to whether this calculation is rigorous or false, extensive or shallow, politics is glorious or dire, great or small. To govern is to foresee!"[39]

The social contract thus takes on the form of an insurance contract. All citizens are now insured. Hence, at once emerges a new type of identification for individuals and new tasks for government. The first will consist of establishing a *statistics of risks*, complete and without gaps. To conceive of politics as insurance goes hand in hand with the burden of exhaustive records, minute controls, a systematic and continuous collection of information. To those who counter that such a regime would exclude all liberty, Émile de Girardin would respond, "No, this will not be the destruction of all liberty, this will be the destruction of all obscurity."[40] The enabling condition of this insurance program, as well as its desired effect, is social transparency: to reduce the grey zones and act in such a way that at any given moment one has an adequate knowledge of each person's identity. To be sure, the contents of this knowledge are precisely defined: the identity of each is not reducible to our current civil status; one is only the risk one represents for others. I am a risk, in an active sense, to the extent I create risks for others and, in a passive sense, to the extent I am a risk that others must bear. Each person's being is thus fundamentally a being for others, a social being.

This regime of identification is the pivot of the system of "universal insurance." Émile de Girardin proposed that each person could be equipped with a sort of *livret* or passport, which he calls a "life registry," which would be both an identity card and an insurance policy and number that, like the present-day social security number, would serve as a national identification number. The life registry not only comprises details about the insured, his "individual bill of health," his "declaration of assets and liabilities," but also, on the opposite side, "the national bill of health," the state's annual budget for expenditures and revenues and a summary of "all of the statistical documents that clarify all interests, all professions, all industries."[41] As an insurance contract, the identity card thus materializes the social contract. The life registry in effect can be understood in two ways: on the one hand, it gives those in power the means of identifying each person; on the other, it shows each individual his or her role and place in universal insurance. Thus each person finds his or her identity in relation to the whole of which he or she is a part. The relationship each person has with his or her self is mediated by others. "It would be easy to demonstrate that life is a great double entry register, where each individual, having his open account, is credited and debited without knowing it. To harm one's fellow man is to debit a quantity equal to the damage that he has either caused or attempted to cause whereas being useful is to earn a credit equal to what your fellow man owes you. In this way the precept of reciprocity only allows for the reciprocity of good and never the reciprocity of evil."[42] This philosophy of insurance involves a concept of the interdependence of individuals that will soon be developed under the name "solidarity"; Girardin designates it by the term "reciprocity." Insurance proposes a modality of the social relation that, through the solidarities it creates, places my own benefit in the benefit of others. It contains the idea that the liberal divide between rights and duties must be effaced. It turns obligations toward others into positive obligations, finding their justification in the very interest of the one who is compelled: "Fraternity imposes on man the opposite of his interest since it demands his disinterest; the reciprocity it provides exonerates him and requires no sacrifice from him."[43]

From this idea of the universal insurance state, Émile de Girardin drew a number of political consequences. Regarding electoral matters, he proposed to "substitute the freedom of opinions for the war between parties,"[44] the formula implying that universal suffrage should not be organized with the aim of establishing the temporary domination of a majority, but as a permanent consultation of opinion. In the manner of our contemporary opinion polls, universal suffrage would become "an instrument to measure or weigh opinion." Regarding social matters, Émile de Girardin recommended an insurance system destined to guarantee the worker a minimum wage whose costs would be attributed to labor itself, rather than to workers. The worker would thus acquire a right that Girardin proposed calling a right *of* work in opposition to the right *to* work.[45] In penal matters, finally, he proposed suppressing prisons (not only because they were ineffective but because they produced criminals) and replacing them with a regime of *publicity* combined with financial reparations. Crime would now only be recorded and marked down on the life registry. "Judges," he said, "no longer *condemn*, they *register*." Freed from all deliberation on what constitutes criminality, penal judgment observes, registers, and lets public opinion respond. The penalty, thus, will always be adapted to social demands. "To observe the fact, without having to qualify it as a misdemeanor or crime, is to punish the perpetrator, since it is to assign blame, contempt, or abhorrence, according to the indulgence or rigor of the time and country. The penalty should not go any further or stop short of this. Thus the punishment of the crime committed is the crime's identification. The criminal's executioner is the criminal himself." The same effect of visibility that Bentham places in the Panopticon Émile de Girardin finds in the insurance society, where each person is definitively placed under the gaze of others and subject to the permanent control of public opinion. Thus penal politics becomes a politics of pure social defense.

Of course, we must not give more importance to Émile de Girardin's speculations than they deserve. Nonetheless, note that, as one of his biographers writes, "his ideas received immense public attention, and, far from going unnoticed, were passionately discussed by his contemporaries, the greatest of whom did not dismiss them," including Victor Hugo and Proudhon.[46] *The Universal Politics* went through numerous editions and was the subject of a long review in the article "Insurance" in the *Grand Larousse du XIXe siècle.* Without a doubt, the work owed its success to the fact that it proposed a profoundly original political idea that had two major characteristics. Insurance offered the means of breaking from liberal individualism without falling into the agony of socialism. Insurance, in effect, presents a dream in the realm of the political: it represents "association happily reconciled with each person's liberty and equality."[47] Insurance is a mode of socialization not bound to any place and compatible with the greatest mobility. It seems able to reconcile the irreconcilable: group affiliation and liberty, solidarity and liberty, "individualism and reciprocity." It proposes an alternative solution to the relationship between security and liberty, a problem that the liberal juridical economy resolved through the separation of rights and duties. That is, with this difference: while the idea of the opposition between security and liberty runs through liberal economy, insurance by contrast establishes the principle of their mutual reinforcement.

The idea of insurance developed in *The Universal Politics* also offered a practical program for a positive politics, resolutely freed of all moral, religious, or philosophical a priori. Better still, it offered the idea of a governmentality without a fundamental guiding principle, a governmentality reducible to a pure pragmatics of the social relation. The universalization of insurance made it possible to annul the divorce between society and state in favor of a society finally reconciled with itself. And society could directly govern itself without any exterior reference: it could *self-manage*, being bound to no rule other than that of maintaining society's harmony with itself. Thus, if insurance had gotten its start in the formation of the politics of social foresight, it could also designate its own political philosophy offering a wholesale alternative to liberal philosophy. This is what Émile de Girardin brought to light in a program informed by probabilistic rationality, the same rationality that Quetelet was so forcefully developing at the very same moment.

PART III

The Recognition of Professional Risk

Over the course of the first half of the nineteenth century, the practices of responsibility were thus singularly complicated. If the legal practice, the immediate endorsement of the principle of responsibility, remained the reference, its prevalence was now contested by the patronal practices of the social economy and by insurance practices. Each obeyed its own type of rationality; a unique strategy, its own manner of thinking about problems of security, runs through each; and each asserted itself as a claim to totality, so that these practices could develop only through conflict. This conflict characterizes the history of responsibility in the nineteenth century.

This conflict of responsibilities was driven by the development of industrial societies. Soon it had appeared that the categories of civil law were insufficient to resolve the problems posed by industrialization. Industrialization imposed the development of a unique industrial legislation that could also really come into conflict with the general principles of common law implicated by the liberal division of obligations. The *patrons*, for their part, confronted with the specific problem of the formation of an industrial workforce, organized their businesses according to an economy of power that was not only foreign to law, but would make it possible to elude the law's control. Finally, the multiplication of the activities and damages resulting from industrialization provoked the birth of damage and liability insurance. In a word, industrial societies developed by questioning the manner in which social regulation had been conceived, which is to say, by questioning the general principle of responsibility. The necessity of reforming the liberal diagram was a part of the industrial process itself.

The question of workplace accidents was the privileged site for the expression and condensation of the conflict of responsibilities.

This was what rendered it so important. The question was symbolic of the problems of security posed by industrialization, and this was a domain where the common law of responsibility demonstrated its inadequacy in particularly striking ways. The desire of the courts to ameliorate the fate of victims could not proceed without exacerbating struggles within businesses and problematized the manner in which the *patrons* sought to govern them. This led the *patrons* to resort to insurance practices, which in turn multiplied the problems rather than resolving them. The debate over workplace accident reparation would also begin with the decisive question of reforming liability law and, more profoundly, with the question of choosing a new diagram of social regulation. The debate was significant and would last eighteen years. It was a matter of agreeing on a new way of thinking about responsibility, one that broke with the philosophy of fault. The concept of professional risk would allow for a distinction between the problem of the causality of damages and the rules for assigning their costs. It was discovered that the problem of attribution was a social problem that did not need to be subordinated to the workings of natural causalities. The schema of insurance offered itself up as a way of conceiving the new regime of responsibility. Thus, the conflict of responsibilities found its solution in insurance.

The philosophy that undergirded this solution to the problem of workplace accidents had a general competence. As a philosophy of insurance and solidarity, it would provide a replacement diagram for the principle of responsibility. It would allow for the planning of a social law, as an alternative to civil law, with the right to life as its basis. At the same time, the problematics of aid, until then thought of as pertaining to morality, were transformed into a problematics of right: the institution of the right to life marked the end of the liberal classification of obligations. Thanks to these new practices of responsibility, a new conception of the social contract took shape, one that was encapsulated in the doctrine of solidarity. A new political rationality, a new way of identifying individuals, of analyzing their behavior, and formulating their obligations appeared under the form of the *welfare state*.

The formulation of this new political positivity, like the formulation of the institution, would be the work of the Third Republic. It was inscribed in the program, belonging to the republicans, of instituting a "democratic government."[1] It marked, in their eyes, the coming of a positive politics, emancipated from the metaphysical dogmas that characterized liberal philosophy. The republicans thought they were accomplishing the French Revolution's unfinished program. But this is a frequent paradox of history, noted by Marx, that "when men appear to be revolutionizing themselves and their circumstances, in creating something unprecedented, in just such epochs of revolutionary crisis, that is when they nervously summon the spirits of the past, borrowing from them names, marching orders, uniforms, in order to enact new scenes in world history, but in this time-honored guise and with this borrowed language."[2] The Third Republic thought their action took place in the revolutionary orbit; but with the institution of the welfare state, another world had begun.

CHAPTER 7

Charitable Profit

First of all, we need to get rid of the idea that until the end of the nineteenth century no one was concerned with the fate of workers who were injured in workplace accidents.

If workplace accidents were formulated as a problem in 1880, it was not in the sense of coming to terms with an urgent and completely new reality, but as reform, modification, and transformation of the array of procedures and institutions through which the accident had to this point been grasped, analyzed, and treated. In the first instance, assuming the problem was posed only because of an increase in the number of accidents, it would have sufficed either to adopt the necessary security policies without any need for further reform or to reinforce or expand the already existing policies. In the second instance, it was the very principles of the existing dispositive that were questioned and problematized.

For workers, the accident means unemployment, perhaps partial or total inability to work, or, in the worst-case scenario, death. In such circumstances, how will they and their families live or escape poverty, homelessness, and the need for assistance?

Workers might first of all bring a civil liability suit against their *patron*. This is the legal route: in practical terms, it makes compensation dependent on procedural rules, particularly regarding matters of proof. They might also benefit from the aid promised to workers employed in one of those industries that had created "prudential institutions" for their personnel—an allocation of aid that belongs to the problematics of benevolence. Finally, if they have demonstrated personal foresight, if they have paid into a mutual aid society or are affiliated with the National Accident Insurance Bank created in 1868, they will receive the compensation they are due.

Such were, in 1880, the elements of the "workplace accidents" dispositive. This dispositive was dominated by the practice of civil liability proceedings and was established as such when the courts recognized that workers have a juridical recourse against their *patron*. Accident insurance—in the form of mutual aid or fixed premiums—did not develop out of direct workers' insurance, but out of civil liability insurance for *patrons*. It emerged from the law, and its destiny remained tied to the law of responsibility. The National Insurance Bank for accidents, created by Napoleon III, sought to offer aid to prudent workers who had not been juridically compensated in order to fill a gap in the system of juridical reparation. As for the *patrons*' relief funds, they were avoided by *patrons* as long as administrative measures tried to impose them. However, as soon as *patrons* saw their workers assign them civil liability, they did not hesitate to favor these funds, to establish them, to organize them, and to personally contribute to them—so much so that we can interpret the main reason for their creation as the fear of going to trial.

This prevalence of liability suits in the dispositive of workplace accidents can be linked back to the strategy of civil security in which, in the nineteenth century, the question of accidents was inscribed, and to the function assigned to the law within this strategy. The practices of patronal benevolence were its complementary and inseparable moral double. And even though insurance treated the risk of accidents according to its own techniques, it operated within a framework delineated by the categories of liability law that it did not dream of challenging. This array of practices and institutions was organized according to the foundational liberal division between "justice and charity."

From Power to Profit

In the juridical sense, *responsibility* does not designate a property of human nature that makes each person responsible for his or her actions, but a particular relation of obligation that, being established between two individuals, makes them debtor and creditor—an obligation whose execution must be ensured by justice. *Civil responsibility* qualifies a juridical relation of indebtedness that is measured by its monetary value and that must be distinguished from the various philosophical, moral, and political reasons whereby people have tried in different times and places to justify and establish it. If, according to the terms of the 1804 Civil Code, we can only be responsible because we possess a will, which, being capable of shaping itself in an autonomous manner, makes us masters of our behavior, this does not imply that a society that uses other categories to identify individuals and their relations would have no concept of juridical responsibility. Far from juridical responsibility being the mere expression of individual responsibility or the sanction of moral rules inscribed in each and every individual's consciousness, we are and must be responsible; we are required to support the burden of responsibility and modify our behaviors accordingly, because a legal judgment identifies us as responsible.

The Civil Code only recognizes two situations where a person may designate another as responsible for a damage the person suffered: the first, when, being connected through a contract, the person does not fulfill his or her obligation; the second, when the person has caused damage through his or her fault. In the first case, one speaks of "contractual responsibility"; in the second, of "tort liability."

The point is that neither of these two regimes of responsibility recognizes the accident, and even less the workplace accident. In precise terms, the accident as such, as a simultaneously involuntary and unforeseeable event, far from giving rise to an obligation and conferring a right on its victim, on the contrary, absolves of all responsibility. It is indistinguishable from what jurists call "an unforeseen circumstance or an act of God." This is because, in the sense that is given to it by the Civil Code, responsibility is based on the principle of the autonomy of the will: an individual is only ever responsible to the extent that he or she *could* have done something other than what he or she did.

Furthermore, to recognize a law of accidents raises the problem of knowing who, if not the person who suffered, will be deemed responsible for it: if the accident is not attributable to anyone, then to whom, and for what reasons, should we assign the burden of reparation? This is a problem of justice that the Code resolves by invoking the relationship of causality connecting the damage suffered to the one who is deemed responsible: damage is only attributable to someone to the extent that the responsible party had the ability and obligation to anticipate and avoid the damage.

The juridical difficulty posed by workplace accidents relates, on the one hand, to the fact that these are truly *accidents*—they have not been caused voluntarily, either by the boss or one of his agents, and they are not misdemeanors (in every instance the problem of their attribution is present)—and, on the other hand, to the fact that these are *workplace* accidents, the result of a human activity produced in a setting created by humans and cannot simply be conflated with natural accidents, such as, for example, a flood or an earthquake. The workplace accident (as, more generally, the ensemble of accidents resulting from social life) escapes the simple system for classifying the causality of damages contained in the Civil Code. It has no assigned place within this system and as such enjoys an ambiguous and equivocal status with regard to the categories of responsibility.

Thus, the first, foundational decision that the courts would have to deliver, and that they would repeat in each of their judgments, would consist of determining what a workplace accident is—its nature, its causes, whether its character is fatal, condemnable, unavoidable, or criminal. For an accident to lead to judicial reparation, it has to be analyzed and dissected so that it no longer rests solely on a predetermined causality, on fate, on chance, on good luck or bad luck, and is inscribed in the field of human causality. The juridical reparation of workplace accidents both presumes and generates a certain objectification of the factory and the labor process, a certain identification of the *patron* and workers, of their behavior and their relations, using the vocabulary, categories, and analytical principles of judicial knowledge. Here we can identify the birth of a type of discourse specific to the factory, both descriptive and normative, that teaches what the factory is and should be. This discourse endowed the factory with a specific shape and reality and existed in competition with other types of discourse such as those of the economist, the sociologist, the *patronat* itself, or those of workers' organizations. So, what will appear just within the categories of juridical discourse and rationality would appear unjust from the point of view of these other types of knowledge. It is precisely this conflict between the rules of juridical judgment and these other forms of judgment about the factory and the relations of production that would give birth to the debate on workplace accidents, where the categories of juridical analysis would seem insufficient and inadequate for thinking about the accident's reality, while the imperatives of justice would discover that these categories are irrelevant for understanding the object they are called upon to judge. Inversely, by virtue of the very fact that the Code is silent on the question of responsibility for workplace accidents, judges would never be able to simply apply the law, but had to always interpret it. They would have to not only speak the law but create it. Thus the possibility of a historical slippage in the law of responsibility opened up, as the law was forced to forget its strict meaning in order to stay true to its spirit. This entailed a divorce between doctrine and jurisprudence, between the practice of issuing verdicts and their grounding in law, between the criteria of justice and the needs of equity.

At the beginning, then, there was a key question regarding the Civil Code's application. Does civil law authorize a worker's juridical action against his or her *patron*? If it does, then which of the two regimes of responsibility is this right based on, contractual or tort responsibility?[1] In the first regime, the worker is connected to his or her *patron* via a contract, the contract for services. It might thus seem natural in this instance to use the rules of contractual responsibility.

But this would mean that the contract for services contains a safety clause obliging the *patron* to safeguard his workers against all accidents that are not caused by the worker or unforeseen circumstances. Yet such a clause figured neither in the Civil Code nor in the contracts as they were actually written. To use the rules of contractual responsibility would thus mean that the judges were not applying the law, but assigning obligations to the parties. In the other regime, penalizing the victims of workplace accidents according to the regime of tort liability would not derive from the letter of the law, either, but would presume on the part of the courts another way of qualifying the relationship between production and working conditions. In addition, the worker's chances of obtaining reparation for the wrong suffered were not the same in these respective regimes of responsibility. The two regimes were not, in effect, equally favorable to the plaintiffs. In any event, whatever the decision rendered, the judges would have to decide on the nature of the wage relation and on the content of the obligations contained within it; they would have to initiate a law of the accident.

Remember that, after a moment of hesitation, this problem of how to apply the Civil Code was resolved, in 1841, through a decree of the Court of Appeals recalling the public order implications of article 1382–86. Working in this framework, and without ever endorsing the idea of a contractual obligation of security, the courts would go on to build a complete doctrine of *patrons'* duties with respect to security.

"It is the duty of the heads of industrial establishments to completely provide for the safety of the workers they employ."[2] Such was the general principle that would guide the courts in their rulings on responsibility for workplace accidents and their interpretation of articles 1382–86 in the Civil Code.

The captain of industry, the contractor, or the "master" had to therefore satisfy, as a matter of public policy, a general obligation concerning the safety of the workers in their employment: "The obligation requires of the *patron* not only to take serious precautions to avoid or reduce work-related risks, but to take all precautions compatible with the necessities of his business."[3] The *patron* was responsible for all accidents that, under examination, could have been foreseen, from the moment he had not taken the measures available to avoid them.

This responsibility was especially strict when it came to work assigned to children and mine workers.

The standard of judgment utilized by the courts presented two immediate characteristics. With regard to the *patron*, the standard not only implied a negative obligation to do no harm to another (an obligation of prudence), but also a positive obligation of care: "He must ensure his workers' safety; he must take all precautions; he must shield them from their imprudence; he must guarantee aid, protection, safety, and coverage for his workers."

In any case, this is not an egalitarian standard of judgment. Until proven otherwise, the fact of the accident suggests that the master had not respected the duty of safety required of him.

The standard of judgment used by the courts, although compatible with articles 1382–86 of the Civil Code, is no less idiosyncratic. It is not obvious from the text; it does not apply the concept of fault to workplace accidents.

The study of jurisprudence reveals that the *patron*'s obligation to provide security rested on an analysis of the factory, its setup, its organization, such that everything was supposed to depend on the *patron*'s will. Both working conditions and workers' behavior express and reflect the *patron*'s will. The *patron* is juridically defined by his own authority, his *power* to arrange things and command men. Not only can he not be relieved of his power or pretend to be powerless over circumstances and men, but he must also exercise his power to avoid being at fault. It is up to him to prevent work from causing damage, so that the process of labor might proceed in total security. *The patron is omnipotent.* His complete power over things and men defines his responsibilities, serves as a measure of his faults, and grounds the obligation to provide safety.

This way of grounding responsibility in the exercise of power in practice excludes all reference to other causes of responsibility. The quest for profit, in particular, does not implicate the *patron*; but neither does it excuse him. The *patron*'s ability to organize labor in a way that produces the maximum profit is not a juridically pertinent argument, no more so than the constraints competition may impose on him. There was a sort of juridical blind spot regarding the individual or social motives behind workplace accidents in favor of only looking for the exercise of power. This was not because the judges were blind to economic laws, but because profit could only be juridically graspable when translated into a certain type of exercise of power.

This jurisprudential doctrine completely contradicts the idea that justice, in the nineteenth century, was in the *patrons*' pockets. It could even appear particularly harsh toward them. This doctrine respected the spirit of the Civil Code, the position of its compilers being completely clear when it came to the protection of the victims of damages: "The law cannot vacillate between the one who errs and the one who suffers." In spirit, the provisions concerning tort responsibility were designed so that all damage stemming from social life found reparation. Additionally, the doctrine of the courts was homologous to the way in which the *patron*'s responsibility with regard to his workers was understood at this time, with a view to a proper government of business. It was the *patron*'s responsibility that industrialization took place without damage. Assigning this responsibility to the *patron* represented a political necessity: pauperism should not have social causes, only individual ones. Imputing accidents and social evils to individual responsibility made it possible to believe that industrial development did not in itself imply degeneration, disorder, and discord—that this depended on the quality of the men who were responsible.

The possible slipperiness of these judgments is understandable. If patronal responsibility is based on the *patron*'s exercise of power, does this mean that, inversely, the sole *fact* of the accident is sufficient to establish that he did not satisfy his obligation to provide security?

Does the obligation incumbent on the *patron* to provide security make him responsible for every accident? Legally, the response is evidently no, since, according to the founding principle of tort liability, one cannot be responsible for something that is beyond one's free will. If the *patron* has the obligation to do everything to prevent accidents, he cannot be held responsible for those things that occur when he has taken every possible precaution. But if the preventative measures that are required of *patrons* are insufficient to avoid accidents, doesn't this invalidate a regime of *obligation* constrained to let "unmerited suffering" pass without reparation?[4]

Accidents whose cause escapes the *patron*'s vigilance, and for which the *patron* cannot then be blamed, can be grouped under the three following categories: the fault of the worker; "inherent danger"; and "unknown cause."

1. *The fault of the worker*. It seems self-evident that any accident due to a fault of the victim should remain at the victim's charge, in accordance with the principle of responsibility that compels each person to carry the burden of his or her faults, and with the imperative of public order that wants each of us to conduct ourselves with the utmost prudence and diligence. Thus, concerning workplace accidents, it would appear just, if not perhaps entirely equitable, that the *patron* is exonerated of all responsibility in cases of worker carelessness or negligence.

This rule establishes the theory of "individual risk." It amounts to saying that it is always the worker who harms *himself*. It assumes: (a) if not that the worker voluntarily harmed himself, that at least he is responsible for the carelessness from which he suffers; whatever the working conditions may be, it must be presumed that they do not affect the worker's volition; (b) an objectification of the factory, of the workshops and their organization, as a neutral, almost inert, setting *in the face* of which free wills need to exercise necessary prudence; (c) an analysis of the wage relation that configures the worker and *patron* as two *equals* in the face of risk. It is up to the *patron* to provide the worker with good conditions. It is up to the worker to be prudent. In sum, each has his or her responsibilities.

This doctrine would not be adopted in the jurisprudence; the worker's fault does not exonerate the *patron*, in accordance with the consecrated formula: "The *patron* should protect his workers against their carelessness." The rule observed by the courts is the following: in the management of the accident's causality, do not stop at workers' behavior, but look into the conditions that made their conduct damaging. The worker's action is a caused cause, a secondary cause. The primary cause must be sought: workers belong to the factory; they are only one cog in a complex labor machine. In a word, their behavior enters into the sphere of the "circumstances" that depend on the *patron*'s will. The carelessness of the worker depends on the *patron*'s will; it is the *patron*'s fault. The judges make the worker's behavior dependent on that of the *patron*, of which it is the consequence. The worker's will is not opposed to the *patron*'s. It does not counter it. It is *subordinate*.

In this way, jurisprudence introduced a fundamental inequality of wills between the *patron* and the worker, a dissymmetry in the distribution of obligations quite far removed from the original framework of responsibility. The jurisprudential doctrine inscribed the wage relation under the sign of a subordination that is not solely economic, but also juridical. It grants a juridical status to the *patron*'s disciplinary power and from here fashions a strict obligation. Out of the *patron*'s social responsibility, a juridically sanctionable obligation to provide public order was formed. As a consequence, in the event of worker carelessness, the *patron* would only be exonerated: (a) if the worker, correctly chosen for his or her experience, had been sufficiently warned of the danger; (b) in the case of an act lacking discipline or extreme insubordination; something that, in any case, implies grave misconduct. In these two cases, workers are reconstituted as subject, and the analysis of their behavior no longer falls under the previous rule.

2. *The "inherent danger."* Labor, in particular industrial labor, occurs in an artificial setting in conditions that the worker has not determined. This setting entails specific risks and heightened dangers. And, as the courts tirelessly recalled, these risks have been created by the *patron*, juridically determined only by him. Hence the following question: Is the fact of a master making a worker toil in dangerous conditions sufficient to render the master responsible for the accidents caused by this danger?

This is a particularly delicate question; tort law, expressed through fault, presumes a limit to the attribution of damages: namely, that a will, being as diligent as possible, cannot prevent. The "inherent danger," or the "inevitable risk," falls under the scope of the unforeseen circumstance that cannot be assigned to an individual will. But this instantly raises a problem of justice: Why must the burden fall to workers rather than the *patron*? Neither one has committed a fault. However, workers alone must bear the burden. This was a considerable point of divergence between law and justice, between the rules of justice and the demands of equity.

This problem was of great importance: it concerned the juridical treatment of industrialization. Was the industrialist at fault for modernizing his workshops by introducing machines?

The doctrine adopted by jurisprudence would stipulate that danger, whether factual or derived from an objective situation, did not in itself entail a *patron*'s responsibility, as long as a series of conditions were met: the master must have correctly chosen the workers for the job; he must have sufficiently instructed the workers of the dangers and provided the necessary means of safeguarding against these dangers; workers must be equipped to conduct themselves in an informed manner and have accepted the risks; and the master must have taken all precautions to reduce them. In other words, the "inherent danger" of work only exonerated the *patron* to the extent that workers were redefined as subjects confronting the conditions of their work, like every individual faced with the inevitable destinies of nature.

Perhaps. But what sense should we give to "all" in the expression *all precautions*? Does this mean "currently used" precautions? Or those that, being merely "possible," would have averted the accident if the *patron* had taken them? This is an important distinction, at least in the practice of court rulings: in one case, the judge would apply a rule of usage, in the absence of a regulation; in another case, he would create the rule and impose it on a *patron* who could not have known it in advance.

Hence a certain hesitation in the jurisprudence, which is nicely illustrated by two declarations concerning a similar type of accident (an iron puddler being injured by molten iron particles) and involving one Wendel and one Schneider. The worker claimed that Wendel had neglected to require of puddlers certain precautionary measures that he had required of other types of workers in his employment exposed to the same risks. Should Wendel then be punished for not taking every possible precaution? The Court of Metz responded that to the extent that no regulation imposed provisions that were not otherwise in general use, their omission was not punishable.[5] The Court of Dijon, whose ruling was upheld by the Court of Appeals, ruled differently:

"The *patron* or industrial manager has the strict obligation to protect workers against any danger that might result from the job in which they are employed. This obligation entails a requirement to anticipate the causes of accidents—not simply the normal ones, but all possible causes—under pain of fault, and to take all available measures to avoid them."[6]

The system of jurisprudence tended to reduce to a minimum the role of "inherent danger," whose excessive application would have implied invalidation of the law. It looked to subjectivize the inherent danger by referring it to the will of the *patron*, who, having created it, should take all possible precautions in order to reduce its effects and manage his personnel so that they would not have to suffer its effects without the means of prevention. Be that as it may, the concept of inherent danger served as a reminder that these were real "accidents," which is to say destructive events that could not be blamed on an act of will. The fact of the accident existed as an irreducible reality involving "unmerited suffering," according to Jules Favre's forceful expression: there were wrongs workers would have to endure where not only were they not at fault, but where they were required to valiantly confront working conditions that, it was known in advance, placed them in a perilous situation.[7]

Of course, one could object that workers, like any other person, had to protect themselves against instances of unforeseen circumstances through individual acts of foresight; that the laws of the market naturally adjusted their wages according to the risks involved. Of course, it could be argued that the *patronat* of big industry, known to be the most dangerous, made sure to provide aid to their workers. But it was precisely not a question of law, and the problem was one of knowing if the law was capable of taking charge of the specific question of workplace accidents.

3. *The "unknown cause."* If the "inherent danger" posed an extreme problem, it remained within the framework of the legal categories of responsibility: the accident had an assignable cause, albeit not one attributable to a will. With the case of *exploding boilers* appeared the problem of the "unknown cause": the knowledge of causality, indispensable for juridically addressing the compensation of damages, breaks down at this point.[8] What is the difference, really, between the cause that is perhaps unknown and the one due to an "inherent danger"? In both cases the result is the same: the worker is not compensated. Note, first of all, that this is an eventuality where the demonstration of proof becomes in principle impossible. Second, note that the machine that exploded is the property of the *patron*; he installed it in order to increase production and profits. With the problem posed by the explosion of steam engines, we

begin to see a problematic of property and *profit* (overtaking the problematic of *power* and overcoming its limits) appearing as juridically punishable.

It is true that, in a decree of 1870, the Court of Appeals had occasion to recall the traditional doctrine—no responsibility without proven fault: "In the case where, as in this incident, a steam engine explodes, and though this explosion is connected to the actions of the proprietor or his agents, the person who pursues reparation for the damages he has suffered must establish, in addition to the accident, that the fault he identifies is tied to their responsibility; such an incident, which might be the result of an unforeseen circumstance and act of nature, by itself does not necessarily imply the fault or negligence of the defendant."[9]

However, the notes that follow this decree indicate that the Court of Appeals, by recalling this foundational principle, intended to put an end to a twofold doctrinal debate. First, over the philosophy of civil responsibility: "This is a system that is vaguely at the back of many minds: it is the idea that the proprietor responds to the damage caused by his property, not because he is at fault, but by virtue of the simple fact that he is the proprietor: you own something, you use it, you reap all of the profit; if it is harmful to another, then you must make reparation. You build, you use an instrument, a very powerful motor; you do so at your own risk and peril. If a third party suffers damage, then you, the one who has reaped all the advantages of the thing's use, must bear the burden of compensation owed to the third party." Jean Étienne Labbé specified that this was not the doctrine consecrated by the Civil Code: "Without fault, there is no obligation."[10] And, as if swept away by his own momentum, he took it upon himself to develop, albeit in a negative manner, exonerating responsibility, a theory of the social division of burdens that some thirty years later would establish the theory of created risk.

Next, on the more technical question of the similarity between boilers and the buildings that are the object of the Civil Code's article 1386, the annotators agreed that the article is suitable for this task, all the while indicating that the assumption it contains only works to the extent that the claimant proves "inadequate maintenance" or a "defect in construction," which is itself declared "very difficult," if not impossible, to prove.[11] Hence these despondent conclusions—"It is the insufficiency of science that forms an obstacle to our efforts to either examine the cause of the accident, or to prevent it"—that highlight the injustice of the solutions offered. Why place the burden of "the imperfection of current knowledge" on workers alone, who can do nothing about it? What is the point of invoking an exonerating clause in workers' favor if it is instantly qualified by the fact that they may never in practice benefit from it?

This problem of the "unknown cause," posed by the explosion of boilers—this situation that makes the worker bear the weight of an impossible standard of proof—would be a decisive element in triggering the reform of tort law. It was in the name of the law that workers found themselves excluded from the law. Such a divorce between the rules of justice and the most self-evident demands of equity was not tolerable, especially because, in the public consciousness, the problem of workplace accidents was generally associated with the development of mechanization. The more the law was needed, the more it appeared powerless. The march of progress led to its marginalization. The situation of the innocent worker, the victim of risks caused by an apparatus that profited another, was unacceptable. At the very least, workers should have been able to find some practical juridical recourse.

Long after the opening of the parliamentary debate, while the Chamber of Deputies and the Senate had opted for professional risk and the Conseil d'État applied it in the Cames ruling, the Court of Appeals would reverse the solution given in 1870.[12] After having accepted the premises laid out in article 1386 with respect to the explosion of boilers, the Court of Appeals would, according to the consecrated formula, discover that the first paragraph of article 1386 declared a presumption of rigorous and general responsibility with regard to damages caused "by the things that one supervises." This was in June 16, 1896.[13] The ruling that invalidated the 1870 solution caused considerable commotion, since the Court of Appeals had recognized, even before Parliament, the principle of professional risk.

Article 1384 of the Civil Code and its sequels had generally been interpreted in the sense of a presumption of fault, thus authorizing evidence to the contrary, while the formula according to which "an individual is responsible not only for the damage he or she causes, but also for the damage caused by those things one has under his or her supervision" had in general been thought to elucidate only the two hypotheses specified by articles 1385 (concerning the responsibility for an animal's actions) and 1386 (concerning the degradation of buildings).[14] Yet the Court of Appeals elevated this second formula to the status of a general rule, autonomous and independent of the idea of fault. This is at least what two authors, Raymond Saleilles and Louis Josserand, would try to demonstrate.[15]

The starting point of the argument made by these two authors was the problem of the "unknown cause": the fact that, in the conditions of modern life, there were more and more accidents whose cause was destined to remain obscure and undetermined. Hence the need to establish a principle for attributing their costs that would no longer depend on the double proof of a fault and, above all, the causal chain connecting this fault to the damage suffered; the need for a rule that could establish this link even though the knowledge of the effective causality of damages was doomed to escape the judge's inspection. What was needed was a rule that would no longer depend on complete knowledge of a situation, but that instead ruled out the possibility of such knowledge while nevertheless retaining the relationship of responsibility. Parliament, the two authors said, had set down this rule in 1804: in the first paragraph, hitherto ignored, of article 1384 of the Civil Code.

Saleilles and Josserand showed that, concerning workplace accidents, this completely sovereign manner of managing relations of causality had first been implemented by the courts. Saleilles summarized the jurisprudence in this formula: "Some fault is proven, and, as punishment of this fault, the risks are attributed to its author," whether or not the "fact of the fault" was the true cause of the damage. Saleilles developed the philosophical implications of these jurisprudential practices in matters of causality. The juridical judgment no longer found its bearing in the idea of a willful causality. Now, one distinguished between the order of facts and the regime of attribution. On the side of the facts, there was now only a completely material chain of causes and effects: the fact of damage now only referred to another fact—the "faulty fact"—more generally, the "thing supervised," without having to make reference to an act of will. Independently, the juridical rule proclaimed that, if such a fact was given, the damage it was materially associated with was juridically attributable to a given estate, the link between fact and the estate being properly juridical, legal, independent of the idea of fault. The rationale behind responsibility was no longer found in the reprehensible behavior of the author of damage, but in the law, the will of the legislator.

What Saleilles demonstrated in these transformations of the management of juridical causality was, of course, the appearance of a new rule of judgment resting on the first paragraph of the Civil Code's article 1384, but along with this, above all, the birth of a new way of thinking about the relationship between humans and things, between humans and humans, a new regime of obligations and identifications. In a word, this was a new rule of justice. The jurisprudence of workplace accidents had a scope completely different from its social one: it attested to the slow birth of another world. This is what was most striking in this new regime of responsibility, the idea that humans could be liberated from the play of natural causalities and set themselves up as the masters of relations of obligation. If, in this case, a regime of attribution without cause was not yet conceivable, the first steps were taken that would allow a purely social and resolutely anti-natural regime of attribution to be considered.

This new responsibility of the "fact of things" could no longer rest on the idea of *fault*. It would instead be founded in the idea of *risk*. In his note to the Court of Appeals ruling of August 24, 1870, Labbé explained that it was not unjust that "some individuals accidentally suffered from the imperfect state of human knowledge." "They suffer," he continued, "from the inevitable conditions in which human life takes place in a determined time. It is in society's interest that certain very powerful means of production might be put to work. The whole world—not merely their proprietor or owner—profits from them, since the products are less costly." Labbé, because he thought in terms of fault, did not believe that it was possible to legally reform the natural economic distribution of profit and social burdens. What Saleilles and Josserand proposed and claimed to the contrary, nearly thirty years later, in the name of equity and a social conception of justice, was that it was unjust that some suffer the losses connected to the dangerous activities that the rest of society profit from. It was up to the legislator to reestablish equilibrium in the distribution of costs and, thus, if not to punish profits—fault is no longer mentioned—at least to assign the burden of damages in accordance with the benefits of profit. While the concept of fault only allowed for the exercise of power and authority to be punished, the concept of risk assumed the juridical seizure of profit: "To use something in one's own interest and to one's own profit, is to take on first of all the associated oversight, and secondly the risk: nothing is more just." The concepts of responsibility, the obligation to keep watch and to oversee, shifted ground: *from power to profit*. In a major shift, responsibility was no longer conceived in terms of cause but in terms of distribution. There were plenty of reasons for this shift beyond the merely juridical ones, reasons that the law, in this case, simply collected and translated.

In their efforts to adjudicate responsibility for workplace accidents, the courts thus developed a jurisprudence that, to say the least, did not stem from articles 1382 and 1383, although these were still cited in judgments and rulings until late in the nineteenth century. Admittedly, the courts had particularly delicate situations to judge that did not obviously involve responsibility. In fact, the opposite was true. The accident as such formed a part of these unforeseen circumstances that would remain the burden of those who suffered them. This position was only tenable so long as the number of accidents remained low. Above all, it was a question of industrial accidents. They were connected to a human activity, increasingly artificial in nature, created by humans for humans. They referred to a will. Political and social imperatives called for their compensation, which required a certain regime of criminal fault, and therefore an obligation to provide security. This assumed a certain type of juridical objectification of the factory, a doctrine of wage relations—in brief, the elaboration of a rule of judgment.

The judges did not so much find this rule in the Code, which was "silent about the question that concerns us,"[16] but in a certain political economy of patronal responsibility that took shape in the 1830s and '40s and that was consecrated by the law of March 22, 1841, concerning child labor. It explained the *patron*'s responsibility through his *power*, private and public, making it a duty for him to exercise his power so that the creation of wealth could occur without damage.

The category of power is not foreign to the Civil Code: it is at the foundation of article 1384, concerning the responsibility for another person's actions. The doctrine unequivocally recognizes that if "masters and their principals are responsible for damage caused by their domestic servants and other agents in the functions for which they are employed," this is not only because of the "free choice of the principal, who, before entrusting the agent with employment, must ascertain his integrity and ability, which is to say his aptitude to fulfill the functions without causing damage to a third party," but above all because of his right to "give the agent instructions and even orders, and to watch over them and ensure their execution." Therefore, it has been argued that with respect to workplace accidents the courts interpreted articles 1382 and 1383 of the Civil Code in light of article 1384—that is, in light of its assumptions about authority, surveillance, and subordination. The jurisprudence's center of gravity would be found in article 1384, even if, for philosophical and doctrinal reasons, the rule that it expressed could only be seen throughout articles 1382 and 1383. The Court of Appeal's decisive ruling of June 21, 1841, where this jurisprudence begins, was concerned with the interpretation of article 1384. It is with reference to this same article that the courts would decide on how to attribute accidents when one works for a firm. The jurisprudence concerning a *patron*'s obligation to prevent the carelessness of his workers could only find its support in positive law in this same article 1384.

The jurisprudence of workplace accidents finds its juridical coherence in article 1384 of the Civil Code. From the outset, the courts assessed the responsibility of *patrons* according to a rule expressed through the categories of power, authority, and management. Articles 1382 and 1383 functioned less as an expression of the rule than as conditions of its implementation. In 1896, the Court of Appeals did not discover article 1384; it proposed a new rule of judgment. The new rule was based on a modification of the old rule's application: it endowed the rule with a presumption of full rights in order to prevent industrial progress (the transformation of the juridical situation) from leading, for the purposes of proof, to the disqualification of the rule. In the same gesture, the idea of power was no longer sufficient to establish this rule, since one could be juridically responsible for damages when all the precautions required to avoid damages had been taken. One thus had recourse to the ideas of profit and the distribution of risks. This presumed a considerable philosophical transformation, one that was at the center of the parliamentary debate over workplace accidents: the reparation of accident-related damages would now be based on a principle of equality rather than the principle of responsibility.

From the social point of view, the jurisprudential construction, however generous, was not satisfactory to anyone. The workers were no more satisfied than the *patrons*. The *patrons'* critique concerned two points. The first point concerned the courts' arbitrariness. The arbitrariness of the judgments, on the one hand: the *patrons* denounced the universally acknowledged drift of jurisprudence, which, to correct the rigors of the law, strove to find patronal faults where, in other circumstances, they would not find them. Arbitrariness, on the other hand, in the calculation of pecuniary damages: "To determine the sum, judges appeal to a whole range of considerations, independent of the seriousness of the damage to be restituted: the *patron*'s fortune, his earnings, special pleas, the more or less serious condition of the victim."[17] There was a dual arbitrariness at work here that placed *patrons* in a state of insecurity that they denounced as most harmful to the good workings of their affairs. To this it must be added that the indemnities that the *patrons* were condemned to pay were often extremely heavy.

If the *patrons* demanded an end to the regime of common law responsibility in matters concerning workplace accidents, this was not only because of the courts' arbitrariness, but, much more radically, because of the trials themselves. At issue here is the manner in which the judiciary's procedural rules oblige the workers to exercise their rights. Workers had to lodge a complaint *against* their *patron*. And in order for the complaint to be admissible, they had to prove that their *patron* had committed a fault, which is to say that, according to the terms of a jurisprudence that linked the *patron*'s responsibility to his power, workers had to prove that their *patron* did not properly manage his business. In practice, the law of responsibility and the rules of procedure led workers to attack their *patron* through his defining trait, which is to say his authority, and to denounce the manner in which he exercised that authority. And this was what the courts sanctioned through their rulings: by condemning this or that *patron*, they officially pronounced, with regard to the workers and the public in general, that this *patron* was a bad *patron*. The condemnation of the *patron*, even when civil, necessarily had a *defamatory* character.

Despite the best intentions of the courts, the juridical regime of compensation for workplace accidents was not favorable to workers either. First, this is because, abstracting from all question of proof, a constantly reproduced statistic established that 88 percent of accidents would legally remain the burden of workers: 68 percent were in effect due to unforeseen circumstances or emergency conditions, 20 percent due to the fault of the worker, and 12 percent due to the fault of the *patron*. It was thus in only 12 percent of cases that workers could hope to be compensated. They would still have to overcome the formidable obstacle of the burden of proof required of them as the ones demanding reparation. Yet, this was practically impossible for a parallel set of reasons. First, for reasons relating to the worker's situation: "Here is a man who is wounded and is knocked unconscious. Most often, he does not know how he was injured. When after his convalescence he looks to gather the evidence and establish the cause of the accident, he is beset with nearly insurmountable difficulties: the state of the environment has changed, the material evidence has become impossible to ascertain. He looks for witnesses, but it may be that the accident had no witnesses, and, if there were any, their memories have become confused. Often these witnesses remain obstinately silent." Secondly, for substantive reasons: the transformations of industry or mechanization have altered the nature of accidents, making accidents "anonymous," which renders the administration of proof not only difficult, but quite impossible.

"To these difficulties are added the difficulties and sluggishness of judicial action."[18]

The debate over workplace accidents opened, in 1880, with this assessment of the impossibility for workers of proving a *patron*'s fault. Auguste Girard, among many others, would take up the argument at the beginning of the parliamentary debate over workplace accidents: "In the majority of cases the worker's rights perish in his hands. And that this right exists does him no good, since he cannot juridically establish it."[19]

Politically, finally, the juridical regime of workplace accident compensation was particularly maladapted: by obliging workers to enter into conflict with the *patron* in order to assert their rights, tort law and its rules of procedure made workplace accidents a permanent source of discord, hostility, and opposition between *patrons* and workers. Liability law encouraged social war. It was not possible for industrial development to be accomplished under the suspicion of presumed patronal culpability. This was to admit that it was wrong to rely on the *patrons'* awareness of their duties to ensure public peace and workers' security. The regime of civil liability that was formulated as a guardian, expression, and sanction of the public order appeared to produce effects that were the inverse of those that had been intended: not only did it not ensure the harmonious coordination of men and activities, but, in the way it was practiced, it completely disabled the exercise of this protective benevolent aid that was supposed to ensure civil security. In addition, the more rigorous jurisprudence became with regard to *patrons*, the more it would be juridically and socially unsatisfactory. Its future was self-destruction. The more it developed, the more the divorce between juridical thought and the needs of business would solidify.

The extension of juridicity in matters concerning workplace accidents was a formidable factor in political destabilization. The law, far from ensuring social regulation in a satisfactory manner, itself created social problems. It fed the antagonism between capital and labor. This was a fundamental critique that crystalized around the question of trials. What was to be done with a law, with universal and timeless principles, if they revealed themselves to be politically and socially harmful? The liability law formulated in the Civil Code might well express the values most essential to human dignity; the government of industrial societies nevertheless called for the establishment of a law that would bring peace and not war. The question of workplace accidents posed a problem of legal politics to which a number of parliamentarians were particularly sensitive, demanding (along with Félix Faure) that one "get rid of trials" as an imperative of all reform.

It is true that the *patrons* did not wait for parliament to take up the question of workplace accidents before trying to put an end to a situation that was so harmful to them. As soon as they felt the threat of trials hovering over them, they would invent a series of tactics calculated to allow them to avoid trials.

The Ruses of Charity

Beyond respect for an obligation grounded in natural law, the first reason for relief funds was to ensure the recruitment and fidelity of the workforce in industrial sectors such as mining that were known for their dangers.[20] As such, they were of interest not only to managers but also to public authorities: as early as 1604, Henri IV issued an edict ordaining

> that in each mine that opens in this kingdom, no matter its quality or type, one-thirtieth of all it produces should be set aside, in order to be placed in

the hands of a treasurer and general receiver of these mines, who will turn it into a separate stream of revenue, which will be the funds used for the support of one or two priests, as need dictates, such as for the saying of Mass at the proper hour every Sunday and holy day of the week, to administer the sacraments, as well as for the support of a surgeon and the purchase of medicines, so that the wounded poor may be freely aided, and through this example of charity, the others will be more encouraged to work in these mines.

Napoleon reformulated this obligation with the decree of January 3, 1813, and the one of May 26, 1813, authorizing, in favor of the Department of the Ourthe's coal workers, the formation of a prudential society. On June 25, 1817, a royal ordinance instituted a prudential fund for mineworkers in and around the town of Rive-de-Gier.

In the two regions in question, the Liège and the Loire, the administration was moved by the sheer number of accidents and would doggedly pursue the creation of two prudential funds.[21] Conceived as separate from the businesses in question, these funds were organized on a local level and administered by committees comprising members of the administration, the clergy, *patrons*, and workers. The funds would be financed by contributions from the state, business owners, managers, and workers. The problem was to obtain everyone's participation (including that of workers and managers), a condition of the fund's success, since there was no recourse to the principle of obligation. Hence the idea of a deduction from employees' wages as a condition and clause of the contract for services. Thus, according to a formula that would find very similar expression in the guise of collective insurance some fifty years later, all workers of every position would be compelled to join the fund.

The problem of obtaining the participation of managers remained unresolved. This was only ever a partial success, for a number of reasons: "cold self-interest and callousness toward the most moving benevolence, above all when it is found scattered among an array of competitive and jealous companies,"[22] the fear of local administration interfering in business, the opposition of the workers and the threat of additional difficulties in personnel management—and above all, without a doubt, the independence of the two funds in relation to the businesses in question. According to the managers, all of these problems made the funds hopelessly expensive, unsuitable, and unjust. These difficulties would disappear as soon as the management of the prudential funds was turned over to businesses. Once this occurred, managers declared themselves favorable to the funds. In this way, they put forward a strategy of security—a strategy that implied subordination to the company and that would be championed by the *patronat* throughout the nineteenth century. But in order for the managers to make this move, the fear of tort litigation and the desire to avoid it had first to provoke them into action.

It should be clarified here that the relief funds were not the only tactic used by the *patrons* to avoid their responsibilities. Others, concerning the payment and organization of labor, sought to place the worker in a position of being juridically in charge of his own security. So from labor to the business, a form of subcontracting practice *avant la lettre* emerged: the employer, rather than hiring workers according to the guidelines of the contract for services, entrusted the job to an independent contractor. If an accident were to take place, it could in principle be attributable only to the contractor. The courts circumvented this sleight of hand and established, as the true criterion of the wage relation, the employer's power of management and the wage earner's subordinate situation.

At the heart of the economy of patronage, the relief funds were originally at the *patron*'s discretion. They obeyed the logic of *patrons*' institutions: not a logic of law, but of generosity, of reward for services rendered. The administration of the fund, controlled by management, reserved the possibility of awarding special aid grants or, on the contrary, reducing or eliminating the disbursement according to the conduct of the injured worker or that of his widow.

In particular, the act of contributing did not give you any rights; aid could not be interpreted as the contractual compensation for contributing. This was inscribed in the conditions of hiring: if one had a "right" to aid, it was as a member of the business, participating in its benefits. In the *patron*'s view, relief funds were moralizing funds, granting, of course, pensions to injured or sick workers, but also financing *patrons*' schools, their teacher, and their clergy.

Beyond the general objective to recruit, train, and retain a workforce, the *patrons* expected a number of particular advantages from the relief funds. Firstly, in the case of mines, the funds ensured that the workers themselves were legally obliged to pay for the maintenance of a surgeon, in accordance with their contributions. Some *patrons* used the funds to cover any compensation the courts might condemn them to pay. More generally, relief funds looked to make accidents an internal affair of the business. One would be treated, compensated, and taken care of by the business, but on one strict condition: litigation would not be sought. Doing so would mean nothing less than waging war against one's *patron*. To bring a legal complaint amounted to excluding oneself from the business. It would doubtless take a measure of courage, a strong will to fight. The patronal market was managed in such a way that it forced workers to accept the transaction offered by the relief fund, which, depending on their enthusiasm, their good will, and their familial responsibilities, would not lack for generosity when it was needed, in contrast to the lottery of juridical reparation combined with the hostility of the patron.

Beginning, it seems, in the 1850s, relief funds were subject to a number of trials. The worker who had a portion of his wages withheld no longer accepted his dependent situation and demanded that his rights be recognized. But which rights, precisely, could he demand? The funds did not fall into any juridical category. The question that was posed, along with the problem of the autonomy of the fund, was the guarantee of the workers' rights in the event that the company stopped supporting the fund, whether by canceling it or through bankruptcy: did the fund have its own juridical character, or was it consubstantial to the operation of the business?

In practice, it fell to the courts to clarify these difficulties until Parliament took up the question.[23] They thus recognized that the funds were constituted on the basis of a *sui generis* contract giving birth to a "society with a peculiar nature," having a unique juridical character. The workers, taken individually, enjoyed a right to aid stipulated in the legal statutes, but did not have any power to seek its dissolution. The funds were of indefinite duration; they would have to be maintained for as long as work continued, even in cases where business ownership changed. But the workers could not claim a right of control that did not exist in the statutes. The work of the courts was then to legislate the relation of dependence at the foundation of the institution, to make the relationship legal while maintaining its character: workers only had rights based on the fact of belonging to the personnel of the business, and the satisfaction of their rights depended on the smooth functioning of the business. Beyond that there appeared, albeit in a tentative fashion, a juridical understanding of business as a collectivity, a legal entity relatively independent of the sum of the contracts for services concluded between the *patron* and his workers, which the institution of accident insurance would go on to perfect.

The *patron*, who is conscious of his duties and exercises them as required, by definition, cannot be responsible for the accidents that befall his workers. In effect, he has taken all precautions to prevent and avoid accidents. In the style of Frédéric Engel-Dollfus, he has created or belongs to an association dedicated to the prevention of accidents. His desire to continually improve the technical dispositives of prevention is constantly on alert.[24] He does not turn away from the sacrifices necessary for his workers' benefit. In this way, if *patrons* come to be condemned, it is only as a result of the courts' "humanitarian fiction."

Accidents would thus only have two categories of causes: in the first place, workplace conditions, to the extent they are of an irreducibly dangerous nature; in the second instance, the workers themselves, who fall in the "field of battle," whether through courage, devotion, self-sacrifice, or, on the contrary, as victims of their own lack of discipline and their immorality. Thus the analysis of the accident that corresponds to the economy of patronage obeys the binary of inevitability (always unforeseeable and unstoppable) and heroism (of workers who confront the accident).[25]

The relief fund would cover all these accidents, whatever their cause. The "right" to aid did not at all obey juridical categorizations: the case of acts of nature—which is to say unavoidable accidents—was compensated in principle, and it was not a question of analyzing workers' behavior in terms of carelessness, negligence, or fault. Without a doubt workers had to be prudent, but they had to also commit body and soul to the task. They were not expected to be prudent in the sense of fearing danger, but in the sense of confronting it with enthusiasm and the spirit of sacrifice.

Here, prudence was called skill, vision, mastery, and intrepidness—all virtues that assume there is no guarantee against danger, but rather that we live with danger, in its company, its familiarity. What was demanded of workers was to not go too far, to know instantaneously how to distinguish courage from recklessness and how to appreciate the imminence of danger. If an accident happened, it might always be said that the worker could have avoided it by being more careful. This would be particularly dishonest. And the juridical punishment for such carelessness would not fail to have the most regrettable effects on production. Workers were not expected to hold back in carrying out their work. Instead, the presence of the relief fund was there to encourage them: the workers knew that if something bad befell them, they and their family would not be abandoned.[26]

This type of analysis in terms of inevitability/heroism was reinforced, amplified, popularized by a whole literature that, until very recently, continued to inspire enthusiasm. This literature inverted the signs and celebrated workers' heroism, courage, greatness all the more when it was painful, dangerous, and degrading. Thus, for example, was born the myth of the miner in love with the mine. When did this rhetoric crystallize? Without a doubt it was the catastrophes at Horloz and Beaujonc in 1812 and the campaign the Napoleonic administration orchestrated around them: Legion of Honor for Goffin, a brochure popularizing the prefect Charles Emmanuel Micoud, a poem by Charles Hubert Millevoye awarded with an extraordinary prize by the Imperial Institute of France.[27] This literature, evidently, also functioned as a patronal institution. A double effect was expected of it: centripetal, to connect the workers to their work, to make them completely invest their dignity and honor in it; and centrifugal, to outwardly assert a discourse about the "field of battle" destined to exonerate the person who was usually found responsible within the juridical categories: the *patron*.

The juridical objectification of workplace accidents had without a doubt lent its schema to a certain type of accusatory discourse: one that attributed the accident to a hierarchical authority individualized and specifically named, manager or engineer, and is focused on describing all of the traits of criminal intent. This is what Yves Guyot would create, for example, in his novel *La Famille Pichot*, directed against the Schneiders and, through their intermediary, against Napoleon III, the empire, and the Bonapartists.[28]

Guyot omits no detail concerning the social context of the accident—neither the engineer's contempt toward the workers nor the workers' hatred of the engineer.

In his writing, this discourse achieves an accusatory violence that the *gauchisme* of the years after 1968, even the most radical, hardly came close to.[29] This is a discourse of maximal individualization, which seeks in the life of the *patron*, his education, his sexuality, his morality, some explanation for the evil he has committed. To this extent, it is a fundamentally optimistic discourse: it allows one to think that the agents of social ills are the men who command, rather than the "system" or social structures. It could be said of Guyot's discourse, an inverted liberal discourse, that it achieves its effects by setting the juridical discourse within the framework of patronal discourse so that the former cancels out the latter: there is no inevitability; responsibilities do exist; these responsibilities belong to individuals; individuals are responsible because they are immoral beings.

The objectification of the accident in terms of its inevitability would give rise to another type of accusatory discourse. Inevitability is an abstraction, a blind, obstinate, and overwhelming process. Denouncing it may well involve giving it a human face: the face of capital crushing human beings, at whatever level of hierarchy they sit and whatever their intentions may be. Émile Zola, who invented what remains to this day the very type of truth discourse on the world of workers and social ills, wrote in an epigraph to the plan of *Germinal*, "The subject of the novel is the revolt of the workers, the jolt given to society, which for a moment cracks: in a word the struggle between Capital and Labor. . . . the most important question of the XXth century." Whereas Guyot gave flesh and bones to those responsible, Zola, on the contrary, did so for the victims. The responsible party is capital, which itself only figures in *Germinal* as "the inaccessible tabernacle where lived the squatting, sated god to whom they offered up their flesh," and never as an identifiable subject.[30]

Zola does not exclude fatalism. On the contrary, *Germinal* simultaneously takes up, uses, and shifts all of the themes of mining literature: the mine as wicked stepmother and ogress, the mining catastrophes, and accidents. These were requisite themes; it is through them that the worker's world could take on its novel-like, moving character. Zola had learned Simonin's lesson: the mine is by itself novel-like; the "effects" do not need to be invented; they are a part of its very reality. He had drawn from it one of his realist techniques: to make something true, stay extra close to reality.

Germinal must thus be aligned with a specific literary, scientific, and political genre that flourished under the Second Empire: the worker's inquest. The investigators of the Second Empire also began from the fact of the workers' misery, but the basis of their perspective was power, in its productive, positive aspects, its moralizing effects, as the thing that allowed for the escape from misery. It was not so much about describing the workers' misery as it was about the dispositives and patronal institutions put in place to ameliorate "their physical and moral well-being." With *Germinal*, the point of view is inverted: it is workers, as exploited, who occupy, through their negative qualities, the center of the discourse. Thus, workers' misery, their brutality, the accidents and the fatalism that hang over them indict capital. They must also be darkly portrayed, with all of their negative qualities the source of their truth. Thus, fatalism no longer designates a hostility constitutive of nature. It becomes a sort of anonymous subject of history.

The force of Zola's discourse, what has perhaps given it its relevance up to today, resides less in the truth it spoke about the mine and miners than in the type of truth-telling to which it conforms. At the moment when Parliament was preparing to turn the accident into a risk and, more generally, to shift the attribution of social evil from individual responsibility toward these anonymous subjects known as business and society, a discourse like *Germinal*'s maintained the fiction of responsibility. This discourse could simultaneously accommodate the new way of objectifying the accident and social evil while being legible as its critique. It is no doubt difficult to live with the idea that evil is normal, that evil is reproduced in a regular and statistical manner. The way in which the philosophy of risk normalizes evil is properly inhuman: it removes all sense from history. Perhaps this is the reason that, beyond the needs of compensation and prevention, we find it so necessary to assign responsibility.

CHAPTER 8

Security and Responsibility

Workplace accident insurance appeared in the 1860s under two guises. The first was a form of collective worker's insurance combined with liability insurance for *patrons*. Adopted by private companies, this combination enjoyed a great deal of success beginning in 1875. The second was a form of individual and collective personal insurance. It was established, in 1868, as a state-run institution and was a decisive failure.

The appearance of a specific branch of workplace accident insurance should be situated within the movement toward the social utilization of insurance that the 1848 Revolution had made official. This also attested to the existence of a market and to the urgency of a problem: the market in question was the financial market for compensation that the "humanitarian" jurisprudence of the courts continually amplified; the problem, doubtless growing with the progress of industrialization and mechanization, was simultaneously political and social. It was political to the extent that the multiplication of accidents fueled wage-labor antagonism through the intermediary of trials. It was social to the extent that there was a recognition of "undeserved suffering" that called for specific measures of assistance and recourse.

Marestaing's Combination

Hippolyte Marestaing, founder of La Préservatrice (1861), is given credit for having invented the combination that private accident insurance companies would go on to use. The idea was to offer the *patrons* a form of collective insurance covering their workers, "combined" with insurance covering their own liability. The main objective was to address the idea not to individual workers—dispersed and lacking foresight, doubtlessly seduced by the hope of obtaining complete judicial compensation in the case of an accident—but to *patrons*, the true strategic linchpins. The *patrons* were important in many ways: as collectors of premiums, first of all, something they could easily carry out by making wage deductions a clause in the contract for services, and as those who had most to gain from preventing the conflicts generated by accidents and transforming the risk of a judicial condemnation into the regularity of a paid premium.

Marestaing invented less than what has been attributed to him. Fundamentally, the proposed combination was only a rationalization of the *patrons'* practice of relief funds. The intervention of insurance offered several advantages: a precise definition of insured risks, a set contractual relationship, and the possibility of accident coverage for businesses whose size did not allow for the creation of a relief fund. Not only did the *patron* see his liability guaranteed, but, in addition, he could hope that placing the fund outside of the business would end the conflicts that went along with the practice of relief funds.

In this way, accident insurance proposed a type of objectification of the business that greatly differed from the one that stemmed from the economy of patronage. Collective insurance is characterized by the fact that the insurer does not know the workers personally; the insurer guarantees a *patron*'s salaried employees as a group, as a whole. The risk value is calculated according to the nature of the profession. Insurance gives a quasi-real existence to the "salaried mass"; the risk in question becomes a business risk. From the point of view of the rationality of risk, the business is no longer identified with the almost monumental figure of the individual person, loved or despised for his personal qualities. Properly speaking, the business becomes a legal entity.[1] And the *patron* himself now only exists as the representative of this legal entity, as its putative site or location.

Civil law, which breaks down the wage relation into as many contracts as there are wage earners, evidently is not able to perceive wage earners as a totality. The *patrons'* social economy doubtless objectifies "the business" but in *reality* confuses it with the real person of the *patron*, who alone can have a reality. Insurance proposes another way of objectifying the business: as totality, as a function of the risk it represents, which is to say by giving it an abstract existence; a sort of incorporeal reality that would enable a new regime of obligations and attribution of blame to be put into place, one that was foreclosed by the two previous modes of objectification, and one that would soon resolve the problem of workplace accidents.

Accident insurance led to the same wage tactics as relief funds: forbidding workers, under penalty of forfeiting their claims, to bring litigation; making the *patron*'s liability insurance dependent on collective insurance, and therefore on workers' contributions; making workers subservient to the business, depriving them of all rights if they quit. Accident insurance offered the *patron* all of the advantages of a relief fund without its inconveniences. But the *patrons* feared that if the fund became too independent with respect to the business, this would undermine workers' loyalty and would lead them to assert their rights. In precise terms, accident insurance, such as it was constituted, proposed a truly ingenious utilization of the law for the *patron*'s benefit, offering him the necessary security, all the while keeping workers in a quasi-nonlegal position.

This status of contributing to a contract in which workers figured only as beneficiaries created a number of difficulties regarding their juridical status. The company stipulated that it had no other contracting party beside the *patron* and thus pocketed workers' money in a somewhat surreptitious way through the intermediary of the *patron*, all the while remaining inaccessible to workers' claims. Did workers, then, only have the right to pay, while remaining dependent, without either right or power, on the transactions between their *patron* and the company?

This raised the problem of *guarantees*. That the insurance contract offers a fixed compensation seems to be a part of its definition, and especially so when it concerns workers' insurance. In what way, then, could an insurance contract that would not offer workers a guaranteed benefit be useful? Doubtless this was how things stood, but in the absence of special legislation on this matter, the satisfaction of these objectives depended on the juridical analysis of the insurance contract. According to the common law of contracts, one had to look for the shared intent of the contracting parties. But this is precisely what workers could not convey: the contract had been discussed solely between the insurer and the *patron* and generally stipulated that "the insurance policy only creates a legal bond between the insurer and the insured. It requires only that the insured pay the contributions due to the insurer, who remains separate from all past or future arrangements between the *patron* and his employees for the distribution of contributions. It requires the insurer, upon deduction of the insured's contributions, to pay to the victim or his beneficiaries the compensation stipulated in their favor by the policy, while protecting the insurer from all other actions except those resulting from garnishments or claims."[2]

The fact is that the juridical analysis of the worker's situation in the insurance contract was in itself particularly delicate. Did the *patron* act as a business manager? Was there any provision for a third party in collective insurance? A mandate? Did workers have direct recourse to exercise their rights against the company? Depending on how the question was posed, these various juridical solutions offered widely different advantages. "The courts," said one commentator, "very favorable to the worker, always seem, amidst numerous systems supported by both sides, to adopt the system that, in the case pending before them, is in the last analysis found to be the most advantageous to the victim of the accident."[3] In other words, the courts' decisions obeyed a finalist rule. Insurance doctrine complained of the obstacles that this procedure put in the way of such a useful technique and, above all, of the fact that the courts claimed to judge a contract according to "abstract principles" at the expense of the explicit intentions of the parties. Was it the job of the courts to legislate the parties? To rule in the place of the lawmaker?

The practice of accident insurance posed, by definition, the problem of the insurability of fault.

The doctrine generally taught was that the insurer could not cover gross misconduct. Justifiable in the case of fire, this doctrine was less so in cases of accident insurance. It was hypothesized that it was difficult to imagine anyone speculating on insurance when the insured would be the first one to pay the cost. The courts seem to have decided in favor of a double extension of workers' protection. First—and this is a rule that would continue to be observed in the case of traffic accidents throughout the following century—they used the existence of insurance, therefore a solvent debtor, to extend the field of responsibilities. And, rather than keeping to a strict understanding of the noninsurability of gross misconduct, they pushed the limit back to the "impardonable," "inexcusable," and "intentional" fault. They thus privileged the resolution of a social problem over a rigorous problematics of individual responsibility. In so doing, they placed the social and legal manners of thinking about security in conflict with each other.

The Failure of Foresight

We recall that Napoleon III "dreamed of making insurance . . . a function of the Second Empire."[4] Well before Otto von Bismarck, he had perceived the political benefits that a government could reap from insurance. In contrast to Bismarck, Napoleon III did not have the opportunity to realize the social insurance program he had clearly envisioned. This was due to the resistance of private interests and the always-constraining character of the doctrine of state nonintervention in economic matters.

In order to overcome the obstacles he foresaw to his business, Marestaing chose to emigrate. Was it not possible to hope for some success by executing Napoleon III's projects? This is what a number of people close to the emperor thought when they formed the project for an accident insurance company, La Sécurité Générale.

The key point: La Sécurité Générale offered to combine Marestaing's personal, individual, and collective insurance operations with civil liability insurance. In sum, it was inspired by Marestaing's combination while seeking to grant official guarantees. Constituted as a corporation, La Sécurité Générale sought government authorization. The Conseil d'État not only forbade it from practicing liability insurance, it also made the corporation introduce into its policies clauses "stipulating in favor of the worker and to his benefit a right to recourse against his *patron*." Not only, then, could the company not insure the *patron*'s liability, but it was also forced to grant the workers the right to recourse against him! As far as workplace accidents were concerned, its operations were reduced to providing direct or collective insurance for workers, along with the reinsurance of mutual aid societies. In its prospectus, the company could hardly hide the fact that it had little to offer for resolving questions of liability.

Despite a strong publicity campaign, La Sécurité Générale experienced a rocky start. The Conseil d'État had changed its statutes in a very unfavorable way. The administration refused its support. The emperor, far from granting it the promised aid, would soon announce that he was in favor of the creation of a Fund for Disabled Workers whose operations would largely be the same as those of La Sécurité Générale. The project would culminate in the law of July 11, 1868, creating both the National Life Insurance Fund and the National Accident Insurance Fund Covering Agricultural and Industrial Labor.

The Napoleonic initiative was part of a program to encourage foresight. Its goal was to allow prudent workers to put together a pension for themselves or their loved ones in case of death or disability, with the help of state funding.

The initiative reframed the problem of state intervention. The principle had been admitted in 1850 with the institution of the National Retirement Fund. But at the time the problem was different: technically, only the state could insure retirements, whereas in this case private companies existed. This was a scenario where state intervention was, by definition, excluded. To this was added the problem posed by the principle of state funding.

Did this funding fall within the traditional framework of benevolent aid, and should it be organized as such, as a voluntary contribution? Or, on the contrary, did the intervention of this insurance fund signify a change in the state's role in the politics of social foresight? The idea of insurance is indissociable from the idea of contract and right; was it a question of giving *rights* to workers, through this insurance, and thus in practice constituting the beginnings of a social right guaranteed by the state?

The provision of state funding was presented as being made possible by the practice of *patrons'* institutions. If the state could intervene in the case of accidents, it could only do so in the manner of a private person, by casting its action in the mold of the *patrons'* actions. The problem was that of deciding how the *patrons'* institutions were to be interpreted with regard to insurance: did insurance imply reforming these institutions according to a regime of rights? Or, conversely, would the eventual insurance-based form of *patrons'* institutions continue to fall within the framework of benevolent aid?

As we can see, the discussion concerned the principle of the divide between rights and benevolence, justice and charity, the organizing principle of the liberal politics of civil security. It would be further pursued in Parliament. The republicans would continually argue in favor of rights. Jules Simon threatened to not vote for the law if the strict character of "justice" was not recognized: "I thus support the idea that this is a right; it belongs incontestably to the worker who saves part of his (often insufficient) salary, and who, through this savings, has come to obtain the insurance you provide him. I maintain that there is neither charity nor benevolent aid at work here, there is only justice, and absolute justice at that; if this act is presented as a form of charity, I will vote against the law."[5]

Against this the Bonapartists responded by continuing to defend the orthodox politics of benevolence. As Pierre Charles Chesnelong specified:

a. there is no conflict between foresight and benevolence; they "complement each other";[6]
b. benevolence is first of all a private virtue, even if it might be supplemented by a public intervention;
c. the fact that it is public does not alter the essential nature of benevolence: the "principle of liberty in duty." And he insisted, "There is a fundamental distinction that must be made between the duties of justice and benevolence: opposite the duties of justice are always found a corresponding right; but as for the duty to benevolence, it is a moral obligation for the one on whom it is imposed; it does not create a corresponding right to the benefit of the one who exercises it";[7]
d. of course, one could think otherwise: "I know opposing doctrines exist, doctrines that tell us: charity has had its time, the duty of voluntary benevolence should be replaced by the principle of obligatory solidarity";[8]
e. but these doctrines are "just as false in their premise as they would be disastrous in their consequences; they would deal a mortal blow to

what is most generous in human nature, the disinterested spirit of voluntary devotion, and to what has been the most productive in social activity, the mainspring of individual initiative. They would replace a principle of harmony respectful of all situations in life (providing aid to all misfortunes) with a principle of antagonism that would quickly unleash the confusion of all rights and laws, the war of interests, and, let me add, the aggravation of all misery."[9]

The debate was ended by Adolphe de Forcade La Roquette, minister of Agriculture, Commerce, and Public Works, who, having "refused to raise any questions about principles," and having recalled the completely pragmatic spirit of the funding, developed a wholesale doctrine of state intervention based on the concept of the *contract*: "The state does not recognize any superior, absolute law, imposed on parliament to obtain state assistance by claiming it as a right. There is nothing comparable in the draft law. What do we find there then? There is a contract, which is to say the negation of an absolute and anterior right, the negation of the right to assistance resulting from general ideas about solidarity."[10] In doing so, Forcade La Roquette took up the terms of the 1850 debate on the Retirement Fund, and proposed as a third way, setting traditional antagonisms against each other, the terms of a *contractual politics* between the state and individuals. The doctrine marked a definite shift with respect to the debates that had hitherto framed the question of insurance in social matters: the will to inscribe the politics of foresight, through the intermediary of insurance, within a certain problematic of rights. Not only did insurance entail the idea of rights, it also allowed for the old question of aid to be reformulated in terms of rights.

The Conflict of Responsibilities

Legal reparation for workplace accidents was beset by a substantial difficulty: the courts recognized a right for workers, and yet workers found themselves divested of this right in practice by virtue of the fact that they were obliged to prove a *patron*'s fault. As early as 1864, Jules Favre had posed the problem before Parliament. And in 1868, over the course of the debate concerning the creation of a "national insurance fund for accidents resulting from industrial or agricultural labor," he developed, as the best means of resolving the problem of workplace accidents, a counterproposal to modify the regime of civil liability: "I would no longer say that whoever commits a wrong owes reparation to the person they have harmed. I would say that whoever demands a service and obtains it from his fellow man must compensate for the harms that this service might lead to, as long as he cannot prove that the harm was caused by the one harmed, or was not caused by an accident owing to an act of God."[11] This was called the "reverse onus" system and was discussed at the opening of the parliamentary debate on "the responsibility for accidents affecting workers on the job" in 1880.

With their regime of responsibility, the *patrons'* institutions (in particular the relief funds) provided, if not a solution, then at least the guiding principle of a solution to these difficulties—the administration of proof, procedural sluggishness, the problem of trials.

However, beginning in the years 1869–70, the patronage regime experienced a multifaceted crisis: on the one hand, the centers of the patronage system were subject to repeated strikes that significantly undermined their promises of social peace; on the other, the republican members of Parliament, building on these strikes, undertook the creation of social legislation explicitly directed against patronage. This was less a matter of destroying the patrons' institutions than of reinscribing them in an economy of security founded on a rights-based strategy in which insurance figured as an essential element. This set of critiques provoked the Réforme Sociale school to undertake its own efforts to reform the patronage regime, also relying on insurance.[12] Thus, in the 1880s, insurance would be mobilized in the service of competing political visions that would come into conflict over the question of its organization. Liberals saw in it a way of resolving the problem of workplace accidents that would compromise neither the juridical regime of responsibility nor the eternal principles of liberty. The *patronat* saw it as a way of reforming the *patrons'* regime while also extending it. And the republicans drew on the technology of insurance to imagine a new strategy of civil security. With what objectives in mind did the Réforme Sociale school advocate for insurance? What were the reasons for this crisis of patronage leading to its reform?

Three main reasons can be distinguished:

a. Firstly, the practices of patronage in no way covered the entire field assigned to them. By definition, patronage rested on the free initiative of the *patrons*, on the consciousness of their responsibilities as "social authorities." The practices of patronage were only the prerogative of certain *patrons* who were held up as examples. Furthermore, whatever patronal voluntarism might amount to, the practice of *patrons'* institutions as it had so far been formulated, which is to say as the fact of individual *patrons*, could not offer a general solution to social problems. Under this form, they were necessarily limited to big business. In this way, the necessary extension of *patrons'* institutions could only happen through their transformation, through the abandonment of individual patronage. Two routes were available: on the one hand, the route that had been taken by Napoleon III when he introduced laws covering mutual aid societies, the National Retirement Fund, and the National Accident and Life Insurance Funds, which is to say the route of state patronage, containing all the risks of state socialism; and on the other hand, the route laid out by *patrons' associations*, which would allow the state to avoid socialism. Of course, it was the second one that the Réforme Sociale school would defend.

b. The patronage regime, as it had been formulated by Le Play, was far from having unanimous support among the ruling class. For the liberals, whichever political camp they belonged to, patronage was not and could not be the solution to social problems it claimed to be. So it was in 1855, the year Le Play published his *European Workers*, that Louis Reybaud, while reviewing John Stuart Mill's *Principles of Political Economy*, denounced the regime's limitations and illusions:[13] being based on generosity, the fact of competition would prevent its generalization; above all, the calculation that workers subject to the patronage regime would be better and more productive "proceeds from a complete misunderstanding of the human heart." "The good old days of patronage are no more."[14] This finding rested on the following two observations: first, the workers refuse it and will always refuse it. "There was nothing unforeseeable here; it was destined to be this way from the day the worker understood what benefits he might derive from a new right, the free debate over wages"; from this point on, social relations would be dominated by strikes, the "war over wages." Second, patronage, far from putting an end to strikes, would be their first victim. *Patrons*, in effect, would convert the "benevolent funds" that they allocated to *patrons'* institutions into "reserve funds" against strikes.

"Must we regret that this war has been unleashed? No," Reybaud said, "because it is the effect and sign of the exercise of liberty and if something does not have burdens and perils at the same time as benefits, it is not liberty. . . ." The example of the English, "who are our masters in these matters," shows how this war over wages could be rationalized, how the "spirit of calculation" could take over the workers themselves and make them consistent with the principles of the economy and the laws of the market. But for this to spread, the workers must have the right to come together collectively. In short, in opposition to the idea that social peace is achieved through workers' socialization under the aegis of the business, which was the form of socialization favored by patronage, Reybaud proposed the idea of workers forming an association amongst themselves, which would no doubt not avoid the war of wages, which was in every way unavoidable, but would "police" it.

On the other hand, in 1861, Jules Simon, in a series of articles published by *La Revue des Deux Mondes*, made a systematic critique of benevolence and, in particular, patronage: "The worker is not himself for the twelve hours that he is chained to a mechanical motor; let him at least return to himself as soon as he leaves the factory's grounds; let him be a husband and a father; let him feel his will and his heart." Having recommended the worker's moralization through the reconstitution of family life as a general solution to the problem of pauperism, and having designated as "the truly painful aspect of the worker's condition . . . the precarious nature of his resources that abandon him as soon as he leaves work," he argued in favor of institutions that, like mutual aid societies, allowed workers to exercise their responsibility and ensure their security on their own.

c. Finally, and this is doubtless the main reason for the crisis that engulfed it, the *patrons'* regime, such as it was effectively practiced, would in a certain sense prove by itself that it was not the solution to the social question that it claimed to be. The important sites of the patronage system—Mulhouse, the mines, Le Creusot—became the center of violent, bitter, harsh, and often bloody strikes that would take on a national dimension, and all the more so since they were connected to the political struggles of the end of the Second Empire and the development of the Workers' International. These strikes, which were like the social balance sheet of the empire, would continue under the Third Republic. At the heart of these workers' struggles, of course, was the question of wages, but also and always the practices of patronage, and in particular the question of relief funds.

Take the example of the miners' relief funds, which would lead to a legislative intervention, sanctioned by the first French law on obligatory insurance.[15] The workers' demands can be grouped under two main headings: under one heading, the control and management of the funds; under the other, their independence with regard to their use. Controlling the management of the fund did not only mean participating in the fund's administration in a nonillusory manner, but also, and above all, authority to verify the use of the funds, to limit their use to the compensation of accidents, to prevent them from becoming moralizing funds, to forbid the *patrons* from shifting the burden of their own indemnities onto the funds—in sum, the authority to ensure that their money would truly be returned to them in the form of indemnities. The demand for independence and autonomy also implied putting an end to forfeiture clauses, the recognition of the principle that contributions to the fund give rise to rights, and, at the same time, the creation of regional funds arranged around catchment zones. All of this would render the *patrons'* contribution obligatory.

These demands, formulated in the *French Miners' Book of Grievances*, would be taken up by republicans in Parliament, who would reformulate them as draft laws that reflected two additional motivations for intervening. The first was that it was not sufficient for the worker to have a right to compensation promised by the fund; this right must also be a *guarantee*. This was to pose the problem of the fund's financial regulation, a problem that would be resolved by using insurance techniques. Furthermore, the republicans in Parliament had purely political reasons for intervening in and regulating *patrons'* aid institutions. What had been one of the essential virtues of the patronage regime, the socialization of workers around *patrons* who were considered politically sound, became a danger with the creation of the Republic. The very same reasons that had served to promote patronage, the constitution of the *patron* as "social authority," responsible for the public order and security of the territory around their business, now meant that patronage had to be abolished. The strikes of 1869–70 had been used to denounce the empire and its politics. The strikes of the Third Republic served a properly political struggle against the enemies of the Republic, whether monarchist or Bonapartist.

Faced with the strikes of 1869–70, whose primary concern had been the question of relief funds, the *patronat* that was directly implicated (in particular, the managers of coal companies) responded that the complaints against them were motivated by the workers' belief that they had a right to the fund and that this was an illusion provoked by the instrument of wage withholding and maintained by certain legal commentators. Social peace would be found again through dispersing the funds and multiplying patronal institutions.[16] The *patronat*, at the time, was unable to find an alternative to its established strategy of industrial government.

This position would be abandoned by La Réforme Sociale beginning in the 1880s. This was doubtless for two reasons. The following years would demonstrate that this solution was not the right one: strikes broke out in places that had been considered models of patronage: Anzin in 1872, 1878, and 1884; Montceau-les-mines, where the unseemly 1882 Black Band affair profoundly weakened the patriarchal patronage of Jules Chagot.[17] In addition, faced with the spirits of universal suffrage, the definitive triumph of the Republic, and the development of public limited liability companies, any effort to keep with the strict principles of benevolence and patriarchal patronage amounted to isolating and, over the long term, condemning the patronage system itself. If it wished to endure, to respond to the ensemble of critiques and contestations of which it was the target, it would have to reform itself, to transition from a "patriarchal" and "militaristic" regime to a "liberal" one. Émile Cheysson became a champion of this reform effort, and the *Report on the Patrons' Institutions* at the Universal Exposition of 1889 constituted its manifesto.

Although it was never a question of compromising on the principles and ultimate aims of the *patrons'* regime—the definition of patronal obligations, the continuity of labor commitments, the stabilization and socialization of the workers through the business—these now had to be achieved through new methods and with new instruments.

As far as the method was concerned, this is what Cheysson had to say: "As under patriarchal patronage, it always and increasingly matters to fundamentally defend the workers against their lack of foresight; but it is a question of doing it almost without their knowledge, to suggest to them the best solution, to entrust it to their carefully guided initiative so that it doesn't go astray, to leave them the illusion (and more and more the reality) of an increasingly complete freedom over the management of their prudential institutions." In applying this method, (a) one would set out to transform the *patrons'* relief funds into mutual aid societies, to replace the *patron*'s benevolence with worker foresight, and to "involve the workers in the management of their funds"; (b) one would distinguish between prudential institutions according to the insurance-based principles of the division of risks, and the institutions would be managed according to the techniques of insurance; (c) forfeiture clauses would be suppressed, particularly with regard to retirement funds, and a system of *livrets* would be established representing the worker's rights to a pension accrued through his contributions; (d) the benefits of *patrons'* institutions would be extended by enriching them from within; (e) in response to the development of public limited liability companies, one would set out to multiply the opportunities to hold meetings; (f) finally, the entirety of these measures would require giving engineers social training; the engineer would no longer be just a technician, but a "conductor of men," a social engineer.

With the transformation of *patrons'* institutions of foresight into insurance institutions, the formation of mutual insurance funds among *patrons*, and the constitution of a worker's right to be guaranteed by the insurance-based management of the institutions, insurance technology became the instrument of liberal patronage. Its aims, at least in theory, coincided perfectly with the new republican politics of civil security. The reformed patronage system responded point by point to the set of liberal critiques directed against it. Was this a reversal? No. Rather, it was an alliance against the common enemy that took shape with the debate over workplace accidents, the enemy that was "state socialism," which also claimed insurance as a weapon. At the end of the nineteenth century, insurance, which everyone appealed to and which everyone saw as the solution to workers' security, thus gave rise to a power struggle over the question of how it was to be organized, a power struggle that set the partisans of the *freedom of insurance* against those of *obligatory state insurance*. The school associated with La Réforme Sociale would of course advocate for the liberty of insurance, a liberty that would alone be compatible with the reform of patronage, but that also involved obligations: in order to preserve liberty, in effect, the *patronat* must offer proof that it could on its own provide a general solution to the main question on the agenda, that of workplace accidents. For the *patronat*, the problem was posed in these terms: what we do not ourselves reform they will change to our detriment. This no doubt explains the very active militantism of the Réforme Sociale school during the debate on workplace accidents. Certainly, the *patronat* was not opposed to the recognition of professional risk and the movement in favor of insurance at the end of the nineteenth century. Quite the contrary. It had anticipated the practice with relief funds, and it was not held back by any juridical respect for the Civil Code. The *patronat* had a decisive interest in modifying the legislation so that it would put an end to trials. For the *patronat*, the problem was not to decide if one did or did not have the right to change the principles of civil responsibility or to decide if fault had to be preferred over risk. The issue lay elsewhere: knowing who, the *patronat* or the state, would have control over the management of the insurance dispositive.

The inadequacy of juridical solutions, the critique of patronal institutions, the general movement in favor of insurance, didn't all of this offer a rosy future for accident insurance companies? Did not the institution of accident insurance as the companies practiced it offer a solution to the problem of accidents, allowing them to dispense with the law, or at least to dispense with the law of responsibility?

Companies' accident insurance practices were the object of too many critiques; they were tainted by too much suspicion. They appeared to represent a form of financial speculation on workers' misery that could only aggravate the social problem posed by accidents. Insurers kept control over the trials; they forbade *patrons* from consorting with their workers. The companies—and this was the reason for their existence—were required to make a profit. No humanity could be expected from them. They did not fail to use all available procedural means to force workers to accept their conditions for settlement. Martin Nadaud, summarizing general opinion, had this to say in a report delivered to the Chamber of Deputies on November 11, 1882: "When an insurance company is party to the trial, one cannot deny the odious and immoral character of this struggle, in which one of the combatants is confined to a bed of misery; one cannot deny the odious and immoral character of this bargaining process, thanks to which the worker, after having been dragged from courtroom to courtroom, war-weary and trying to avoid starvation, settles for paltry compensation."

The trials no longer placed the injured workers face to face with their *patron*, but instead placed insurance companies face to face with a disreputable class of person scornfully designated as "claims agents" in parliamentary debate. These latter, particularly feared by the *patrons*, canvassed industrial estates and suggested workers hire them for their legal battles, in which the agents would receive, in the event of a success, a substantial portion of the increasingly generous compensation allocated by the courts.

It was in the interest of insurers, as well as claims agents, to see every accident as an occasion for litigation. For the former this was because litigation might force a worker to compromise; for the latter this was because litigation would help extract a maximum amount of money from the accident. Legal debates ended up covering for pure financial speculation. The moral question of fault, practically undecidable, blindly arbitrated the sordid haggling. One of the nonnegligible reasons for the initiation of the parliamentary debate and one of its immediate objectives were to put an end to these practices. All speculators, claims agents as well as insurers, had to be removed from the process. The reputation of the latter was so dubious in the eyes of the public that, when the parliamentarians sought to expand the insurance program for workplace accidents, they would do so in defiance of insurers, in order to drive them out.

As for the National Accident Insurance Fund, it was a failure: out of more than three million workers nationwide, the fund included 2,214 insured in 1874 and 1,812 in 1880. There were first of all technical reasons for this failure: only accidents causing permanent disability or death were insured; these were the least frequent. The premiums were calculated on the basis of mining accidents, one of the most dangerous industries. The administration had done nothing to publicize the law: the existence of the fund doubtless remained unknown to those who might have benefited from it. Administrative formalities, finally, made it almost impossible to implement. Each side saw it as a political operation, but there was no political force to sustain it: the "economists" saw it as "state socialism"; the Bonapartists, who had expressed their lack of enthusiasm during the debate, would be removed from power; the republicans could not be expected to become the defenders of a Napoleonic initiative.

Above all, neither the *patrons* nor the workers had any interest in insuring themselves. For the workers, this was because the modest aid promised by the fund could not compete with the hope of legal reparation. Neither did the *patrons* see much interest in the fund, since they sought above all to guarantee their civil liability. One of them wrote, "For the entrepreneurs, the question of responsibility is the only truly important issue."[18] Whether or not a *patron* affiliated his workers with the National Fund in no way altered his responsibility.

This failure would first of all serve the arguments of those who opposed state intervention, in particular in matters of insurance. It also proved that nothing of value could be expected from the worker's free exercise of foresight. This observation was commonplace at the end of the nineteenth century, and this was of a considerable political importance, since it undermined the foundation of a liberal politics of security: the solution to social problems would not depend on liberty. One would now have to depend on obligation and therefore on the law. Finally, it appeared that these two regimes of juridical and moral obligations, which Roucher in 1864 still thought of as complementary, in practice functioned in an antagonistic manner: at bottom the failure of the National Accident Insurance Fund stemmed from the overgrowth of the juridical sanction of responsibility.

The same observation could be made for each element of the workplace accident dispositive. Each element provoked its own burden of critique; none appeared individually as a possible solution to a problem that industrialization each day made more severe. Above all, far from working together harmoniously according to the principle of the liberal divide, so that in every case compensation or aid was offered to the affected worker, each one developed in a way that contradicted the others according to a logic of conflict. There was conflict between the juridical regime of compensation, the courts' humanitarianism, and the needs of a peaceful industrial governance, a conflict between the will to extend the field of insurance and the respect for the principles of civil responsibility. The solution to the problem posed by workplace accidents thus could be achieved only through the reform of the dispositive that had been in charge of them, through the modification of its architecture inasmuch as it was structured around the liberal regime of responsibility. At stake was the very principle of the liberal divide concerning civil security. The *juridical* and the *social* did not function, as they were supposed to, as a unified pair. Industrialization had placed them in opposition. One could no longer dream of combining the one with the other; one would have to choose between them.

It is much too simplistic to locate the problem of workplace accidents only in their existence and their quantity. The problem of accidents is indissociable from the practices that manage them and from their own type of rationality. The solution did not primarily depend on some institutional invention, but on a transformation in the way the accident was problematized. Workplace accidents challenged liberal political rationality and its way of posing the limit between law and morality. This was a conflict of rationalities that would over the course of the parliamentary debate focus on the problem of *trials*. Here was the biggest sticking point, the true line of opposition: must one continue to subordinate workers' compensation to a trial-based legal practice? Should trials be maintained? Must we subordinate workers' rights to a legal procedural exercise? Every solution, every proposal for reform would be judged according to this standard: would it lead to a trial? Thinking within the framework of classical liability law amounted to maintaining the prevalence of the judge and judiciary. This is what the reformers wanted at all costs to avoid. The invention of professional risk was tied to this imperative: create rights for workers, but rights that would not lead to a trial, rights that would put an end to the antagonism between capital and labor, rather than feeding into it—a body of law, then, where the judiciary function would be purely declarative, *expertise-based*. Social law, since this is what will emerge, was initially conceived as a nonjudiciary law.

Regardless of the envisioned solution, notably the development of an insurance-based system of reparation, the problem implied a transformation of the juridical regime of responsibility and thus a legal crisis. But this transformation also required and assumed a redefinition of the politics of civil security, in keeping with the principles of a new political economy, and with it, the set of mechanisms destined to insure, along with the public order, the regulation of economic and social life. In this regard, Léon Say was right to suggest, during the debate on the law of April 9, 1898, that this was "first and foremost, a political law."[19] More profoundly, the fact that the problem of workplace accidents was posed, that a regime of justice appeared as unjust, and that it became necessary to modify this regime, and, with it, the politics of civil security—all this assumed that the admirable economic, political, and juridical harmony that had to this point guided thinking about the problem of society's governance was dislocated. In order to resolve this problem, one needed to analyze and conceive of it with another type of rationality. There was not a solution to the problem of workplace accidents that did not leave behind liberal political rationality.

CHAPTER 9

First and Foremost, a Political Law

The political stakes of the parliamentary debate that began in 1880 are enough to explain its longevity.[1] One needs to look to the nature of the problem posed rather than the already-existing political and social divisions to find the underlying reasons for the duration of the debate—eighteen years. Even if it can be established, in view of the text finally adopted, that the left was favorable to a law that the right rejected, keeping to this explanation for why the debate lasted so long would make us miss the debate's essential features. There were not supporters on one side and opponents on the other. There was, based on a general inclination toward reform, competition among projects. The left and the right did not debate each other according to a proposition-opposition binary, but rather through two ways of posing the same problem. The *patronat*, at least the one representing big business, was the first group in favor of reforming the regime for compensating workers injured in workplace accidents. It was even one of the main driving forces of reform: it collaborated on the technical aspects of the reform projects, proposed solutions, and created institutions. The *patrons* defended the theme of professional risk. Were they not practically its inventors? They were naturally favorable to an insurance-based solution to the extent that the organization of workplace accidents would remain in their hands. Some did not hide their approval for the most radical solution proposed: the one favoring obligatory insurance. The workers and their political and syndical representatives did not participate (or hardly) in the technical debate. Evidently in favor of a reform, they only envisioned it in the most ideological terms: the *patrons* must be made responsible for accidents.

If there was considerable debate inside as well as outside of Parliament, this was not unique to France. The same problem was simultaneously being dealt with by all of the industrialized nations: Germany, Switzerland, Austria, England, Russia, Italy, and the United States, to name only a few. Beginning in 1880, on the occasion of the different universal expositions, representatives of these nations met in congresses of workplace accidents to discuss reforms and exchange their experiences. These congresses were a sort of general assembly where the industrialized nations sought to conceive of a postliberal era[2] with the social policies that would become those of the welfare state. As early as 1891, it was decided that the event should be called the *Congress of Workplace Accidents and Social Insurance*. As a result of international competition, social progress proceeded through the simultaneous adoption of measures. There was both simultaneity in the posing of problems and solidarity in the solutions. For this reason, legislation over workplace accidents and, more generally, social insurance would be based on comparative law, with reflection on foreign legislation playing a decisive role.

The experience of Germany, which, under Bismarck's leadership, adopted a system of social insurances—in 1883, a law on health insurance; in 1884, a law on workplace accidents; and in 1889, a law on disability—would play a decisive comparative role. It was soon understood that reform would be implemented according to the German model and would lead to the same organization of insurance, even if this was not to be accomplished by the same means. At least in France, German statistics, the only ones available, were used as a point of reference. In Parliament, people argued in the name of Germany. For some, denouncing a project as being inspired by the German model amounted to condemning it. For others, it was not possible that France, as innovator in matters of liberty, might cede the initiative to the Germans. Amidst the numerous critiques that members of Parliament leveled at this bureaucratic piece of legislation, denouncing it as the most horrible expression of socialism, state socialism, it is nevertheless possible to discern a certain fascination for an imposing architecture whose success would soon become undeniable. It would not be wholly incorrect to say that the problem for French members of Parliament was: How do we avoid being German?

The Contractual Hypothesis

On May 29, 1880, Martin Nadaud submitted a first-draft bill containing only one article: "When a man contracting his labor to another man is wounded or killed at his service, the employer will be fully responsible, at least if he cannot prove that the accident resulted from the fault of the victim."[3] A second project, submitted by Louis Peulevey, expressed the view that accidents due to unforeseen circumstances (68 percent, according to the statistic always cited) must be covered by society, and he proposed a reform of the National Accident Insurance Fund created in 1868.[4] A third one, authored by Félix Faure, put forward the principle of a systematic and all-inclusive form of compensation.[5] A fourth, finally, proposed a procedural reform: the establishment of a special jury.[6]

Such a variety of proposals attests that, at the time, there may have been agreement concerning the necessity of reform, but there was no agreement on the solutions. If there was evidently a problem concerning workplace accidents, it had not yet been formulated. What was the aim? Was it to reduce the most blatant abuses of the juridical regime of compensation by modifying the rules of judicial procedure? Or, by contrast, was it to make the law on workplace accidents the first piece of a complete social insurance dispositive? Was it to resolve the painful problem of the burden of accidents due to unforeseen circumstances or unknown causes, or to completely rethink them within the problematics of civil security? The first decade of the debate would be spent trying to understand how the question of workplace accidents should be formulated rather than discussing solutions. And it is only during the two deliberations of 1888 that the Chamber of Deputies finally agreed on what would then become the problem of workplace accidents: the organization of insurance covering professional risk.

Initially, one gravitated toward a solution of the juridical variety, involving the duty of the worker to provide proof of a *patron*'s fault. Liability law in itself was just; there was no need to modify it. However, it was unacceptable that, for factual and procedural reasons (concerning the burden of proof), the worker was in practice deprived of a right that the law should have granted. To successfully recharacterize the worker in juridical terms, a simple procedural modification seemed to suffice: shift the burden of proof to the *patron*. A presumption of responsibility would be imposed on the *patron*. The operation seemed to be relatively simple and need not pose significant problems. According to Nadaud's formulation, it would be enough to add a presumption clause to those already found in the Civil Code.

This idea of *the reversal of proof* was conducive to winning over the jurists. It allowed them to think that one could resolve the problem of workplace accidents by not wasting time on a law that, "in the current mindset, would be a political law." The means for doing this were available—namely, turning the *patron*'s obligation to ensure security into a contractual obligation: the contract for services would contain an obligation for the *patron* to provide security; the occurrence of an accident would attest, until proven otherwise, that the *patron* has not respected this obligation.[7] No one questioned the contents of the *patron*'s obligation to provide security that had been formulated in jurisprudence. Quite the contrary, it was claimed that the obligation's true juridical foundation was now established. Invoking dual juridical and sociological lines of argument, it was assumed that the courts had taken "a wrong turn" by turning the responsibility of *patrons* into a tort liability.

The obligation to provide security that was endorsed by jurisprudence represented a sort of obligation of care that did not square with a provision like that of article 1382 of the Civil Code, which required only that one do no harm to another: "The law commands abstention, it prohibits wrongdoing, it does not command care. By contrast, the contract's raison d'être is precisely to force someone out of abstention by offering a benefit. This ensures active participation through personal interest."

Granted, the accident in question was a *work accident*;[8] the question of responsibility should therefore be judged within the terms of the contract for services. But how, on this new juridical foundation, does one generate a *patron*'s obligation to provide security, since it could also be argued that by entering into a contract, workers take upon themselves the risks of their profession and furthermore that the wage is proportionate to the risks their work entails? Doesn't one lose the contract's contents as they have been defined by jurisprudence when the *patron*'s obligation is turned into a contractual obligation? How does one avoid reinstating the thesis of individual risk when also reinstating the framework of the contract for adjudicating accidents? It was assumed that the difficulty could be resolved through a sociological type of argument.

It was argued—the theme would be constantly revisited over the course of the parliamentary debate—that industrialization, mechanization, and the modern organization of labor had completely overturned the respective positions of the worker and the *patron*, what some called the "juridical environment."

In the modern conditions of industrial labor, the wage relation is a fundamentally asymmetrical and inegalitarian relationship. The workers lose control over their labor; what is sought is less their initiative than their obedience. And the *patron*'s power to organize, supervise, and dispose of people and things increases in the same proportion: "The worker has no power over the direction of industrial development; this control belongs to the one who commands, to the one who supervises, to the one who pays, to the *patron* alone. One burden of this role of manager and supervisor is the obligation to ensure that work is performed in conditions that are as perfect as possible for the safety and health of the worker."[9] Thus, we have arrived at the rule that, according to the supporters of the contractual thesis, expresses both the foundation and metric of *patrons'* responsibility with regard to workplace accidents: "The more the worker's independence is restrained, the more his activity is subject to the control of another, the greater are the *patrons'* duties: responsibility is a consequence of the authority exercised."[10]

Such was, in brief, the argument that supported the contractual thesis. It was the same one that supported the jurisprudential doctrine. The only thing that changed was its juridical object: the contract took the place of the tort.[11] The stakes of the contractual thesis were clear. It amounted to a conservative thesis aiming to give problems as difficult as workplace accidents a solution that did not affect the edifice of the Civil Code. This is, evidently, what made it successful.

The thesis would fail for two different reasons: theoretical and practical. The doctrine of contractual obligation to provide security that it expressed could be drawn neither from the Code—which was silent about what the *patron* must do besides paying a wage as well as about taking care and precautions to prevent accidents—nor from the expressed intent of the parties. It necessarily had these two equally contestable elements. Or else one had to invoke a sort of objective interpretation of the contract concerning its nature or its essence, from the point of view of equity, that would be set against the explicit will of the parties. This would entail turning the contract for services into a special type of contract—one began to speak of "employment contracts"—that would fall outside of the common law of article 1134 and would contain, almost inherently, mandatory provisions. The contractual thesis was all about turning the obligation to provide security into a legal obligation and making the contract for services a legal contract. Firstly, this partially contradicted the project to avoid the recourse to Parliament; secondly, this was not acceptable at a time when the idea of the contract could not be conceived independently of the principle of free will.

Otherwise, workers had to be deprived of their wills, denied any use of their liberty in their labor. The contract for services would be identical to the lease of objects or the transportation of merchandise. One can imagine the objections: How can you compare the worker to a piece of merchandise? Moreover, such an objectification of the worker was at the very least at odds with the will to redesignate the worker as a legal subject. Finally, the idea of burdening businesses and industrialists with a general presumption of guilt was philosophically very unsatisfying.

The contractual thesis, which was theoretically contestable, was full of practical unknowns. In the best-case scenario, it only offered a limited solution to the problem of accidents. The biggest confusion among the authors concerned the system of obligation that derived from the contract. Some protested that the desired reversal of the burden of proof could not be derived from the contract. Nor was there agreement over the substance of the *patron*'s obligation that was supposed to derive from the contract. And one was confronted with the serious problem that the contractual hypothesis seemed to validate agreements absolving responsibility. Finally, the very idea of reversing the burden of proof seemed like an overly large sacrifice, considering the practical results that could be expected. It did not change the scope of compensation: workers remained responsible for their own faults (20 percent of accidents), as well as for unforeseen circumstances (68 percent of accidents). Only accidents due to an unknown cause would be, in the most rigorous scenario, covered by the *patron*. Supporters of the thesis responded that this objection conflated two separate problems: the *juridical* problem of responsibility and the *social* problem of covering unforeseen circumstances. The latter was the purview of insurance. Such an argument could not count as a solution, given the criticisms of insurance company practices.

Above all, the foreign legislative experience (Germany, 1871; Switzerland, 1878, 1881) was at hand to prove that, far from resolving the problem of workplace accidents, the establishment of such a provision instead exacerbated it. Because of the proliferation of trials that resulted, trials that would unfold in more and more pathetic terms due to *patrons*' recourse to insurance, Louis Ricard declared in the Chamber of Deputies that the system of reversing the burden of proof was odious. The goal was to avoid trials: every solution that ended up encouraging them was automatically disqualified. To obtain a dubious amelioration of the worker's judicial status at the price of aggravating the relations between workers and *patrons* was truly a prohibitive cost.

The thesis would eventually be abandoned by its own supporters. The French courts declined to accommodate it. The debate that it provoked did not prove useless, however. Its merit had been to pose the problem of workplace accidents as questioning the nature and the regime of the labor contract. To regulate the problem of workplace accidents, the law could not be avoided, and this law would be a way of legislating the contract for services.[12] Moreover, it was proven that there was no solution to the problem of workplace accidents in the framework of the common law of obligations: the criminal route had been exhausted; the contractual route seemed illusory. A new law would have to be invented, a law that would entail a totally different judicial modality, since, in principle, it would not lead to a trial—a formidable conclusion to the extent that it signified a final divorce between the political imperative to provide security and social harmony, on the one hand, and the juridical authority of the Civil Code, on the other.

"A New Law"

It is in these terms that Alfred Girard described the project submitted by Félix Faure on February 11, 1882, which advanced (without yet using the term) the thesis of *professional risk*.[13] Girard specified that this law "lay outside the scope of current legislation" and that it constituted a "parallel legislation." It would be conceptualized under the category of *solidarity*, which doubtless here found its first institutional foothold. Léon Say specified, "Between civil law and the new law, there is no interaction; the one is based on the principle of responsibility; the other on the principle of solidarity."[14] This clearly situated the relationship between the new law and the common law of liability: they were less contradictory than heterogeneous. They belonged to two epistemological configurations whose differences the members of Parliament would continue to expose over the course of the debate.

In the parliamentary debate, the concept of professional risk was used in two poorly distinguished senses. Professional risk is first of all a risk to be insured. From this point of view, its definition raises a problem of insurance technique: it is a matter here of determining risk's setting, the population of beneficiaries, the cost of indemnities, who will cover the premiums, and which institutions will reinsure the risk. A whole segment of the parliamentary debate, the lengthiest one, would be devoted to reaching consensus on the definition of professional risk as insurable risk. And it is this concept that would be enshrined in the new law where one searches in vain for any statement of general principles comparable to articles 1382–86 in the Civil Code.

Professional risk also designates a way of posing the question of workplace accidents, a way of envisioning their reparation, which, without relying on the examination of the worker's or *patron*'s behavior, generally attributes the problems to labor. "All labor has its risks; accidents are the unfortunate yet inevitable consequence of labor itself."[15] In this sense, "professional risk" refers to a principle of attributing damages and a specific regime of obligation. According to the canonical definition proposed by Émile Cheysson, "Professional risk is the risk pertaining to a particular profession independently of the fault of the workers and the *patrons*." According to the principle of professional risk, the burden of workplace accidents is to be attributed to the head of the business, no matter their cause, whether they juridically are due to an unforeseen circumstance or, better, to the worker's own grave misconduct. "To make the *patron* responsible for the fault of the worker he employs, I do not hesitate to say, affronts the conscience. It seems to me that a cry of justice is raised against such theories," Louis Peulevey indignantly exclaimed in the Chamber of Deputies.[16] Senator Lebreton would go even further: "This is the reversal of all of our legal principles. . . . This is not a law of justice, since it strikes even the innocent and irreproachable *patron*."[17] Such hostility only attested to the fact that the new rule of professional risk had no meaning within the categories of the law of responsibility. The idea of professional risk emerged through a split between causality and attribution and the indifference of the second toward the first, which is to say through the intuition of a principle of attribution that no longer referred to the objective causality of damages. The invention of professional risk consists of conceiving a principle of attribution that, freed from the old dependence upon nature, would find its reference in a social relation. This is what made the category both valuable and difficult to conceive.

In the explanatory statements for these projects, as in his interventions in the Chamber of Deputies, Faure gave two arguments in favor of this "juridical heresy": on the one hand, was the idea of profit—"In every instance where an accident is produced in the service and to the profit of a business venture, the business should bear the consequences of the accident"—on the other hand was the idea that the burden of workplace accidents should be counted amongst the general costs of business, under the same designation as "the factory and the destruction of its resources, the degradation of its equipment, the risks of fires, risks of liability, and many others."[18] These two arguments do not have the same weight. The idea of making the *patron* bear the risks of a labor process that he supervises and from which he reaps profits had the seductive quality of being inscribed in the traditional framework of responsibility; it maintained the fiction of a causality, except that it substitutes an objective causality for the subjective causality of fault. It is known that beginning in the 1890s a certain juridical tradition would develop this theory under the framework of "created risk." But this does not sufficiently explain the new legislation. Converted into a legal proposition, it would place a presumption of responsibility on the *patron* to cover even unforeseen events; it does not mean that the "grave misconduct" of workers would be attributed to him, although this would be accomplished by the law of April 9, 1898.

The idea that the burden of workplace accidents is to be counted amongst the general costs of business is, despite its bean-counting image, much richer than the previous argument. First of all, the establishment of professional risk marks the realization of the objectification of the business through insurance: businesses are characterized by the risk of accidents, and, inversely, it is the risk that constitutes them as such. Under the purview of the 1898 law, the "captain of industry" represents a legal entity. The principle of professional risk does not make the *patron* responsible for the fault of his workers—no more than accidents due to unforeseen circumstances. Professional risk is anonymous; it characterizes a collectivity; individuals are not the cause, but only a certain part of the cause, more or less determinable in advance. While the theory of created risk remains a realist theory, connected to the sociological reality of industrial transformations and condemned for that very reason to remain limited, the theory of professional risk is, by contrast, expressed as a fiction. It contrasts what has thus far passed as the only reality with the equally real reality of risk, though this latter has no other existence than as a category of thought. Whereas the theory of created risk or the risk of profit is inscribed in the framework of a type of classic juridical truth-telling, the principle of professional risk presumes a new one.

The rationality that is at the foundation of professional risk changes the way of thinking about the problem of the juridical attribution of damages: no longer in terms of *cause*, but in terms of *redistribution*—redistribution within the business, between profits and costs; more generally, the social redistribution of costs. Professional risk, like every other risk, only exists in society. Léon Say had seen this. The idea of professional risk is at the end of the day only a means of transferring to the whole of society, which benefits from industrial labor, the burden of labor's associated damages.[19] It reestablishes a broken equilibrium. In this sense, the concept of professional risk obeys a rule of equity.

The idea of professional risk proceeds from a statistical and probabilistic type of thought. The regularity of risk is independent of the behavior of individuals. The faults they commit, whatever they may be, are only partial factors that do not affect risk's statistical reality. Thus, when it is a question of professional risk, one can insure all workplace accidents up to and beyond the worker's (or *patron*'s) inexcusable fault. This is one of the main benefits of the concept: to derive workers' rights from the very fact of the accident, from the damage sustained, whatever the cause may be. The key difference is that whereas a principle of responsibility based on an idea of cause implies a selective distribution of burdens, professional risk, on the contrary, brings *solidarity*. Solidarity, on the one hand, between the *patron* and the worker in the business setting: professional risk could put an end to the antagonism between labor and capital that liability law fed. On the other hand, social solidarity: professional risk, by shifting the burden of workplace accidents onto society, ensures a new equilibrium between producers and consumers. It reconciles society with industry by offering an intellectual tool adequate to its development. Industry is not to blame for modernizing itself; accidents no longer indict industry, and professional risk brings with it a conception of the good and the evil that the philosophies of solidarity would develop. Beyond ideas of culpability and inevitability connected to fault, professional risk will allow the accident to be conceived in accordance with the categories of *normality* and *abnormality*.

The type of rationality at the foundation of professional risk does not ascribe it any limit.[20] In terms of professional risk, every workplace accident can be compensated, for all industry, for all personnel. Professional risk could cover what Say called the "risk of humanity."[21] It naturally extends to cover "social risk" as such. However, for it to become practical, it must be properly delineated. Since this could only be done from a position outside itself, there would not be any practical definition of risk that was struck by a constitutive *arbitrariness*.[22] The category was truly very confusing: the debate would not end with its recognition. It would rather begin with it, to the extent that professional risk is nothing until it is defined. And this necessary definition—How far does it go? Who benefits? What are its rates of compensation?—could rest neither on a conceptual constraint nor on objective criteria drawn from natural circumstances. It would irreducibly stem from a decision that could not be applied to an exterior objectivity but that instead came down to the object to be defined and its particularity.

The recognition of professional risk also involved a remarkable inflection in the nature of legislative decision-making and in the rules for producing norms. It was no longer only about conferring a juridical status on a hitherto unknown social reality—the fact of industrial transformations—after deciding on its true objectivity. The debate over professional risk would rather allow legislators to free themselves of the obligation to refer to some kind of nature—of things or of the law—so as to elaborate the rules through a legislation that would now be called "social." The supporters of the new law would not look to express a new principle of responsibility that could replace civil law's principle of fault; they would look rather to free themselves from the idea of thinking about law through universal and timeless principles in order to conceive of it in terms of social objectives: in this case to put an end to the antagonism between labor and capital by allowing every worker injured in a workplace accident to be compensated. Through its neutrality with regard to the workings of natural causalities, professional risk opened a sort of non-oriented space where the different economic, social, and juridical interests concerned would be able to freely balance out and find a point of composure. The form of a *compromise* would thus replace nature in the production of juridical objectivity.

Hence the very particular character of the law of April 9, 1898: its character as a law of *transaction.*[23] Workers would abandon their rights to full restitution of damages sustained in the event of the *patron*'s proven fault and gain the certainty of always being compensated; the *patron* would be juridically responsible for all workplace accidents, the portion of his responsibility being rigorously limited. The concept of professional risk is indissociable from the concept of transaction at its foundation. And inversely, it is as a synonym of *legal transaction* that its adversaries would combat it.

If there is truly a regime of professional risk, it has no juridical foundation in the sense that this expression implies the idea of a general principle. What establishes professional risk is not to be found in a sociology of industrial labor, either, even if it involves a recognition of one; it is based on a new politics of the law that is now called "social." This happens in such a way that the debate over professional risk unfolds on two always conflated levels: (a) Must accidents be conceived in terms of risk, from the vantage point of a new law? and (b) How is the insurable risk to be defined? Or further: Must we, Parliament, establish ourselves as the agents of these transactions? And if the answer is yes, how is justice to be defined in these transactions? Moreover, to recognize professional risk would not only mean establishing a new principle for attributing costs, but more generally finding both a new way of legislating and a new mode of discharging juridical norms. In a word, it would mean establishing a new type of *jurisdiction.*

The Game of Transactions

The law of April 9, 1898, concerning the "responsibility for accidents affecting workers in the workplace," is divided into five sections: I.—Compensation in the event of accidents; II.—Accident claims and inquiries; III.—Authority—Jurisdictions—Procedure—Revision; IV.—Coverage; V.—General provisions.

Let's set aside the fifth section, which only concerns how the law is to be applied. Sections II and III broadly treat the problem of compensation. Compensation then comprises three parts. No part, not even the first, outlines the principles of professional risk; but all of them presume it and manage it. The first part (section I) defines professional risk as risk that is insurable from the point of view of those affected (articles 1 and 2) and the cost of compensation (articles 3, 4, and 5). The first five articles thus state the rule, article 20, rejected in the part treating procedures, outlining an exclusion of intentional and inexcusable faults. The second part (sections II and III) defines the conditions for implementing the new law from the standpoint of the accident: Parliament defines the conditions of a procedure that should be as brief as possible and take the form of a conciliation (article 16). The last part is dedicated to the problem of covering the worker's claims: access, insurance, and the creation of a guarantee fund (articles 23 to 28).

The drafting of each of these three blocks led to a debate not only within each of the two assemblies—the Chamber of Deputies and the Senate—but more importantly between them. As in the German and Austrian models, the Chamber conceived of professional risk from the standpoint of the organization of insurance. Its approach to the problem of workplace accidents was less juridical than social. It is the inverse with the Senate, which did not want to hear about the organization of insurance and conceived of reform as only needing to fulfill the timeless rules of liability law. The definitive text, adopted with the greatest urgency at the end of the legislative session, when all arguments had been exhausted, would be the result of a compromise between the two social and legal manners of envisioning the problem. The Senate accepted the definition of professional risk elaborated by the Chamber, the Chamber abandoning its projects for a court of arbitration and obligatory insurance. Fittingly, section IV of the law was not titled "Insurance" but "Coverage." This is a text, then, that was predictably seen as a bastard. However, precisely, what might appear unsatisfying from a purely rational point of view is not necessarily so if the legislation obeys the social principle of harmonization amongst diverse interests.

The Fixed Rate

According to the common law of articles 1382–86 in the Civil Code, the reparation of damages obeys two rules: its amount is sovereignly determined by the judge, not on the basis of a set scale, but on a case by case basis; it must be comprehensive, which means adequate to the harm suffered. The rule used by the courts to determine the amount of compensation obeyed a principle of *individualization*. Two harms might appear to be similar, yet they do not affect the same individuals in the same situation, do not have the same consequences, in a word do not cause the same harm. Hence the infinite variance in the total damages set by the courts in cases that might appear analogous. And the serious accusation of *arbitrariness* was brought against judicial accident compensation.

Certainly, for reasons simultaneously relating to competition but above all security, the *patrons* would not tolerate the (often drastic) variation in compensation that they observed from one court to the next, and sometimes within the same court, for what appeared to them to be the same accident. The *patrons* did not hide the fact that they preferred the certainty provided by a fixed scale of compensation even if this meant accepting their own accountability. It is a remarkable fact that this serious critique of arbitrariness was widely taken up by the members of Parliament, very few of whom defended the principle of individualizing compensation. It seemed abnormal that what was recognized to be the same damage could continually lead to different compensations. In fact, a new conception of equality and justice was being formed. The concept of professional risk was emblematic of this, and the parliamentary debate would be the occasion for reflecting on it.

The judicial mode of compensating workplace accidents was not compatible with the idea of professional risk. The burden of professional risk would not fall on the *patron*; it must be controlled by insurance. This assumed that its amount must be fixed in advance, that a rate of compensation should be determined—at the very least that judicial discretion should be rigorously controlled. But also, in the logic of professional risk, reparation no longer found its cause in the fault of an overseer, but, directly, in the harm suffered. Compensation could no longer have any other metric than a social one: "It cannot be a question of comprehensive reparation," Girard and Nadaud would say, "since true attribution does not exist."[24] Faure specified: "Since we recognize that there is no true fault, that there is only risk inevitably resulting from labor, we are justified in limiting responsibility."[25] Finally, above all, trials must be avoided to put an end to the uncertainties of the judicial procedure: workers by ceding a portion of their hypothetical rights for the certainty of aid; the *patron* by accepting a principle of accountability, albeit predefined and limited.

This ensemble of requisites naturally led to the idea of a fixed rate and the legal structuring of compensation. The rate would be the very expression of this compromise known as professional risk.[26] As Senator François-Marie Thévenet summarized at the end of the debate, "Professional risk necessarily entails a fixed rate: there is a fixed rate for the accident and a fixed rate for the compensation."[27] This principle in itself contained nothing particularly new: it was used for military pensions; it was at the foundation of damage insurance compensation; the German and Austrian legislation had adopted it. Yet it did pose formidable problems. First of all, it implied the restriction of the judge's role in deciding over the multiple elements that constitute liability. Marc Sauzet saw in it "the sure sign of a public weakening of the concept of law, or a surge in public passions that threaten to snuff out all feeling of impartiality and justice."[28] Senator René Bérenger himself interpreted it as a return to barbarity:

> Parliament substitutes itself for the judge, and the law is a true judgment rendered in advance, blind to each case. It will be a case of this amount for temporary disability, this amount for permanent partial disability, this amount for complete permanent disability, this amount for an eye, and this amount for a tooth. You wish to return us to the legislation of the Visigoths. I contest this set of legal provisions. Persistent in thinking that the principle advantage of contemporary justice, so fortuitously founded on the debris of the arbitrary and diverse justice and byzantine procedures that existed before 1789, is this complete freedom of discretion left up to the courts, this suppression of multiple obstacles that prevent the judge from listening to the cry of his conscience, I ask that the courts not be deprived of the right to discretion.[29]

Above all, the principle of professional risk confronted Parliament with a decisive difficulty: it required determining a new metric for compensating damages, thus a new rule of justice distinct from the self-explanatory idea of equalizing damage and compensation.

In practical terms, compensation could not have any standard aside from the damage itself. For equal damages there would be equal compensation. But how does one construe damage? How is it defined, since the same disability—the loss of an arm, a leg, an eye—does not have the same consequences for every profession, or for victims of different ages, or for the different family sizes supported by the workers? With regard to so many parameters, the character of a set rate appeared supremely unjust, in particular if the system of the insurance companies was adopted, where injuries were in a certain sense appraised in advance. How does one put a price on the body? One spoke of appraising the worth of human flesh, the return to the *wehrgeld* of the Franks and Burgundians.[30] Wasn't the search for security and social peace being pursued at the price of a considerable injustice in solutions, a sort of judicial regression where one might wonder if the most legitimate rights of workers were being sacrificed solely for the *patrons'* interests? According to Senator Bérenger's strong formulation, "Wasn't the fixed rate the very negation of justice?"[31]

No. The fixed rate, in itself, could not be called just or unjust. That depended on the scale that would be used to calibrate it. The insurance companies' system was found to be unjust because it compensated a sort of abstract damage, accident in general and not a workplace accident where the damage specifically involved loss of one's ability to work, the latter finding expression in the victim's wages. The fixed rate would be just as soon as it was calibrated to the victim's *wages* and would be determined, according to a certain scale, as compensation for the loss of wages due to the accident. Disabilities would be calibrated as a percentage of the total inability to perform any labor (set at 100 percent). In cases of death, the worker's widow and children would also receive a certain percentage of the wages that the worker would have received had the worker not been in an accident, but under the form of an annuity. But at what level should these different compensations be fixed? How much should be the compensation for permanent disability?

Having conceived of compensation as "assistance," "aid," or "relief," and having toyed with the idea of adopting the National Accident Insurance Fund's rates, it would be agreed that the worker's right should be based on the idea of a transaction reflecting the concept of professional risk. By using statistics on the causes of accidents, the full value of permanent disability came to be fixed, though not without contestation, at the rate of two-thirds of the worker's wages. This solution was only adopted after long discussion. Of course, there was the problem of the financial costs that would be placed on industry. But the economic problem did not especially affect the principle of the fixed rate, which was the biggest obstacle. "It is not possible to place the imprudent, risk-prone worker on the same footing as the cautious and seasoned worker. It is not possible to place the *patron* who has done everything he could to shield his workers from accidents on the same footing as the *patron* who may have indirectly courted accidents through his lack of care," Deputy Ernest Camescasse explained, summarizing a general opinion.[32]

At one point, it was thought that a satisfactory compromise was to be found between the necessities of insurance and those of individualized compensation by stipulating that the judge could set rates within the limits of a legal maximum and minimum. But if this solution satisfied a feeling of justice to which many still clung, it jeopardized both the principle and the aims of the new legislation. In principle, this was because the idea of professional risk consisted of setting compensation rates based only on damage, independent of circumstances, and any consideration of the workers' behavior. In its aims, it was because it entailed making every accident a reason for litigation, and this in a context where one precisely sought an end to the confrontation between insurance companies and claims agents.

Thus, despite the resistance of those who would only want to see justice in the hands of the judiciary, the principle of the fixed rate was eventually adopted as the only solution compatible with the new legislation's social objectives (article 3 of the law of April 9, 1898). Parliament became the representative of the interests of the contracting parties; it compromised in their name. It thus endorsed the practice of transaction that *patrons* and insurers had used for a long time, while carefully controlling its conditions. The decision was important. Parliament had established a new way of proclaiming law. The judge saw his discretionary power significantly reduced.

Parliament, finally, had established a new rule of justice. In the case of classic judicial compensation, there was no sense in comparing the compensation of one person with that of another: the rule of individualization in principle made them incommensurable. From now on, in matters concerning workplace accidents, one would no longer look to equate reparation with the harm committed. The metric for compensation was no longer found in the objectivity of the harm, but in a certain obligation that society recognizes toward some of its members. This metric is variable; it is fundamentally arbitrary in relation to the harm, even if, in the present case, Parliament wanted to legitimate this arbitrariness through the idea of the transaction. The metric for compensation was nothing other than a social relation. Its amount was determined by the sum that society was able to devote to the compensation of damages, according to the state of the economy. The fixed rate for professional risk was nothing other than the code for redistributing this "social" sum. Justice meant that two individuals placed in the same legal situation would be treated equally. This new mode of compensation was adequate for the concept of workplace accidents that professional risk objectifies: the wealth produced by labor serves to repair the damages connected to its own production. In a word, professional risk designates a dispositive that allowed the economy to regulate itself by avoiding recourse to morality.

The judge, then, gave way to the expert. Ideas of punishment and condemnation disappear, to be replaced by the sole objective acknowledgment of the damage suffered and the application of a preestablished rate. In the judicial system, compensation was a way for workers to make known their rights, their just rights, to assert not only the physical loss they had suffered, but also their moral worth, to reinstate their scorned and despised dignity, to wage a battle where they employed, in the face of the *patron*'s will, their entire being. From this point on, the pursuit of justice would be a battle between experts, where everything was beyond the worker's will. It would mean pursuing a maximal rate of disability and increasing the amount of the pension. If the law instructed workers to demand the power to work without being either wounded or killed, they could now only obtain compensation through insurance. The judge assessed behavior according to faults committed. Insurers and doctors looked to unmask *pretenders*.[33] This marks a singular shift in the class struggle. There was a general desire for an end to the actions of "the rabble of case agents" that speculated on workers' misery. Workers were transformed into speculators of the self, as it were, with their own suffering as the object of speculation. There was good reason for workers to present themselves as the most gravely wounded, as the most mutilated. It is true that this was perhaps the price that had to be paid to transform workers into owners of capital: one now represented, thanks to the new law, by their own bodies.

Risk and Danger

The definition of the fixed rate of compensation doubtless brought with it the principle of professional risk; yet this was not enough to make it practicable. It remained to be determined who would stand to benefit. Would the new law apply to any type of artisanal, industrial, or agricultural labor? Or should the benefits be limited to those working in industries that, since 1804, had experienced the transformations giving rise to the new class of risks designated by the term *professional risk*? Was it the very fact of the workplace accident that gave access to the law's provisions? Or the fact of working in an environment reputed to be particularly dangerous? The drafting of the first article of the law—the delineation of the scope and field of application of professional risk—was one of the most intensively debated points in the parliamentary debate. What meaning should be given to the concept of professional risk? Is it a category of thought, a new way of envisioning the problem of accidents, applicable no matter the industry or type of labor concerned? Or, on the contrary, does the category of professional risk only describe the reality of a danger specific to certain industries, in order to provide the danger a juridical existence? Theoretically, this was not at all the same thing, and it did not entail the same practical consequences.

As a category of a new body of law, professional risk, we have seen, is also a category of thought: as such, its genesis did not refer to reality but to epistemological transformations. The existence of professional risk does not depend on the nature of the industry or labor in question. It stems from the application of the type of rationality informing insurance practices to workplace accidents, a rationality that itself has a somewhat limitless application. It is a manner of envisioning the compensation of damages that, free of the knowledge of their cause, pictures it in terms of a social redistribution of costs. Professional risk can help one think about accidents in every type of labor; its extension is in principle limitless. This is what Faure explained, desiring to avoid connecting professional risk to concepts of danger and mechanization: "The professional risk has absolutely no origin in the development of mechanical instruments. It has always existed. Although it was not appreciated in the way we appreciate it today, it existed no less in the previous century."[34] This opinion was corroborated by the statistics: the most dangerous industries were not, despite general opinion to the contrary, the most mechanized. It was thus perilous to want to connect the recognition of professional risk to the fact of industrial development.

In this perspective, to adopt the new legislation was not only to recognize a hitherto misunderstood reality, but to choose between one type of thinking and another. This was to take account of the reality of the workplace accident as such, rather than reducing it to the fact of industrial transformations. In addition, once this decision was made, Parliament could reserve the option to progressively implement this legislation in order to ensure its success. This is the position that was adopted by Parliament in the first article of the April 9, 1898, law.

Although simple in appearance, this position, which could be called broad, would provoke considerable opposition. Bearable for large businesses, which did not wait for legislative intervention to practice it, professional risk would be ruinous for small ones. It was denounced as a measure of industrial consolidation with politically disastrous effects; it definitively discouraged workers from establishing themselves as patrons; it would lead to the disappearance of the small *patronat*, which was, after all, the cradle of democracy. The argument forgot that professional risk was an insurance risk, that it was not meant to be directly borne by the *patrons*, and that, to the extent that small businesses were often the most dangerous, the premium of professional risk would be certainly less costly for the small *patron* to bear than the comprehensive compensation called for in article 1382.

A second objection of the juridical-constitutional variety would join the economic argument. To proceed as the Chamber of Deputies had done, by enumerating in the first article of the law the list of industries or kinds of work to which the law would apply, amounted, with a singular arbitrariness, to enacting a law of *privilege*. Why these industries and not others if the goal is to protect workers against the very fact of accidents? The law should be general. This is a fundamental principle of republican legislation. If the extent of professional risk must be limited, this should only be done as a function of a universalizable principle: identical treatment for an identical situation. The limiting principle of the new legislation could only be found in an objective reason, not in the sole will of Parliament. One senses the shift: the critique led to a transformation of professional risk into an objective cause of responsibility as understood by traditional law, which was exactly what one wanted to escape.

This drift was natural. It attested less to the ill will of certain members of Parliament than to what, in Gaston Bachelard's vocabulary, would be called an epistemological obstacle. One could not help thinking that if professional risk must be recognized it was because it really existed, as a fact of industrial transformations that defeated the law of proof and multiplied inherent dangers resistant to all preventative measures. Professional risk could not only be a name. What mattered was the thing. People did not realize that the new reality was only the occasion for a different way of thinking, even if thought and reality could not be conflated.

It is also true that Parliament would not justify its decision to establish a new law based on its own sovereignty: it, too, needed to believe in the reality of professional risk. It was necessary to correlate the new rule with a certain objectivity, at the risk of conflating the motivations for the creation of a new law—industrial transformation, the desire to not leave injured workers without aid—with the law itself: at the risk, then, of inscribing the new law within the old law's categories and creating a new cause of responsibility, a law particular to certain industries and certain forms of work. It was decidedly difficult to leave behind the type of thought that informed the Civil Code.

The persuasiveness of Senator Bérenger's very legalistic interventions, with which he repeatedly lobbied his colleagues of the upper chamber, attests to this. Bérenger did not refuse the principle of creating legislation in favor of workers injured by workplace accidents. On the contrary, he put forward projects and counterprojects. He claimed to be a defender of "professional risk"; he nonetheless proposed an interpretation of professional risk that made it simply a complement to the common law of responsibility, not an alternative. The transformations that industry had experienced since 1804 could not as such invalidate the principle of responsibility formulated by article 1382 of the Civil Code and thus only justified limited measures destined to fill in the law's gaps where a new reality was apparent. The new source of responsibility that would be recognized had to be generally applicable.

It was thought that the concept of *danger* would allow one to respond to this series of requirements. Danger was adaptable to the causal framework of responsibility. Conflated with unforeseen circumstances, its recognition as a specific cause of responsibility did not affect the traditional way of punishing the faults of the worker or *patron*. Moreover, it was a universalizable category: wherever danger could be found, the worker who was recognized as its victim would benefit from the law's provisions. Thus Senator Bérenger's proposals foresaw that "all dangerous labor" would provide a right to compensation,[35] with the understanding that "labor" should not mean industry or profession in general, but the express designation of a precise occupation—this alone allowing one to define labor as dangerous.

The strength of the thesis resided in its universality: the workplace accident was conceived as independent of all consideration of fact concerning industrial modernization.

This solution seemingly benefited from a high degree of coherence. It nonetheless fell prey to the two reproaches of injustice and impracticality. Firstly, abstracting from the question of how to define danger, this thesis was as discriminatory as the one it contested: among the workers who were victims of workplace accidents, only those who worked in an occupation labeled dangerous would be able to benefit from the new law's provisions. In what way, it was asked, were these workers more important than the others? One then arrived at situations of a flagrant injustice. One consequence was that any *patron* who had the misfortune of seeing his business recognized as dangerous or involving dangerous elements would at the same time also be penalized with the cost of professional risk. This did not encourage industrial modernization.

All of this assumed that there was some agreement over the definition of "danger." But how can "danger" be defined? "Danger" is the very paradigm of a false objective category. How can you know if something is dangerous when it has not been experienced, when the danger is not manifested in an accident? A statistical grasp of danger is possible. Yet this proposition was unacceptable within the perspective described here, since it amounted to making the very fact of the accident and not danger the basis of the law. Some would have liked to propose an objective definition of "danger": danger would reside in the machine or the presence of a mechanical instrument. The solution was overly arbitrary: it amounted to excluding the statistically most dangerous industries from the law (mining, construction, transportation, for example). Lacking an objective criterion of danger, one had to proceed by enumeration. This was such a meticulous task, so subject to revision, that it could not be the work of Parliament. Who then would come up with the list of dangerous labor, given that this entity would practically be the master of the law? The Conseil d'État? It was not possible for Parliament to establish it as a legislator. So the judge was left. This was the solution that Senator Bérenger ended up embracing, after some hesitation.

The result: having wanted to suppress Parliament's arbitrariness, another even more contestable form of arbitrariness would be reintroduced, that of the judge. The judge-legislator was established: "If we accept the commission's system," Senator Maxime Lecomte explained,

> it is not we who will make the law, it will be the courts; so that, sirs, in the place of the law, which should be immutable, equal for all and applying equally throughout all of our territory, you would have something absolutely unstable, which is to say jurisprudence, which varies according to each court and in each part of the country. Sometimes jurisprudence will make the new principles of risk triumph, other times the old principles of personal responsibility, and this will happen everywhere on a daily basis.[36]

Worse, the number of trials would increase. Every accident would lead to a double trial, the first a preliminary hearing to determine if the accident was due to dangerous labor, the second to apply the relevant law. These different objections, in particular the last, without a doubt socially prohibitive, have only small relevance from a strictly juridical point of view. That the law did not cover certain industries, however high their accident rate, was not in itself juridically objectionable if in these industries the workers' situation had not changed. In these cases, it was simply supposed that accidents resulted from the workers' (or the *patron*'s) lack of foresight. That the law led to a trial and that it implied a judge's individualized appreciation could not count as a juridically pertinent objection, either. The thesis came down to instating a presumption of delimited responsibility under the rubric of "professional risk," restricting to the sole hypothesis of danger the presumption that had been expressed through the labor contract or the first paragraph of article 1384 of the Civil Code. This was like basing the old idea of the reversed burden of proof on tort law.

After having repeatedly considered the problem, the senators agreed to recognize that dangerous labor is labor that leads to accidents, that danger could only be practically defined through the very fact of the accident: "What allows us to distinguish dangerous industries from nondangerous industries is the accident itself," Senator Alfred Poirier, the bill's rapporteur, would state.[37] One could distinguish dangerous labor or industries from those that were not dangerous. There were only differences in danger's intensity. This amounted to establishing the accident as the foundational condition of the new law and abandoning the idea that professional risk had to describe an objectivity in favor of the idea that it was a category of thought. All labor—artisanal, industrial, commercial, or agricultural—was liable to fall under the new legislation, even if, initially, a declarative but nonlimiting list of relevant industries was kept.

> Thus the first article of the April 9, 1898, law stipulates that accidents arising from the fact of workers' and employees' labor in industries concerning construction, factory work, manufacturing, building sites, land and water transport, loading and unloading, public stores, mines, mining, quarries, and, in addition, in every operation or parts of an operation in which explosive materials are either fabricated or put to use or in which is used a machine powered by a nonhuman or animal source, provides a right to compensation covered by the head of the business, to be paid to the benefit of the victim or his beneficiaries, on the condition work has been interrupted for more than four days.

The expression "accidents arising from the fact of labor" carries the trace of the long discussion over the concept of "dangerous labor" and the difficulty the members of Parliament had in freeing themselves from the imperative to connect the attribution of damages to an objective causality. Such was the compromise: every accident in the listed industries would lead to compensation, but on the condition that it was truly a *work* accident, which is to say an accident that could be connected to labor through some relationship. Parliament thus maintained, in a somewhat loose and imprecise fashion lending itself to multiple interpretations, the idea of a necessary causality between the accident and labor. In practical terms, this entailed entrusting the courts with the task of precisely delimiting the law's scope. We will see that, to do this, they would abandon the idea of a causal criterion in favor of the criterion of a contract for services. In doing this, far from denaturing the spirit of professional risk, they rigorously respected it.

The Inexcusable Fault

The former transaction dealt with defining the scope of professional risk. A final transaction was necessary for professional risk to become operational: this transaction was concerned with defining its logic. Would the principle of the fixed rate, in the framework of the relevant industries, be applicable in every case, independent of an examination of the worker's or *patron*'s behavior? Would it cover their faults, even their gross misconduct?

It was part of the logic of professional risk to conceive of compensation with a sort of indifference to the causality of accidents. The worker should be compensated in every case, whatever the accident's cause. "The very foundation of our project," Ricard, rapporteur of the 1888 bill, declared, "is that in every case, the injured worker would be compensated."[38] This came down to making damage the very source of the law, to recognizing in the very fact of the accident the cause of the worker's right. It also corresponded to the logic of the fixed rate, to the social objective of professional risk, "to ensure the victim's means of existence," all the while avoiding trials.

Nonetheless, this quite practical idea of a compensation that was indifferent to the consideration of faults, which would have satisfied many patrons and workers, collided head-on with the principle of responsibility, an inescapable principle, since it was constitutive of social order. "This system of responsibility," Georges Graux, for example, recalled, "not only conforms to the principles of our civil law, but to the eternal principles of justice, which wants each to be awarded according to his works, and conforms to the principle of liberty, which desires for each to be responsible for his actions."[39] Félix Martin, would go one further:

> How is this just a theory, this primordial principle that each should be responsible for his faults and above all for his gross misconduct? Where would we be, in what state of barbarity would we not still be immersed if this guiding principle had not been put into practice since the beginning of societies, if it had not instructed, enlightened, corrected, and civilized us? Truly, I fear, I am insulting the Senate by insisting on this point, but it seems to me that to attack this primordial principle, which is not only a juridical principle, but which is the cornerstone of the social pact; it seems to me, I say, that to attack this fundamental principle, one must truly be blind; one must forget or misunderstand that it is the very condition of liberty, progress, and public security.[40]

In other words, the problem that confronted Parliament was to decide if the principle outlined in article 1382 of the Civil Code was one of those maxims of natural law that could not be ignored without disqualifying oneself as legislator. To put it slightly anachronistically, did article 1382 have constitutional value?

The most resolute supporters of professional risk agreed: accidents caused by the victim's *intentional fault* should be excluded from the benefit of the law.

Conversely, the intentional fault of the *patron* would make him completely responsible for any damage inflicted on his workers. But would it be appropriate to go even further: to exclude from the benefit of the new law those accidents that were due to *gross misconduct* on the part of the victim, with the understanding that it was agreed that any slight negligence on the victim's part would be acceptable? In other words, it was a matter of knowing if Parliament could ignore the principle that responsibility for gross misconduct could neither be debated nor insured—a founding principle of the law of obligations that the courts constantly endorsed.

The question of professional risk's meaning was again posed in relation to the question of fault. Was it the same thing as coverage for accidents due to unforeseen circumstances or natural disasters? Was it only a matter of legalizing, in the case of workplace accidents, the old moral obligation to provide benevolent aid, a principle outlined in article 1382 of the Civil Code? Did it mean, on the contrary, creating a principle of compensation that would be based on the very fact of damage and therefore independent of all consideration of fault? At the Congress of Brussels, Bruno Chimirri, deputy of the Italian Parliament, stated in his report on gross misconduct, "In workplace accidents, there is no fault to be punished, but rather misfortunes to be remedied."[41] Specifically, can "misfortune," the simple fact of being the victim of an accident, bestow rights?

For many, both deputies and senators, it was not possible in any event for the new legislation to ignore the fault of the worker or the *patron*. It was already considerable, with regard to the principles of law, that *patrons* were expected to cover accidents due to unforeseen circumstances or the slight negligence of the worker, that they were made responsible for something that was considered an uncontestable cause for exoneration with regard to common law. It was generally agreed that changes in technology, the mechanization of workshops, and the new forms of organization of labor exposed the worker to constant, inevitable odds of being involved in an accident that should be covered by the business or the profession. "The worker," explained the Count Albert de Mun, "without anyone being at fault, is in the presence of continual risk, inherent in the very fact of industry and the normal conditions of work. . . . Once such risk exists, it creates, for the one who is exposed to it, a right to compensation when he is injured."[42] How could workers be reproached for their lack of foresight? "Lack of foresight," he continued, "is forced, it is inevitable, it results from labor itself; the laboring worker is exposed to peril at every instant, he does not think of the peril, he cannot think of it; if he thought of it, he would not confront it. . . . Every precaution has been taken, the workers have been warned, regulations have been displayed, and yet, despite everything, the accident happens, since the worker, who lives in danger, becomes familiar with it and forgets the recommendations of prudence."[43] Moreover, as Tolain recalled, "The most precautious workers are not the best."[44] This is surely true, but that does not mean that examining and punishing each person's contribution to the causality of accidents should be abandoned.

Plenty of reasons were given for excluding gross misconduct. First of all, there was the nearly natural sentiment that it was impossible for the author of such a fault to be compensated in spite of everything. "Is it possible," Ricard asked in his report to the Chamber of Deputies,

> to conflate accidents due to the ordinary or slight fault of the worker with those caused by gross misconduct, by a worker's serious foul play? Does the operator have the right to plead his case after not listening to the strident call of the whistle indicating high pressure in the boiler and is burned by a jet of steam? Should a roofer who, on the pitch of a roof, wishes to perform acrobatics for his friends, be declared eligible to request compensation when he breaks a limb? . . . And, on the other hand, is it enough to impose obligatory insurance on the captains of industry in order to remove them from all oversight and all responsibility? Is it just for the *patron*, who has resisted all calls to modify or change dangerous and worn-out machinery, who has caused through his negligence the death or serious injury of many of his workers, to be liberated by the payment of his contribution, based only on the figure of the wages paid by him, multiplied by its risk coefficient?

He concludes,

> The majority of your Commission has not thought so. The proposed law should be a law of justice, but not degenerate into a cushion of indolence for all interested parties.[45]

It was added that to not consider workers' fault would encourage their lack of foresight; the number of accidents would surely increase. The statistical results of the German legislation registered a sharp growth in the number of requests for compensation: was this not incontestable proof? The strongest argument consisted of charting the multiple injustices that would necessarily flow from any solution indifferent to the consideration of faults. How could one treat *as equals* two workers wounded in an accident due to the fault of one, the other being innocent? How could workers who, through a serious lack of foresight or an act of indiscipline, had caused the ruin of their *patron*, be allowed to claim, despite everything, compensation? Moreover, how then could workers eligible for a criminal conviction under articles 319 and 320 of the Penal Code, at the same time, in nearly the same circumstances, be compensated under the new law? Senator Bérenger had summarized this contradiction, which he believed to be unanswerable, with the often-repeated formula "Condemned and pensioned."[46]

Those who supported the exoneration of gross misconduct in the framework of professional risk were not themselves lacking in arguments. They relied on statistical observation to conclude the independence of the causality of accidents in relation to individual factors. It was noted, in effect, that the rate of accidents varied as a function of objective factors like the duration of work, that it remained constant for a given industry despite changes in personnel. From this was drawn the idea of the objectivity of professional risk: this would designate so-called inevitable, unavoidable accidents, a sort of accident fatalism. In the modern conditions of industrial labor, the causality of accidents should no longer be analyzed in terms of freedom, but rather process. Only the process, which is to say the economy, could be culpable. Referring to the theory of the average man, Cyrille Van Overbergh did not hesitate to attribute to society itself the sum of accident damages that might befall workers:

> It has to be conceded that, each year, the working class pays a tribute to the accident, to death, that is as regular as it is terrible. In the face of this formidable debt of injuries and lives liquidated each year by the collectivity of workers, the question of individual responsibility loses its importance; it disappears from the foreground; the isolated case disappears in this multitude; individual damage only appears as an infinitesimal part of an evil that strikes society; the reparation of all damages, even the one caused by fault, becomes legitimate because the fault itself, as has been observed, is conceived from the social point of view, which is to say as the inevitable mark of human imperfection.[47]

In these conditions, it becomes supremely unjust to wish, through the obsolete idea of fault, to make the worker alone bear the burden of damages that are essentially social—especially since workers, the accident's victims, are by this same token considerably penalized since they must suffer, through their wounds, a lifelong punishment:

> I ask myself if all of us who are here, if we always suffer the full consequences of our gross misconduct. Do we not often escape a deserved pun-

ishment for wrongdoing: does a punishment always weigh on us, and are we and our friends not happy if the punishment does not immediately follow from guilty action? Well, let's grant the same to the worker who puts his body, life, health, and existence on the line. Where in the world could we find, for even grave misconduct, a punishment that applies to the entire life of the guilty? Let's not expect too much of them. Let's act nobly as true friends of the workers! I affirm that this is not only wise and political, it is also Christian; it is equitable and just to leave no worker guilty of gross misconduct without compensation and to not risk abandoning him and his family to misery.[48]

It was thus incorrect to say that, by not taking the workers' fault into account in the compensation of accidents, they were not punished for gross negligence. They were always the first to be punished and the most severely punished, and this punishment was incomparably more severe than what justice could do. Workers, it was still argued, were the victims of economic warfare. It made no more sense to want to reproach them for their wounds than to reproach soldiers for dying on the field of honor.

It was also argued that the exoneration of gross misconduct could not be seen as discouraging foresight, given that workers were the primary victims. Wasn't the instinct for self-preservation the most effective instrument of prevention? The German statistics did not prove an increase in the number of accidents, only a greater insistence on the part of workers to assert their rights. But above all, it was recalled that to introduce the consideration of gross misconduct into compensation would end up turning every accident into a trial. Yet it was well known that the impossibility of penetrating the cause of accidents was precisely what had motivated legislative intervention in the first place. It also led by necessity to the idea of expressing compensation through the very fact of damage. And, moreover, given that gross misconduct was in practice indefinable, wanting to punish it amounted to establishing Parliament as judge and submitting the law to their arbitrariness.

The substance of the debate occurred at the indeterminable level of the philosophical assumptions behind the juridical solutions. Two types of thought stood in genuine opposition over the question of fault, and the discussion only accentuated an awareness of their differences. For one group, it could be assumed that despite all the possible transformations of industry, despite the most profound changes in the conditions and organization of labor, and all possible excuses for the worker's eventual lack of foresight, it was inconceivable that workers not remain free. "The worker cannot be compared to a thing," Senator Lacombe recalled, to much applause from his peers, "since he has the liberty that is man's prerogative, and the responsibility that is a consequence of this liberty."[49] Evidently, this affirmation was not the same as a psychological observation. It had a dual status. First of all, it was disciplinary in nature. Of course, compared to artisans who are masters of their labor and tools, modern workers are characterized by intense subjectification. No doubt, the modern labor process first of all required workers be rigorously disciplined, rendering them defenseless against professional risks. That did not mean one shouldn't set aside those cases of indiscipline or boastfulness, unfortunately all too frequent, where workers were precisely no longer dependent and subordinate, but the subjects of their own experiences. How, in these conditions, could one still talk of professional risk? This is what was at stake in gross misconduct, where punishment was in every respect necessary to maintain discipline. Furthermore, this affirmation of workers' liberty was invoked as a sort of philosophical foundation allowing one to talk of rights and responsibility. How, then, could transformations in labor conditions, a question of fact, affect the very thing that made the workers people, the subject of hypothetical rights? From this point of view, the existence of gross misconduct appeared as the a posteriori proof of the irreducible existence of workers' liberty.

The other group stood on completely different terrain. The ontological status of workers mattered little to this group, or rather, from their perspective, the question of compensating workers who were injured by workplace accidents had to be posed independently of such considerations. It mattered little whether workers were or were not free; there was a social problem to be resolved, whose solution should not be impeded by each person's philosophical convictions. The problem was framed in this way: put an end to the antagonism between capital and labor by allowing workers injured in workplace accidents to be compensated, without making them go through a legal battle to ensure that their rights are upheld. In practice this assumed the necessity of abstracting from all consideration of causes and faults, of associating compensation with the very fact of the damage, and thus, if not forgetting, at least putting in parentheses the principle posed by article 1382. On matters of gross misconduct, the opposition between the juridical and social types of thought manifested itself in its most radical form. The former appeared in binding the law to specific philosophical doctrines and reasoning, yet at the same time, *in abstracto;* the latter appeared as pure practical thought, free of the constraint of principles and governed by the knowledge of facts, such as those, for example, that statistics could deliver. The conflict involved two modes of evaluating the law, two ways of reflecting upon the politics of law, which Émile Cheysson would summarize by posing the question "Must one say as some do 'let social peace perish at the expense of a principle' or, conversely, that social peace is a principle that is superior even to the one in article 1382?"[50]

The compromise would be reached, not without difficulty, over the expression of *inexcusable fault*.[51] Article 20 of the April 9, 1898, law stipulates, "The court has the right, if it is proven that the accident is due to the inexcusable fault of the worker, to reduce the pension established in section I. When it is proven that the accident is due to the inexcusable fault of the *patron* or those who supervise in his stead, the compensation can be increased, as long as the annuity or the total of annuities allowed does not surpass either the reduction or the amount of the annual wages." The inexcusable fault would not deprive workers of compensation. The insurability of faults had increased by one degree. And, at the same time, the concept of professional risk in its social acceptance had been recognized: workers would be compensated, whatever the accident's cause; the field of application for professional risk would not stop short at the inexcusable fault. This fault, on the contrary, was only a regulatory instrument.

Gross misconduct or inexcusable fault—the difference would appear difficult to appreciate. The expression's merit lay precisely in its vagueness. Some, in particular the juridical minds who had supported the exclusion of gross misconduct, thought that the change in words concealed an essential identity. For the others—and this is the thesis that would prevail in jurisprudence—the inexcusable fault designated a fault greater than gross misconduct, just shy of intentional fault. Nominally indistinguishable, gross misconduct and inexcusable fault pertained less to two severities of fault than two ways of judging it. According to Roman jurisconsults, gross misconduct consisted of the fact of not having understood and not having perceived what everyone else had understood and foreseen.[52] Gross misconduct was, by comparison, assessed from what is supposed to be the least diligent behavior in the same situation. As serious as it may be, it implicitly refers to an abstract model of behavior: gross misconduct designates the intolerable, the unacceptable. Frédéric Passy spoke of the "aberration of the moral sense."[53] The inexcusable fault—the word "unpardonable" was also used—did not refer to moral thresholds but rather to a psychosociology of behavior. One begins with the idea that the lack of foresight or the negligence of workers is explained by fatigue, stress, routine, a complete pathology of the will formed that implies they are not quite their own subject, but rather a caused cause. The inexcusable fault appears when, in attempts to explain workers' behavior, all excuses having been exhausted, there remains something that does not necessarily relate to a liberty but a cause that public order forbids covering. Gross misconduct or inexcusable fault, the difference lies in the management of causality and in the correlative objectification of workers' behavior. The rule of judgment that founds the concept of gross misconduct excludes the concept of professional risk. The rule that founds the inexcusable fault is on the contrary consistent with its own rationality and with the objectification of the accident as inevitable, implying an interaction between causalities where there is only ever a caused cause.

Insurance

Under the heading of professional risk, the members of Parliament looked less to pose a principle of responsibility in the juridical sense than to establish a practical dispositive for covering damages. What could be called the method of professional risk, the social method, does not look for a solution to a problem by applying a general rule, but rather by establishing an institution. The risk defined by Parliament in 1898 was an insurance risk. Even if the senators sought to reinscribe it within the juridical problematics of principles, it had no meaning without the insurance dispositive that framed it. The concept of professional risk encounters, announces, and presupposes the concept of *social insurance*. The two are indissociable. Without a doubt, the French Parliament of 1898 had not proposed (in contrast to its German neighbor) the principle of obligatory insurance: it had not erected a vast organization of insurance covering accidents. Nevertheless, the law of April 9, 1898, was fundamentally an insurance law: the first social insurance law. It is true that if the new legislation is conceived within the opposition between public and private law, it must be conceded that the French solution derives from private law. But, precisely, the law of April 9, 1898, to the very extent that it forms a new kind of law, social law, perhaps removes the relevance of the opposition between public and private. The fact that Parliament maintained the organization of insurance within the problematics of an insurance of responsibility should not deceive us: the concept that founds professional risk is that of social insurance.

The question of insurance was problematized under multiple headings over the course of the parliamentary debate. First, the type of rationality that characterizes its technology was interrogated. The category of professional risk refers to an insurantial type of thought. In fact, it is through the concept of professional risk that the rationality of insurance appears as a possible alternative to the rationality informing liability law. Insurance thinking, which is a thinking of mutuality and contract, implying that no one is a stranger to another, allows the establishment of relations, exchanges, equivalences where, on the contrary, the problematics of responsibility divides, opposes, subtracts. The concept of the business, as principle of totalization and redistribution of risks—the problematics of allocating the cost of damages on the basis of solidarity—all of this derives from the rationality of insurance. From this point of view, one could speak of the philosophical appeal of insurance, or of insurance as the philosophy informing the law of April 9, 1898.

Insurance, furthermore, was considered the only technical dispositive capable of making professional risk practicable. The goal of the law was to organize a sort of solidarity-based security between the *patron* and workers. The law granted security to workers, certain to be compensated for every workplace accident; it granted security for the *patron*, who would know in advance the cost of his liability. Certainly, these are contradictory demands when they are considered in their bare elements, owing to the new costs the *patron* is made to cover, but that become compatible and reciprocal when the idea of insurance is introduced. According to an expression often used over the course of the debate, insurance allows "the maximum coverage for the worker at minimum cost for the *patron*."[54] Insurance alone makes the burden of the new law amenable to small businesses; it allows small businesses to maintain, faced with the risk of accidents, a certain position of equality in relation to big businesses. Moreover, insurance offers small businesses a more secure position than the one offered by the common law of article 1382. More generally, insurance presented itself as the very instrument through which the new law could and would be practiced, as a clear alternative to liability law and judicial procedure: in a word, as the adequate institutional expression of the compromise that was professional risk.

From the political point of view, finally, insurance offered a way of organizing industry distinct from both liberal individualism and the old corporative organization that the 1789 revolution had suppressed (and to which there was no question of returning). Bismarck had made the organization of social insurance an instrument in the battle against socialism and a unifying principle for the new German Empire. Since 1848, at least, there was no lack of reflection on the political benefits that could be expected from organizing social insurance in France. The debate over the law of 1898 once again gave rise to intense reflection on the politics of insurance and the central place that was now generally accorded to insurance within the politics of social foresight. Insurance appeared as the natural instrument of the juridical solidarity between *patrons* and workers in which one now sought the governmental principle of industrial societies. Nadaud, claiming both Émile de Girardin and J. S. Mill for his cause, from the outset of the debate declared, "Our principle is that of universal insurance."[55] The debate gave rise to a great proliferation of programs—insurantial utopias mixing with the great political themes of the day. Of course, there was the theme of *association*, insurance being one of its major modes, but also the theme of decentralization. Such was the ubiquity of a technology that could serve the realization of the most varied political programs. Wasn't insurance, essentially, the most appropriate method for territorializing individuals in industrial societies?

It is this triple (philosophical, technological, and political) problematic of social insurance that provides the true frame of reference to the concept of professional risk. Already the partisans of the contractual thesis, Marc Sauzet, Charles Sainctelette, and Joseph Émile Labbé, recognized that the juridical problematic of responsibility could not by itself, at least not without being distorted, offer a satisfactory solution to the social problem of workplace accidents. This problem had to be managed by insurance. Say, in his own way, said much the same thing when he declared that what needed to be established was an insurance law. In a certain sense, it was agreed that the solution to the problem of workplace accidents would come less through a liability law than through an insurance law; but people were divided on how to envision the organization of insurance. Must one maintain insurance as a form of liability insurance (the benefit of its coverage depending on judicial sanction), or, on the contrary, was it more appropriate to make the worker the direct creditor of an insurance fund created by industry associations? Should the *patron* retain the liberty to insure himself, as well as the liberty to choose the means of insurance, or, inversely, should an obligation to insure be created and, consequently, an insurance dispositive destined to make the stated obligation practicable? All of these questions were intensely debated. People were searching for a concept of social insurance.

It is telling that although the debate, both in the Chamber of Deputies and in the International Congress of Workplace Accidents, was engaged with the theme of responsibility, it would quickly find its true focal point in the question of how to organize social insurance. This was moreover the most revolutionary thing about it, and what the French senators stubbornly refused to concede, this shift from a problematic of responsibility toward a problematic of insurance—or, more precisely, this way of posing the question of responsibility no longer in terms of law but in terms of the organization of insurance. According to this logic, in effect, the debate over workplace accidents was a pretext for setting up the political and financial organization of the welfare state. Each person, in France as well as abroad, knew that this was what was truly at stake in the question of workplace accidents, a vehicle for embracing the future. How could industry be united in solidarity? On a territorial basis or through the type of activity? Should the workers participate in the management of insurance or contribute to its financing? Another subject of discussion was: how would the sums pledged to cover the new rights of the workers be used? It could not be a question of freezing such a vast amount of capital in the state's coffers. It should be invested in industry and thus contribute to the development of its activity. All these debates were left hanging on the fundamental question of the *obligation to insure.* Generally demanded by those principally concerned, *patrons* and workers, its political cost was considerable. Indeed, it was thought that the transition from the liberal state to the welfare state would pivot around the outcome of the debate concerning this obligation. Once the principle of obligation had been accepted in matters concerning accidents, it was hard to see what would prevent it from spreading to matters concerning sickness, disability, fires, or any other cause of misfortune.

After Félix Faure's 1882 project, all projects based on professional risk collectively proposed the organization of an insurance dispositive intended to make the new *patron*'s responsibility bearable. Thus, Faure proposed reforming the National Accident Insurance Fund. At that time, only voluntary insurance was discussed. The legislature of 1885–89 saw the first projects for obligatory insurance. It is this question that was addressed by the extraparliamentary commission on manufacturing accidents presided over by Tolain. Its findings would serve as the basis for two draft laws, one submitted by Édouard Lockroy, then minister of Commerce and Industry. These projects would founder before the Chamber of Deputies' commission: to impose an insurance obligation on the industrialist "would be for the state to see itself as a better judge of the purely private interest of the citizens than the citizens themselves. . . . The role of the state being essentially to regulate the legal relations between men, it seems to us," the rapporteur Duché wrote, "that the state goes beyond its mission when it takes upon itself to judge private interest as such and substitutes itself for the liberty and responsibility of individual action."[56] The Chamber followed the commission, leaving the *patron* free to decide on insurance, while offering him the possibility of coverage either by creating mutual insurance unions or by affiliating with the reformed National Accident Insurance Fund. By contrast, during the following legislature (1889–93), the Chamber of Deputies, joining forces with the general movement in favor of a social insurance organization, adopted a project of considerable size (eighty-three articles), outlining both the principle of obligatory insurance for patrons and organizing as a consequence a vast system of mutualities divided among regional districts. *Patrons* could remain self-insured, either individually or by joining unions, though this was only ever the exception. This project, which practically dried up the market for accident insurance, represented the French version of social insurance against workplace accidents. The rapporteur, Émile Maruéjouls, defended it by explaining that obligatory insurance would place the full weight of professional risk on the whole of society. "The state," he specified, "is both the instrument and organ of national solidarity. It is the born defender of the poor, the unfortunate, of the victim of social ruin; it alone possesses, moreover, the necessary powers to impose collective duties and assign to each the obligations that stem from them."[57] One understands why accusations of state socialism were hurled against this project, or worse, the charge of "bourgeois socialism," leveled by Say.[58] The idea of *mutuality*, endowed with every virtue, was thought to be a way of escaping these claims. A principle of social organization that allowed one to go beyond liberal individualism without falling into the rut of corporatism, mutuality made possible an organization of social insurance corresponding to the Latin temperament and escaping from German statism.

This project was torn to pieces by the senators, who were opposed to both obligatory insurance—the state could not, in principle, impose foresight on industrialists—and the organization of patronal mutualities where a troubling tendency toward a welfare state was detected. "By acting thus, the state would promptly arrive at the annihilation of individual initiative, thanks to the aid and protection the citizens in every circumstance would have come to expect of it. And when this fatal end would be achieved, the welfare state would quickly be seen as responsible for all disappointments, all catastrophes. Are these the morals we should introduce into our democracy?" asked Senator Poirier, rapporteur of the bill.[59] And he added, reprising the old problematic of patronage, "What is most serious is that this system, in order to regulate disputes arising from accidents, ends up replacing the business leader with a subscription mutuality, which is to say a financial organization having as its head not a man but a steering committee that would have no other desire than the interest of the fund. Where once the *patron*'s humanitarian sentiments have ironed out plenty of difficulties, we will now only find anonymous defenders of the fund's coffers."[60] The obligation to insure presumed a sort of "legal presumption of the industrialist's insolvency" that was deemed perfectly unacceptable. Finally, the Chamber's system was reproached for "removing from industry, where it is found to be relatively useful, considerable sums that are often needed," to be left unused in the state's coffers. The critics took up the old liberal argument. They agreed with the idea of conceiving professional risk in terms of juridical responsibility. Of course, one must "avoid any circumstance where those concerned would experience the cruel disappointment of their rights annihilated by the business leader's insolvency." Of course, there were "no creditors as deserving of interest as the victims of accidents deprived of all labor, these unfortunates who are deprived of the only capital that nature had given them at birth: their power to work and their limbs," but why not cover their claims using the framework already laid out in the provisions of common law, under the terms of security? This is the solution that the Senate agreed upon in the debate of 1890.

Both the measures for juridical guarantees and the system of insurance coverage adopted by the Chamber in 1893 shared the defect of freezing the industrialists' capital and thus restraining its possibilities for productive investment. If one desired to effectively cover the worker's claims, then in every instance dispositions other than those provided by common law had to be imagined. This is what allowed the Senate and Chamber to find a point of compromise between their very different positions. The idea of joint coverage for the *patron* and the worker implied in the project for obligatory insurance would be abandoned: if Parliament wanted to guarantee the worker's claims, it could not, therefore, impose on industrialists a particular manner of honoring their new obligations. The industrialists would remain free to cover claims as they saw fit, but on the condition that the worker did not suffer from this liberty. To do this, Parliament, somewhat presuming the general solvency of industry in general, gave itself the right to organize the solvency of industrialists by requiring them to contribute to the operation of a *guarantee fund* intended to cover the estimated 1 percent of defaulting employers. Thus, one moved from a system of obligatory coverage to a system of redistributed insolvency through the creation of a "joint *patrons*' responsibility."[61] The insurance companies had saved their skin. Even better for them, an immense market opened up to them, without any requirement besides intensified oversight by the administration. They would not waste any time before profiting from the situation. The threats Parliament made against these companies had led them to organize. The day after the vote on the 1898 law, they looked to profit from their quasi-monopoly by raising their rates, thus provoking the reform of the National Accident Insurance Fund in order to make it competitive and for its rates to serve as a market regulator.

This dispositive, that some would deem a bastard, would continue to operate until the law of October 30, 1946, turned the general social security regime into the principal provider of services in place of commercial and industrial employers, thus extinguishing the bond of responsibility between employer and victim. Through this law, the funds became directly payable to the worker, and private companies found themselves simultaneously excluded from the coverage of risk. In a certain sense, the 1946 law put an end to the divorce between the concept of social insurance informing the 1898 law and the institutions intended to put it to work. Yet this interpretation reflects a will to apply overly rational schemas to a reality that resists such simplifications. It would be false to say that, concerning workplace accidents, one would have to wait for 1946 for insurance institutions to finally embody their concept. First, this is because the concept of social insurance does not designate anything essential or substantial, but rather a program or a politics amenable to multiple institutional forms. And second, because it would doubtless be fairer to envision the institutions set in place by the 1898 Parliament as an initial form of organization (a private one) for managing social insurance.

a. On April 9, 1898, in the urgency of a closing session of Parliament, the Chamber of Deputies definitively and unanimously adopted the law on "the responsibilities for accidents that affect workers in the workplace." Parliament had created, outside of the Civil Code, a new law of obligations and a first code of the accident. The accident, one of the Civil Code's blind spots, found itself juridically constituted on its own terms. It conferred a right, independent of any analysis of its causes. According to the strong phrasing of the Paris lawyer Louis Sarrut, "The accident is equivalent to entitlement."[62] More precisely, now one would distinguish between treatment of the causes of workplace accidents that related to the dispositive of *prevention* and one of the effects, posing the problem of their reparation and subject to a social framework. The gesture was as important as that gesture of one of the Civil Code's original compilers, outlining, a century earlier, the general principle of article 1382. The connection to nature had been severed. Industrial society, becoming aware of its power as infinite and limitless, gave itself the possibility of creating obligations based on itself and without any other reference than itself. Along with the concept of professional risk, a principle was now available that opened up the future of social obligations, to be grouped a half century later under the heading "social security."[63]

b. The law in itself was innovative. Not only through its provisions but also through its presentation. It was a *social law*, not only in its object but also in its very form. Parliament was established as a transactional agent. The law did not draw its value from the universally valid principles that it put forth, but from the objectives it aimed at and the means of attaining them. Professional risk had allowed Parliament to liberate the legislation from its dependence on principles that were discovered to be inescapably divisive because they stemmed from necessarily distinct philosophies. Social thought is a way of thinking that recognizes these doctrinal divisions and looks to get past them in a sort of pragmatic beyond. Thus, the success of the German legislation was recognized: of course, it had not allowed for a reduction in number of accidents; it had not in fact made litigation disappear; but it satisfied the *patrons* and workers; it had put an end to the antagonism between capital and labor that was fueled by the question of workplace accidents.

The 1898 law had been voted on as an experimental law that could be modified, extended, or transformed, if one felt the need to do so. As early as 1883, Faure had proposed, "Absolute principles have nothing to do with these questions. Legislation is not a science. It is no more a science than the construction of a house, or the construction of a machine. Legislation is a labor that creates human institutions; it is a series of conventional regulations, based—at least I believe so—on experience, regulations that can change from one century to the next, for the purpose of allowing men to live in the best possible way in society."[64] "Absolute principles" versus "experience": this opposition spanned a debate that ended up confirming the victory of experience as a principle of legislation, an experience that could be gleaned from the statistics as well as foreign legislators. This was the beginning of a sort of legislative pragmatism. The law no longer desired timelessness or generality.

The 1898 law only concerned workers—and only some of them at that, at least temporarily. With regard to the principles of 1789, this was without a doubt a law of privilege. It did not legislate for an abstract subject. One imagines the emotion that such a break was sure to provoke. To all intents and purposes, a new rule of justice was in formation. The three great debates concerning the definition of professional risk—the principle of the fixed rate, the extension, and the purview of professional risk—centered on the question of *equality* and two different ways of envisioning it: an equality before misfortune or suffering (where equality of risk means abstracting from the individual's responsibility) came to replace the idea of equal behavior as a rubric of justice (where two individuals of different merit cannot be treated equally).

But how was the worker defined? Several definitions were put forward over the course of the debate. According to the Civil Code, workers are contracting parties: they do not lease themselves, but their labor power. According to this analysis, the risks of labor are borne by the workers, the wage serving as compensation for those risks. To protect workers, one had to abandon this framework. The supporters of the contractual thesis did so by erasing the division between workers and their labor power: workers placed themselves and their wills under the dependence of their patron: "The worker abandons his will and his initiative in the exercise of his profession and gives up protecting himself against the dangers of exploitation," explained Labbé.[65] This was a completely militaristic and disciplinary objectification of workers that meant they were recognized as a subject only through their acts of indiscipline. One passed from one extreme to the other: from the absolutely free worker to the radically subjugated worker. The 1898 law defines its beneficiaries outside this way of thinking. It mattered little whether workers were or were not free. The law indexes compensation for the accident through the victim's wages; in a sense, it collapses all of the harms suffered by workers into the sole fact of lost wages and lost capacity to work. The 1898 law gives a juridical status to the *wage earner*, an alternative persona to both the master and the servant. Wage earners are not someone's object but are incapable of saving and foresight. For this reason, their lives are completely dependent on the conservation of their ability to work and the possibility of employment. The 1898 law and the new politics of security informing it operate through the juridical and social recognition of wage labor as a sort of stable, normal, irreducible, and generalizable state, coming, in a certain way, to complete the status of the citizen, if not to actually replace it.

c. The law of April 9, 1898, a law that recognizes a right of the accident, a social law, also marks the birth of *labor law*. At the end of the nineteenth century, the Civil Code's silence on the question of the worker was often highlighted. It is true that the Code said nothing other than that the wage relation should be analyzed as a contract. This did not exclude the existence of an abundant industrial legislation. Beginning with the law of Germinal, Year XI, a complete industrial policy was developed that regulated labor conditions. A characteristic of this legislation was that it did not conceive of itself as overriding common law. It specified it, limited it, organized it. By contrast, the body of law that emerged with the April 9, 1898, law was of a new kind. This new body of law did not only add new provisions to the existing legislation, it inaugurated a specific form of law that would now be called "labor law." The April 9, 1898, law did not fill a gap within the law; it proposed another way of conceiving the law. It involved a transformation of juridical rationality that would express itself, in particular, in the shift from the concept of the *contract for services* to that of the *employment contract*. Labor law is the law of the employment contract.

The courts had initially analyzed the wage relation as a contract consisting of the exchange of remuneration for labor. By contracting, workers took upon themselves the risks involved in an act of labor. This was the theory of individual risk. Beginning in 1841, in order to compensate the victims of workplace accidents, jurisprudence disassembled the wage relation into two types of obligation: contractual—the wage-labor exchange—and criminal, imposing on the *patron* an obligation to provide security. For a long time, these two obligations existed sided by side without ever interacting—until the April 9, 1898, law brought them together, thus giving birth to the modern definition of the employment contract.[66] The same move would allow the courts to extract the concept of the subordinate relation as criterion of the employment contract and derive from it the principle for defining the scope of the April 9, 1898, law. The first article of the law seemed to assume the existence of a relationship of causality between the accident and labor as a condition of receiving benefits. The criterion—"through the fact or the occasion of labor"—was inapplicable because it lacked sufficient precision. Jurisprudence would interpret it as meaning that professional risk was not located in a relation of objective causality, but rather in the contractual relation itself. There was a sort of reciprocity between the concept of the employment contract and professional risk, a point that Deputy Léon Mirman highlighted as early as 1901 in the explanatory statement of a draft bill looking to extend the benefits of the law concerning workplace accidents to all wage earners:

> It is the fact of working in the service of an employer and being victim of an accident, which has resulted from the fact of such labor or during its performance, that confers the right to compensation. This right is implicitly contained in the employment contract (written or tacit), and this contract retains the same value no matter the employer and whatever uses he might make of the products of the labor performed; it matters little whether the employer sells his products, whether he consumes them himself, or whether he dedicates them to a work of public interest: professional risk, freed of the idea of fault or offense, and based on the contract, is the same for all categories of wage earners, and this is precisely what the modern idea of law consists of, as demonstrated by its initial expression in the law of 1898.

The thesis, consecrated by the Parliament of 1938, was consistent with the concept of professional risk, which, as we have seen, is characterized by the fact that it does not base its attribution of costs on a relation of causality (whether of danger or fault).[67] Professional risk can have no other juridical cause than the contract. Furthermore, contracts are its foundation: the idea of redistributing risks, in effect, can have no other foundation than a contractual one, and inversely, professional risk inscribes the contract for services in this problematic of redistribution that transforms it into an employment contract. The two concepts of professional risk and employment contract stem from the same epistemological regime.

d. Thus, through the long detour of professional risk, Parliament effectively endorsed the thesis of those who, at the beginning of the debate, had sought to locate the *patron*'s obligation to provide security in the contract for services. The same distance separated the contract for services from the employment contract and the contractual thesis from professional risk. The contractual thesis floundered because it was not juridically possible to derive the *patron*'s obligation to provide security from the civil law theory of the contract. This is also to say that it was impossible to derive the concept of the employment contract from it, and that beyond the common use of the word "contract" the employment contract was something much more than a simple regulated contract and more than a civil contract that Parliament endowed with specific obligatory clauses.

The concept of the employment contract is indissociable from the concept of social insurance; it could almost be said that it is one of the attributes of the concept of social insurance. The employment contract does not draw its source from either the agreement between wills or even from the law. It depends on an autonomous concept of the contract, which is manifested in the idea of the redistribution of risks and costs that is at the foundation of the concept of social insurance. Professional risk and social insurance refer to a sort of objective social contract at the basis of individual contracts, a social contract that unites all social activities, losses, and profits alike. The social contract precedes individuals, and these same individuals now only embody the social contract in their juridical relations. The social contract generates an autonomous social regime of obligation in which individual contracts find their defining principle. The foundational act of labor law, the April 9, 1898, law is also the first social insurance law. Labor law and social insurance: you cannot have one without the other. The concept of professional risk that belongs to each of them also unites them.

The presence of insurance in labor law is manifest in particular in the concept of the business. It is only through the objectification of the factory as a business that the type of exchange stipulated in the employment contract becomes thinkable. This is so to the extent that the business is at the interface of the individual and the collective. The business is the fiction that allows one to think of the ensemble of individuals who contribute to the process of production as a whole. But, at the same time that it reveals the business, insurance brings different businesses together in solidarity and socializes industrial activity. The fact of workplace accidents could have led to the condemnation of the business as guilty of so many damages. By redistributing risks in a certain way, insurance allows for the business to reintegrate into society. Furthermore, insurance makes this reintegration the focus of its development, the norm; it truly transforms modern societies into industrial ones. The concept of the employment contract is tied to the concept of the social redistribution of costs. It is simply one way of activating the vast solidarity of risks that characterizes the social contract in industrial societies.

A certain tradition has taken to denouncing the ideological and deceptive character of the Civil Code's provisions with regard to the reality of the relations of production: the dogma of the equality between contracting parties, for example, never ceases to be belied and contradicted by the reality of inequalities. It has also been said that on the contrary, the social legislation at the end of the nineteenth century represented an initial acknowledgment of the facts, even if this was not yet sufficient. The doctrine of labor law, whether it be positive or critical, is thus bathed in a sort of realism: the value of labor law is judged by its proximity to the facts. This is a sociologist's approach, without a doubt attractive to minds enamored of the real, but it ends up missing what is essential. Labor law is as much composed of fiction as civil law. This is conceivably why its pronouncements retain legal status. The difference between civil law and social law is not one of fiction versus reality, but rather a transformation in the type of fiction. For the fictions of will, equality, and fault are substituted those of risk, business, and society. Psychoanalysts might say that we have gone from one symbolic order to another. Nor does this bring us any closer to the real: our imaginary simply ceases to be the same.

e. Workplace accidents opened up dual formative paths for *social law*. The first was the juridical path of civil liability: the social law appeared in its impasses, as liability's inverse, as the need to fill in its gaps. It fell to a new body of law to banish the "unmerited sufferings" that common law was not able to reduce. The other path derived from benevolent practices: *patrons'* funds for relief and insurance. From this angle, social law emerged as a form of workers' resistance. Faced with the *patron*'s will to make the business a site of non-law, subordination, and subjectification, workers' demands for liberty took place through the juridical implementation of institutions seeking to construct their dependence. It was less about obtaining rights than legalizing *patrons*' security practices. In practical terms, this occurred through insurance. At first implemented on the model of a *patron*'s institution, after the creation of the National Accident Insurance Fund, workplace accident insurance would give rise to a contractual shaping of the politics of civil security that was consolidated, as it were, by the law of April 9, 1898. This law accomplished the dream formulated by Émile de Girardin when he opposed the right *to* work to labor law (or the law *of* work).

Although imagined as complementary within the primitive terms of the liberal divide, juridical practices of civil liability and the aid practices of states or *patrons* soon found themselves in competition with one another. The history of workplace accidents unfolds as a formidable conflict of responsibilities, one that will be settled in 1898 with the victory of the social logic of entrepreneurs and insurers over juridical logic. The patrons, it will be said, had won. In a certain way, yes: Parliament at the end of the nineteenth century did nothing other than generalize the *patrons*' practices that had served as a model for all social nineteenth-century social thought. But this was also a pyrrhic victory. The Parliament of 1898 reformed *patrons*' social practices as much as it acknowledged them. One even envisioned a sort of expropriation of the *patrons*' power of management over their own institutions. Insurance, which made it possible to give a legal form to workers' demands, was the instrument of this reform. Thus, insurance could simultaneously be, at the end of the nineteenth century, the form, the instrument, and the stakes of political and social struggles. It was simultaneously driven by these struggles and by the notion that they could be brought to an end. Thus, one and the same movement made it possible and necessary to conceive of social law as a substitute for civil law and ousted the old state of law in favor of a society that would be called, for better or worse, insurantial.

NOTES

Translator's Preface

1 Behrent, "Accidents Happen," 585–624.
2 On these terms' specificity, see Kolboom, "Patron et patronat," 89–112.
3 Kotkin, *Magnetic Mountain.*

Risk, Insurance, Security

1 Ewald, "Risk, Insurance, Society," 6.
2 Foucault, *Discipline and Punish.*
3 Foucault, *Security, Territory, Population*, 20.
4 Foucault, *Society Must Be Defended*, 246.
5 Ewald, "Risk, Insurance, Society," 2.
6 Defert et al., *Socialisation du risque et pouvoir dans l'entreprise.* A summary of Ewald's contribution to this publication can be found in Lenoir, "La Notion d'accident de travail," 77–88.
7 Donzelot, *L'Invention du social.*
8 Procacci, *Gouverner la misère.*
9 Castel, *La Gestion des risques.*
10 Ewald, "Risk, Insurance, Society," 2.
11 Cour de Cassation, ch. civ., June 16, 1896, D. 1897.1.433. The Teffaine case was brought by the widow of an engineer who was fatally injured by the explosion of a tugboat boiler. Prior to this case, French case law had only recognized two instances in which ownership of a thing (*chose*) could justify liability. These instances were enumerated in article 1385, which mentions damage caused by animals, and article 1386, which refers to damage caused by the collapse of dilapidated buildings.
12 Article 1384(1) Code civil: "On est responsable non seulement du dommage que l'on cause par son propre fait, mais encore de celui qui est causé par le fait des personnes dont on doit répondre, ou des choses que l'on a sous sa garde."
13 There is no consideration of the unequal gendered distribution of risks in Ewald's account of the social insurance state. For a germane history of the French and British welfare states that does take this into account, see Pedersen, *Family, Dependence, and the Origins of the Welfare State.*
14 Foucault, *History of Sexuality*, 1:144.

15 Ewald, "Norms, Discipline, and the Law," 138–61. In this article, Ewald seems to want to attribute his own account of legal transition to Foucault. Yet the thesis is uniquely his own. In France, the term "social law" or *droit social* refers to a specific branch of law—namely, the ensemble of rules pertaining to workplace relations: labor law, social security law, and public assistance laws. Ewald, however, wishes to deploy the expression in a broader sense to cover any kind of legal intervention that is informed by the framework of social insurance, standardization, and normalization.

16 Horwitz, *Transformation of American Law, 1870–1960*, 213–46; and White, *Constitution and the New Deal*, 94–127.

17 The Communist Confédération générale du travail unitaire (CGTU) that was active in France between 1922 and 1936 denounced social insurance as a capitalist deception. See Finkel, "Workers' Social Wage Struggles during the Great Depression and the Era of Neoliberalism," 113–40.

18 Michael Behrent argues that Ewald's *Histoire de l'état providence* is entirely shaped by the proposition that social insurance precluded revolution; Behrent, "Accidents Happen," 585–624. However, it seems to me that this interpretation is more evident in Ewald's interviews and miscellaneous writings of the time than in his monograph, which suggests a notably more agonistic reading of social insurance.

19 Dutton, *Origins of the French Welfare State*, 66–96.

20 Steinhouse, *Workers' Participation in Post-Liberation France*, 9–56.

21 Crozier, "Western Europe," 11–58. Interestingly, Ewald completed the last two years of his doctoral thesis under the supervision of Michel Crozier after Foucault's untimely death in 1984.

22 On the political activism of the long-term unemployed in France, see Bouget, "Movements by the Unemployed in France and Social Protection," 209–34; for a study of seasonal performance workers (*intermittents du spectacle*) that contextualizes their recent activism within a much longer history of struggles, see Grégoire, *Les Intermittents du spectacle.*

23 Quetelet, *Sur l'homme et le développement de ses facultés.*

24 Desrosières, *Politics of Large Numbers*, 9–10.

25 For a complete history of this period, see Dutton, *Origins of the French Welfare State.* The second edition of Ewald's *Histoire de l'état providence*, which we translate here, stops short at 1898. The longer version, published as *L'État providence* in 1986, includes material on the subsequent evolution of the welfare state up until the law of 1946. See Ewald, *L'État providence*, 335–45, 395–405.

26 Loi no. 46-1146 du 22 mai 1946.

27 Witt, *Accidental Republic.* See also Fishback and Kantor, *Prelude to the Welfare State.*

28 Quoted in Witt, *Accidental Republic*, 44. For a comparable history of workplace accidents in Britain, see Bronstein, *Caught in the Machinery.*

29 Witt, *Accidental Republic*, 11–12.

30 For a small sample of this literature, see Hilary Land, "Women, Work and Social Security," 183–92; Nelson, "Origins of the Two-Channel Welfare State, 123–52; Barbara Harrison, "Are Accidents Gender Neutral?," 253–75; Pedersen, *Family, Dependence, and the Origins of the Welfare State*; Quadagno, *Color of Welfare*; Mettler, *Dividing Citizens*; Klein, *For All These Rights*; Witt, *Accidental Republic*, 126–51.

31 Of course, this may also be the reason the book was not translated. Notoriously, the reception of Foucault in the English-speaking academy often served to justify a deliberate marginalization of labor politics.

32 See, for instance, Baker and Simon, *Embracing Risk*, and O'Malley, *Risk, Uncertainty, and Government*. Ewald's *Histoire de l'état providence* seems also to have inspired, directly or indirectly, a number of subsequent histories of workplace accidents. See, for example, Witt, *Accidental Republic*, and most recently, Moses, *First Modern Risk*.

33 After the election victory of the Parti Socialiste (PS) in 1981, social Gaullism became less influential on the parliamentary right, while a resurgent Orléaniste faction turned its attention to the neoliberal arguments of the so-called nouveaux économistes. On this period and the influence of neoliberal think-tanks in France, see Denord, "La Conversion au néo-libéralisme," 17–23. This decade saw a spate of publications attacking the welfare state from the neoliberal right. See, for example, Baccou et le Club de l'Horloge, *Le Grand Tabou*; le Club de l'Horloge, *Les Racines du futur*; and Bénéton, *Le Fléau du bien*. But the left also produced a critical literature of its own. In 1981, the historian Pierre Rosanvallon published a highly influential polemics purporting to offer a "third way" between the bureaucratic-statist model of welfare and the neoliberal attack on welfare as such. This "third way" model of welfare would involve widespread decentralization and the devolution of responsibility to local, communal, and familial solidarities. See Rosanvallon, *La Crise de l'état-providence*. Despite this intellectual assault, the French welfare state continued to enjoy immense popular support throughout this period, and neither of the mainstream parties dared to attack it openly in their campaign rhetoric. Resorting instead to the argument that social security needed to be saved from bankruptcy, they carried out incremental budget consolidations throughout the 1980s, mostly consisting of hikes to individual contributions. More extensive cutbacks to medical, pension, and unemployment benefits were undertaken from the early 1990s onward, under the impetus of the Maastricht Treaty and the prospect of formal membership of the European Monetary Union. See Palier, "De la Crise aux réformes de l'état-providence," 243–75.

34 Ewald, "Two Infinities of Risk," 221–28. See also Ewald, "Return of Descartes' Malicious Demon," 273–301.

35 See Rosanvallon, *La Crise de l'état-providence*, 13–108, for a critical overview of the French-language literature diagnosing the limits of the welfare state.

36 Hacker, *Great Risk Shift*.

37 Pauly, "Economics of Moral Hazard," 531–37.

38 O'Malley, *Currency of Justice*.

39 McGarity, *Freedom to Harm.*

40 A 2012 roundtable organized at the University of Chicago brought together Gary Becker and François Ewald to reflect on Foucault's late lectures on neoliberalism. Becker, Ewald, and Harcourt, "Becker on Ewald on Foucault on Becker American Neoliberalism and Michel Foucault's 1979 'Birth of Biopolitics' Lectures."

41 Foucault, *Birth of Biopolitics*, 259–60.

42 "The question of the norm in Foucault's work has always been very closely linked to the idea of producing a common standard of measurement. Today, and I believe this to be the specific difficulty of the present moment, we are precisely experiencing a crisis of measure without precedent"; Ewald, "Foucault et l'actualité," 209. My translation.

43 See Zamora and Behrent, *Foucault and Neoliberalism*, and Sawyer and Steinmetz-Jenkins, *Foucault, Neoliberalism, and Beyond.*

44 Behrent, "Accidents Happen."

45 See Ewald's recent interview with Johannes Boehme for a frank recounting of this trajectory: Ewald, "What Do You Want Me to Regret?"

46 See Ewald, "La Providence de l'état." My translation. This interview offers an interesting insight into Ewald's own reinterpretation of his earlier work.

47 The argument is made in some detail by the Foucauldian Robert Castel in an excoriating commentary on Ewald's work for the MEDEF. See Castel, "'Risquophiles' et 'risquophobes.'"

Part I. The History of Responsibility

1 The French word *juridique* is sometimes translated into English as "legal." However, Ewald consciously distinguishes between the terms "juridical" and "legal." The term "juridical" relates to the administration of legal codes and systems as an expression of social and political power, whereas "legal," in English, usually refers to anything more generally relating to the law. This distinction is especially important for tracing Ewald's adaptation of Michel Foucault's work on the history of law, norms, and sovereignty. See, in particular, Ewald, "Norms, Discipline, and the Law," 138–61; Foucault, "L'Extension sociale de la norme," 3:74–79. *Trans.*

2 The *patronat* is the sum total of all employers in society, regarded as an interest group. Later, there would be actual organizations responsible for guarding and advancing employers' interests, such as the Confédération générale du patronat français (1936–40), the Conseil national du patronat français (1945–98), and the current Mouvement des entreprises de France (MEDEF). *Trans.*

3 *Contrat de louage de services*, a form of labor contract that is usually governed under private law and lacking many of the provisions of the modern employment contract. The difference is similar to the modern distinction between individual or part-time contractors and formal employees. For a brief overview of this distinction in Britain and the United States, see Wilkinson and Deakin, *Law of the Labour Market*, 42–109. *Trans.*

4 Foucault, *Discipline and Punish*, 195.
5 Deleuze, "Écrivain non," 1215.

Chapter 1. Civil Law

1 The corporate bodies of prerevolutionary France banned by the Le Chapelier law were workers' guilds and *compagnonnage* (apprenticeship programs). Aside from setting up social distinctions that revolutionary legislators wished to abolish, it also aimed to eliminate barriers to free trade. *Trans.*
2 Marx and Engels, *Manifesto of the Communist Party*, 475. *Trans.*
3 Schaller, *De la Charité privée aux droits économiques et sociaux du citoyen*, 36.
4 Turgot, "Fondation," 73.
5 Cousin, *Justice et charité*.
6 See with regard to David Hume, Leroy, *David Hume*, 253; Deleule, *Hume et la naissance du libéralisme politique*, in particular 74; Smith, *Theory of the Moral Sentiments*; and more recently the confirmation of this tradition, Hayek, *Law, Legislation, and Liberty*, in particular vol. 1, *Rules and Order*.
7 On the formulation of natural rights, see, for example, Pufendorf, *Les Devoirs de l'homme et du citoyen*; Burlamaqui, *Élémens du droit naturel*; Lepage, *Éléments de la science du droit*; Oudot, *Conscience et science du devoir*.
8 The French term *juridicité* is close to the English term "legality," but the two are not exactly the same concept. Whereas "legality" implies conformity to the law, "juridicity" implies the perception of the ways legal instruments operate. See Duxbury, "Juridicity as a Theme in French Legal Philosophy," 85–95. *Trans.*
9 For a synthetic presentation of this argument and its historical context, see in particular Bloch, *L'Assistance et l'état en France à la veille de la révolution*; Lallemand, *Histoire de la charité*; Foucault, *History of Madness*; Castel, *Regulation of Madness*.
10 Jourdan, *Le Droit français*, 32. "One does not make devotion by decree; one does not organize sacrifice and sympathy"; Troplong, *De la Propriété d'après le code civil*, 67.
11 Say, *Cours complèt d'économie politique pratique*, 2:358–59. Say continues, "But even making charity an abstraction of this sentiment of sympathy, prior to Christianity, and one that asks of each (nondeprived) person to combat the maladies of his peers, it is not in the interest of the social body to tie this to the severity of the law."
12 Duchâtel, *Considérations d'économie politique*, 158.
13 Duchâtel, *Considérations d'économie politique*, 187.
14 Duchâtel, *Considérations d'économie politique*, 188; to which we can add Thiers, *Rapport présenté par M. Thiers au nom de la Commission de l'assistance et de la prévoyance publiques dans la séance du 26 janvier 1850*, 11: "But it matters that this virtue, when it moves from the particular to the collective, from private to public virtue, preserves its character as virtue. This means that it remains voluntary, spontaneous, and lastly free to act or not act, because otherwise it will have ceased to be a virtue and will become a constraint, and a disastrous one at that. So, in effect, instead of receiving, an entire class could demand, taking on the role

of beggars who ask while holding guns. This would give occasion to the most dangerous violence."

15 Bastiat, *Justice et fraternité*, 114.

16 Proudhon, *Les Confessions d'un révolutionnaire*, 175.

17 Portalis, *Discours, rapports et travaux*, 83. Elsewhere, Portalis writes, "One governs poorly when one governs in excess. A man who deals with another man should be attentive and wise. He should mask his own interest, take in all available information, and pay heed to everything useful. The office of the law exists to protect us against other fraudulent people, but it does not exist to make us use our own reason. If it were otherwise, under the oversight of the laws, the lives of men would be nothing but a long and shameful immaturity. And this oversight will itself degenerate into an inquisition" (53).

18 Kant, *Metaphysics of Morals*, 387. Translation amended. *Trans.*

19 "Men are born and remain free and equal in rights."

20 Kant, *Metaphysics of Morals*, 388. Translation amended. *Trans.*

21 "What are those things which men have the right to impose on each other *by force*? I only know one such case, and that is *justice*. I have no right to force that which might be religious, charitable, instructive, laborious; but I have the right to *force* it to be *just*; this is the case of legitimate defense"; Bastiat, *Harmonies économiques*, 18.

See Article 4 of the 1789 Declaration of the Rights of Man and of the Citizen: "Liberty consists of the freedom to do everything that injures no one else; hence, the exercise of the natural rights of each man has no limits except those which assure to the other members of the society the enjoyment of the same rights. These limits may only be determined by law."

22 See Kelsen, *Introduction to the Problems of Legal Theory*. *Trans.*

23 Thiers, *Rapport*, 6.

24 Vailland, *Choderlos de Laclos par lui-même*.

25 The French original reads, *La moindre transaction gripperait cette belle mécanique et ruinerait l'ensemble du dispositif* (The smallest transaction will jam this beautiful mechanism and ruin the whole of the framework). Based on the context, it seems likely that "transaction" is a typographical error. Thanks to Melinda Cooper for pointing this out. *Trans.*

26 "If the providential laws are harmonic, it is because they act freely. Without this freedom they would not be harmonic by themselves. Thus, so long as we can speak of a default with harmony in the world, it can only correspond to a default of liberty, to an absent justice"; Bastiat, *Harmonies économiques*, 18.

27 Gérando, *Traité de la bienfaisance publique*, 163. NB: Ewald has slightly altered Gérando's text. I have followed the text in Ewald's book. *Trans.*

28 Gérando, *Traité de la bienfaisance publique*, 164.

29 Duchâtel, *Considérations d'économie politique*, 330.

30 Duchâtel, *Considérations d'économie politique*, 177. "Prudence is an eminent virtue, the most important of all"; Cousin, *Du Vrai, du beau et du bien*.

31 Duchâtel, *Considérations d'économie politique*, 37.

32 See Fenet, *Recueil complet des travaux préparatoires du Code civil*, 13:474, 477.

33 On these three characteristics of liberal inequalities, see for example, Thiers, *Du Droit de propriété*, 61; Passy, *Des Causes de l'inégalité des richesses*, "Inequality is bound to the laws of the world," 9; Cousin, *Justice et charité*, 24.

34 Gérando, *Traité de la bienfaisance publique*, 1:166.

35 See Rousseau, *Discourse on the Origin and Foundations of Inequality among Men*, 64.

36 Duchâtel, *Considérations d'économie politique*, 306–7.

37 Duchâtel, *Considérations d'économie politique*, 29.

38 Duchâtel, *Considérations d'économie politique*, 207–8.

39 Chevallier, "Assistance," 74.

40 The French term used here is *institutions patronales*, which is based on the French word *patron*. The French word *patron* is often translated as "boss." However, in the nineteenth century it is also distinguished from *maître* [master], which is also close to the modern English word "boss," and the much rarer word *employeur* [employer], which gained in use after the nineteenth century. I have chosen to use *patron* in order to best approximate the specific connotations (paternal, patronizing, etc.) of the French word in its nineteenth-century context. See Kolbloom, "Patron et Patronat," 89–112. *Trans.*

41 Concerning the history of assistance, in particular at the close of the eighteenth century, see Foucault, *History of Madness*, 55–77, 406–18; Lallemand, *La Révolution et des pauvres*; Bloch, *L'Assistance et l'état en France à la veille de la révolution*; Bouchet, *L'Assistance publique en France pendant la révolution*.

42 Montesquieu, *Spirit of the Laws*, book 23, chapter 29.

43 "The legislation that governs this class [the poor] must form a necessary part of the Constitution established for this society; otherwise, it will be beautiful in theory, but it will not be legislation adapted to a country governed by a Constitution where this legislation will only be an hors-d'oeuvre"; La Rochefoucauld-Liancourt, *Premier rapport du Comité de Mendicité*, cited by Bloch, *L'Assistance et l'état en France à la veille de la révolution*, 431.

As one of its fundamental provisions, the Constitution of September 3, 1791, states, "A general establishment of *public aid* will be created and organized to raise abandoned children, help the disabled poor, and provide work to the abled poor who have not procured it for themselves."

44 See the Constitution of September 3, 1791; Constitution of June 24, 1793, Declaration of the Rights of Man and of the Citizen, article 21; Constitution of November 4, 1848, Preamble, article 7; Project of the Constitution of April 19, 1946, Universal Declaration of Human Rights, Chapter II: "On Social and Economic Rights"; Constitution of October 27, 1946, Preamble.

45 La Rochefoucauld-Liancourt, *Quatrième rapport du Comité de Mendicité*, cited by Lallemand, *La Révolution des pauvres*, 45.

46 La Rochefoucauld-Liancourt, *Premier rapport du Comité de Mendicité*, 1.

47 Foucault, *History of Madness*, 413.

48 Cited by Bouchet, *L'Assistance publique en France pendant la révolution*, 121.
49 The Convention was the legislative body that succeeded the National Assembly after Louis XVI was deposed and the first Republic of France was created. One of its main tasks was to create a new constitution. *Trans.*

Chapter 2. Security and Liberty

1 Liberal philosophy, which is a moral vision of the world, obeys a logic proper to such a vision: "The freer self-consciousness becomes, the freer also is the negative object of its consciousness"; Hegel, *Phenomenology of Spirit*, § 599, 365.
2 Bastiat, *Harmonies économiques*, 13.
3 See, by way of example, Humboldt, *Essai sur les limites de l'action de l'état*, 23: "All state interference in the private affairs of citizens is to be rejected where there is no immediate violation of the rights of one by others."
4 Gérando, *Traité de la bienfaisance publique*, 1:167. Also, Duchâtel, *Considérations d'économie politique sur la bienfaisance*, 352: "Such is the nature of this world, that good cannot grow without evil developing at its sides at the same time."
5 Gérando, *Traité de la bienfaisance publique*, 1:165.
6 See Kant, *Idea for a Universal History from a Cosmopolitan Perspective*.
7 "Events led by the combination or the encounter of phenomena that appear from independent series, in the order of causality, are what we call *fortuitous* events, or the results of happenstance"; Cournot, *Exposition de la théorie des chances et des probabilités*, 73.
8 *L'accidentalité généralisée*. This is one of Ewald's neologisms. *Trans.*
9 Kant, *Idea for a Universal History from a Cosmopolitan Perspective*, 3–4.
10 F. A. Hayek has reprised this thesis in "Results of Human Action."
11 On the begging-pauperism opposition, see Hatzfeld, *Du Paupérisme à la sécurité sociale*, 7–8; Castel, *Regulation of Madness*, 106–7.
12 See Rigaudias-Weiss, *Les Enquêtes ouvrières en France entre 1830 et 1848*.
13 Chevallier, "Pauperism"; Leroy-Beaulieu, *Traité théorique et pratique d'économie politique*, 4:457.
14 Gérando, *Traité de la bienfaisance publique*, 1:342.
15 On the institution of this relation of tutelage as general form of government, see Castel, *Regulation of Madness*, 77–83.
16 See Guéneau, "La Législation restrictive du travail des enfants," 421.
17 As Guéneau notes, the French legislator was inspired by numerous English laws adopted in these matters, and especially the bill of August 19, 1833. We should also specify that the movement in favor of regulating child labor traversed all of the states of Europe at the same time; Guéneau, "La Législation restrictive du travail des enfants," 422.
18 Under the French Restorations, from 1814 to 1848, the government legislature was split, similar to the English government, between an upper house, the Chamber of Peers, and a lower house, the Chamber of Deputies. *Trans.*

19 Chamber of Peers, *Moniteur universel*, February 22, 1840, 428.

20 "Today it only concerns young children; but you can be sure, not long will pass before it also includes regulating the work of adults. Is this good? Is this evil? I do not say. I am inclined to believe that it is good; but you can be sure it is serious"; *Moniteur universel*, April 11, 1840, 2487; Count Portalis, Chamber of Peers, *Moniteur universel*, February 22, 1840: "I fear that by dealing with the fate of these children, these future men who should replace the voids left in society by the loss of such children cut down by death, that we may be led to deal with all those who might contribute to the existence and well-being of humanity"; 443.

21 Charles Dupin, Chamber of Peers, *Moniteur universel*, February 22, 1840, 458. "You declare a public good that which, to this point, has only ever been considered a private good," Gustave de Beaumont, *Moniteur universel*, April 11, 1840, 2487.

22 Charles Dupin, Chamber of Peers, *Moniteur universel*, February 22, 1840, 350, 426; Renouard, Chamber of Deputies, *Moniteur universel*, April 11, 1840, 1292.

23 Montesquieu, *Spirit of the Laws*, book XI, chapter 3. *Trans.*

24 *Recueil Sirey* (1838), 70; *Recueil Sirey* (1839), 432; *Recueil Dalloz* (1839), 2:168.

25 In virtue of article 1384 of the Civil Code: "One is responsible not only for damage one causes themselves, but also for that damage caused by persons to whom one is responsible, or for things that one has in their custody. . . . Masters and their principals, on the damage caused by their servants and employees in the functions in which they have employed them."

26 *Recueil Sirey* (1838), 70.

27 A principle of the will's autonomy, of which Rousseau and Kant were the honored theorists. See Gounot, *Le Principe de l'autonomie de la volonté en droit privé*, 58. On the "liberation" represented by the Civil Code, see Saleilles, "Le Code civil et la méthode historique," 116; Ripert, *La Régle morale dans les obligations civiles*, 37.

28 "Beneath every legal obligation there is an implicit will that motivates and grounds that obligation. . . . By making will the essential element of crimes and torts, we place them within the domain of the contract"; Gounot, *Le Principe de l'autonomie de la volonté en droit privé*, 67, 69.

29 Articles 1156–64 of the Civil Code.

30 *Recueil Sirey* (1838), 70; *Recueil Sirey* (1839), 432.

31 This interpretation of the contract for services, reduced to the simple exchange of a wage for a service, would remain the interpretation of the courts until the end of the nineteenth century. In addition, compensation for workers who are injured in workplace accidents could not be legally based in contracts for services. More generally, this is to say that the contract for services, inasmuch as it is a contract and obeys the general regime of contracts, is resistant to something like a labor law, which is to say to the formulation of obligations, exceeding the simple exchange of work-remuneration, that presided over and ruled the liberty of salaried agreements. The stipulations that would be those of labor law do not have contract law as their birthplace, but are exterior to it. They come from other juridical sources. For the appearance of our modern employment contract, with

the juridical relationship of subordination that characterizes it, in order to be inscribed in the principles of a new juridical economy, the contract for services had to be extracted from the general regime of contracts.

32 *Recueil Sirey* (1838), 70.

33 Guyot, "La question des accidents de travail et le Congrès de Milan," 300.

34 Léon Say, Senate, *Journal Officiel*, 232.

35 Morisseaux, in *Congrès international des accidents du travail et des assurances sociales*, 768. NB: The reference given in Ewald's original is to page 763. The correct page is 768. *Trans.*

36 Report and commentary reproduced in *Histoire des accidents du travail* 4 (February 1978): 9.

37 We should point out that the question of the security of labor had been one of the central points of debate concerning the law of 1841 governing child labor.

38 See chapter 3. The *livret* was a booklet carried around by workers that kept track of their work and employment history. In modern-day terms, it is a cross between a résumé and a passport. *Trans.*

Chapter 3. Noblesse Oblige

1 Engel-Dollfus, cited by Mamy, "Mesures préventives prises contre les accidents," 5.

2 Le Play, *La Réforme sociale*, 301.

3 Literally, "Socialists of the Chair," a German economic school. *Trans.*

4 Cheysson, "Le Devoir social et la formation sociale du patron," 49–50.

5 An English approximation of the terms *patronat* and *grand patronat* would be "the business/managerial organization" and "big business organization." However, I have kept the French due to the specific nature of the term (and for reasons similar to the term *patron*). On the specificity of the terms *patronal, patronat, and patron* in nineteenth- and twentieth-century France, see Kolboom, "Patron et patronat," 89–112. *Trans.*

6 Le Play, in the history that he provides for his own studies, emphasizes that he has only ever published in response to direct orders: *Les Ouvriers européens* (1855)—that would receive the statistics award from the Academy of Moral and Political Science—under the pressure of Thiers, Tocqueville, and Jean Reynaud, in the moment of 1848. *La Réforme sociale* was published at the request of Napoleon III himself; see Le Play, *Les Ouvriers européens*.

7 The Society of Social Economy had been founded in 1856 by Le Play, J. B. Dumas, Villermé, Charles Dupin, Mathieu, M. Chevalier, Gasparin, and the vicomte de Melun. It will publish a bulletin and, beginning in 1881, a review, *La Réforme sociale*. The Unions of Social Peace will be created in 1872 in response to the collapse of the empire and the Commune.

8 "The word patron only applies to the leaders who assure peace and security to their subordinates. The moment this role is not fulfilled, the patron falls into the category of *master* and is only an *employer*, following the barbarous term that

tends to be substituted for that of the patron in the regions where instability reigns"; Dubreuil, "Le patronage," 466. See also Le Play, *La Réforme sociale*, chap. 1; the program of the *Réforme Sociale* school, in *La Réforme Sociale* 1 (1881): 4.

See n.5 for the differences between *patron* and "employer." *Trans.*

9 See in particular Chaptal, *Essai sur le perfectionnement des arts chimiques en France, an VIII*; Chaptal, *Quelques réflexions sur l'industrie en général*; Chaptal, *De l'Industrie française*; Chaptal, *Mes souvenirs sur Napoléon*. See also the works in which Claude-Anthelme Costaz has systematized the principles of this politics of industrialization, in particular the *Essai sur l'administration de l'agriculture, du commerce, des manufactures et des susbsistances*, and *Les Lois et instructions ministérielles sur les manufactures, les ateliers, les ouvriers et la propriété*.

10 Chaptal, *Essai sur le perfectionnement des arts chimiques en France, an VIII*, v, vi. On the decisive role of the wars with England in France's industrialization, see Viennet, *Napoléon et l'industrie française*; de Jouvenal, *Napoléon et l'économie dirigée*.

11 Chaptal, *Quelques réflexions sur l'industrie*, introduction. This text, written after the Congress of Vienna, is a critical commentary.

12 Chaptal, *De l'Industrie française*, 2:205.

13 Chaptal, *De l'Industrie française*, 2:217–19.

14 Chaptal, *Essai sur le perfectionnement*, 88.

15 Costaz, *Les Lois et instructions ministérielles*, 3.

16 Girardin, Report on the Law of April 21, 1810, cited by Locré, *Législation sur les mines*, 421.

17 Locré, *Législation sur les mines*, 295. NB: In the French text, Ewald quotes Locré as writing, "A force de sollicitude, il mine et la liberté et la propriété." Locré's text, however, reads, "A force de sollicitude, il *ruine* et la liberté et la propriété" (my emphasis). I have translated according to Locré's original text. The translation of Ewald's original sentence with the different verb would read, "Through overconcern, it undermines both liberty and property." *Trans.*

18 Chaptal, *De l'Industrie française*, vol. 14.

19 Maximilien de Béthune, Duc de Sully (1560–1641) was an adviser to King Henri IV (1553–1610). *Trans.*

20 Costaz, *Essai sur l'administration*, 10.

21 Le Roux, *Exposition universelle de 1867*, 23–24.

22 Costaz, *Essai sur l'administration*, 336–37.

23 On the worker's *livret*, see, in particular, Sauzet, *Le Livret obligatoire des ouvriers*, and Plantier, *Le Livret des ouvriers*. The text of the law of Germinal Year XI is reproduced in Sauzet: "Essai historique sur la législation industrielle de la France," 1133.

24 "A worker should have the ability to leave his master at any time if only so that his master might turn him away at any time: but as this ability should lead to serious inconveniences, since it might lead to the dissolution of the factory, a means of reconciling the interest of business with the right of individuals must be found; now, these means will be those that, by assuring for a determined time the labor of a worker to the entrepreneur, will secure the worker against an unexpected

and undeserved dismissal. It follows from these principles that public security, business, and morality desire that a worker should only be received in a workshop if he can deliver a certificate of good conduct from his former workshop to the hands of his new supervisor. These are the wise and conservative measures that assure the prosperity of businesses and establish always-precious friendly relations between the supervisor and the workers. These are measures that, giving the supervisor the assurance of dependable manual labor, and assuring the worker a well-being that is always dependent on his conduct, permit the former to give his business speculations the appropriate scope and reassure the latter of his means of subsistence"; Chaptal, *Essai sur le perfectionnement*, 55–57.

25 It is known that Napoleon visited workshops.

26 On the concept of "social authority," see Le Play, *L'Organization du travail*, 18.

27 Chaptal, *De l'Industrie française*, 2:236.

28 For a synthetic view, see Trempé, *Les Mineurs de Carmaux*, and Murard and Zylberman, *Ville, habitat et intimité*.

29 These practices are directed first of all to the management personnel who are principally concerned with attracting and retaining workers; Saint-Léger, *Les Mines d'Anzin et d'Aniche pendant la Révolution*; Rouff, *Les Mines de charbon en France*, part III, chap. 4, "Les ouvriers."

30 Burat, *Les Houillères de la France en 1866*, 293.

31 Leroy-Beaulieu, *La Question ouvrière*, 177–78.

32 According to which company managers will justify child labor in mines: "It's principally through the child that workers are recruited, work in the mines requires a long apprenticeship to which it is useful to become acquainted at a young age"; *Comité des Houillères du Nord et du Pas-de-Calais*.

33 The Lens Company spoke of this as a "creation": "From the beginning of the exploitation of Lens' mines, in 1852, the problem was posed of creating a mining personnel in a region entirely devoted to agriculture"; Société des Mines de Lens et de Douvrin (Pas-de-Calais), *Habitations ouvrières*, 5.

34 "Literally, the company takes the mineworker from the pram and accompanies him until the grave"; Reybaud, *Le Fer et la houille*, 190.

35 "Two rules emerge from the preceding: (1) the worker's productive power is in direct relation with his morality . . . ; (2) the patron has an immediate interest to have at hand an upstanding and regular worker. From this it follows as a rigorous consequence that the patron should encourage everything that works toward the development of the worker's morality"; Picot, "Les Institutions patronales."

36 Le Creusot is a commune in east-central France that saw massive industrial development over the course of the nineteenth century, particularly through the steel factories run by Adolphe and Eugène Schneider. *Trans.*

37 Reybaud, *Le Fer et la houille*, 35.

38 *Villes politiques*. Ewald uses this term along the same lines as French philosopher and geographer Henri Lefebvre; see Lefevre, *Urban Revolution*. *Trans.*

39 The managers of the Béthune Mining Company constructed brick walls to properly designate the company's boundaries.

40 Ewald uses the medieval expression *charge d'âme*, which referred to a church official's duty to keep care of his congregation's spiritual well-being. *Trans.*

41 Le Play, *La Réforme sociale*, book 4, chap. 34, p. 236.

42 Michel and Renouard, *Histoire d'un centre ouvrier*, introduction.

43 Le Play, *La Réforme sociale*, book 4, chap. 34, p. 244.

44 One can imagine the problems that the development of publicly held companies [*sociétés anonymes*] are going to pose to the patronage regime's disciples; Cheysson, "Le Devoir social et la formation sociale du patron," 80.

45 Cheysson, "Le Devoir social et la formation sociale du patron," 31–32.

46 Le Play, *La Réforme sociale*, book 6, pages 176–88.

47 The term *famille souche*, or "stem family," derives from Le Play's theory of family forms. In his classic empirical studies of the mid-nineteenth-century family, Le Play identified three basic family structures that he thought could account for all historical kinship variations around the world. Le Play referred to the first type of family as the *famille patriarcale*, or "joint family," in which all sons remained living and working with their parents into adulthood. This type of family could still be found among Eastern nomads, Russian peasants, and the Slavs of Central Europe. In the second type of family, the *famille souche* or stem family, one child alone was chosen by the father to work in the parental household and eventually inherit it, thus continuing the family line. According to Le Play, this type of family was common among peasant communities throughout Europe. The third type of family, the *famille instable* or nuclear family, represented a degraded kinship structure that was predominant among the working-class populations of industrializing Western Europe. Because industrial workers had little property to hand down, most children left home at an early age and established their own households, leaving the parents without support in their old age and the family without continuous heritage. See Le Play, *L'Organisation de la famille*; Le Play, *Les Ouvriers européens*. *Trans.*

48 On this point, see Le Play, *La Réforme sociale*, book 6, chap. 44, "L'inégalité et liberté"; *L'Organisation du travail*, § 56: "La corruption du langage et l'abus des quatre mots" (*liberté, progrès, égalité, démocratie*), 337.

49 Cheysson, *Oeuvres choisies*, 2:89.

50 "The wage is a right: by hour or by day, by cubic meter of land worked or by kilogram of coal, the worker must reach an agreed-upon sum. By paying the wage, the patron clears a debt: the price of labor delivered. This is the purely economic contract in all of its justice, but also all of its callousness. On the contrary, when the patron preoccupies himself with propriety, the worker's needs outside of the workshop, to try to satisfy them, he goes beyond his role as strict procurer of manual labor. He benevolently does more and better. He brings himself closer to the man he employs as well as his family, instead of only seeing his role as an abstract source of labor"; Cheysson, *Oeuvres choisies*, 2:87.

51 Latin for "I give so that you might give." This is a type of contract where one party gives something up so that the other party can provide something else in return. *Trans.*
52 Cheysson, *Oeuvres choisies*, 2:88.
53 "The subsidy produces the results most beneficial to the families of workers, by subtracting them, for the satisfaction of certain needs, from the consequences of the worker's lack of foresight. Even though the worker is overindulgent or extravagant, his family will not lack for heating, housing, care, if they benefit from heating, housing, and medical care, via subsidies"; Cheysson, *Oeuvres choisies*, 2:88.
54 Guérin, "Du Salaire et des moyens d'existence," 118.
55 "The principle, this is what should interest the personnel in the prosperity of the workshop"; Cheysson, *Oeuvres choisies*, 2:31. "Labor is incumbent on the worker: we search for the mode of remuneration of labor that ensures the worker, generally lacking foresight, the greatest standard of well-being and we found that it is in the wage combined in such a way that the interest of the worker should be always tied to the interest of the person or persons who employ him"; Gibon, *Des Divers modes de rémunération du travail*, 23.
56 Foucault, *Discipline and Punish*, 222–23.
57 Cheysson, *L'Économie sociale à l'Exposition universelle de 1889*, 17–18.

Part II. Universal Insurance against Risk

1 Condorcet, *Mathématique et société*, 104.
2 Gouraud, *Histoire du calcul des probabilités*, 5.
3 Chateleux and Rooijen, *Le Rapport de Johan de Witt*. Christiaan Huygens (1629–95) was a Dutch astronomer and physicist who wrote an early work on probability theory, *On Reasoning in Games of Chance* (1657). Pierre Rémond de Montmort (1678–1719) was a French mathematician known for his *Essay Analyzing Games of Chance* (1708). The Grand Pensionary was the second most powerful office in the Netherlands, second only to the Stadtholder. De Witt (1625–72) occupied this office from 1653 to 1672. *Trans.*
4 Condorcet, *Mathématique et société*, 104. *Ars Conjectandi* is Latin for "the conjectural arts." *Trans.*
5 Gouraud, *Histoire du calcul des probabilités*, 38.

Chapter 4. Average and Perfection

1 Quetelet, *Recherches sur le penchant au crime aux différens âges*, 4.
Pierre-Simon Laplace (1749–1827) was a French statistician, philosopher, and astronomer. *Trans.*
2 Quetelet, *Du Système social*, 8.
3 Quetelet, *Lettres à S. A. R.*, 47.
4 Quetelet, *Physique sociale*, 1:93–94.

5 William Petty (1623–87) was an English anatomist and political economist. *Trans.*

6 Ewald does not provide a citation for this quote, and I have not been able to locate it, but it does echo sentiments present throughout Quetelet's body of work. It is also similar to the epigraph by Laplace on the cover page of Quetelet's *Sur l'homme et le developpement de ses facultés*: "To the political and moral sciences we apply the method based on observation and calculation, the method that has served us so well in the natural sciences." *Trans.*

7 Ménard, "Trois formes de résistance aux statistiques," 419. NB: Ewald here quotes a passage from Ménard's essay that quotes a line from Say. *Trans.*

8 Ewald here refers to the French "Information Technology and Liberties" law of January 6, 1978 (loi no. 78-17), which protects individuals from harm related to amassing digital information. *Trans.*

9 The Gauss curve, named after mathematician Carl Gauss (1777–1855), is commonly referred to in Anglophone mathematics courses as a "normal distribution" or "bell curve." *Trans.*

10 Quetelet, *Lettres à S. A. R.*, 133. NB: The pagination for this and the following citation corrects the pagination provided by Ewald. *Trans.*

11 Quetelet, *Lettres à S. A. R.*, 137.

12 Quetelet, *Du Système social*, 13–14.

13 Quetelet, *Du Système social*, 18–19.

14 Quetelet, *Sur l'homme et le développement de ses facultés*, 1:20, 2:250.

15 Antoine Augustin Cournot (1801–77) was a French philosopher, economist, and mathematician. Alphonse Bertillon (1853–1914) was a French police officer and forensic theorist who established techniques of human measurement to identify and track criminal suspects. Maurice Halbwachs (1877–1945) was a French philosopher best known for his theory of collective memory. He also wrote a book-length critique of Quetelet: Halbwachs, *La théorie de l'homme moyen*. For the ancient Greek Stoic philosophers, incorporeals were qualities, such as time, place, or speech, that existed but could not be reduced to specific physical matter. *Trans.*

16 Foucault, *Discipline and Punish*, 184. *Trans.*

17 Bidiss, *Age of the Masses*. *Trans.*

18 Quetelet, *Physique sociale*, 1:96–97. "The result," Quetelet says, "is that the person who carries his head to the scaffold or is going to finish serving the remainder of his days in prison is in a certain way a sacrificial victim of society."

19 Quetelet, *Sur l'homme et le développement de ses facultés*, 1:14.

20 Quetelet, *Du Système social*, 69.

21 Quetelet, *Du Système social*, 96.

22 Quetelet, *Du Système social*, 97.

23 Quetelet, *Recherches sur le penchant au crime aux différens âges*, 81.

24 Quetelet, *Du Système social*, 258.

25 Quetelet, *Du Système social*, 9.

26 Quetelet, *Études sur l'homme*, 12.

27 Quetelet, *Du Système social*, 95; Quetelet, "De l'Influence du libre arbitre," 3:145.

28 The French word is *chute*, which can mean a physical fall as well as a metaphoric downfall. Quetelet and Ewald play on both senses in this paragraph. *Trans.*
29 Quetelet, *Physique social*, 2:248.
30 Villermé, "Sur l'hygiène morale," 46–47. NB: In the French edition, Ewald gives "Sur l'hygiène sociale" as the title of this essay. *Trans.*
31 Quetelet, *Du Système social*, 291.
32 Machiavelli, *Prince*, 85. *Trans.*

Chapter 5. An Art of Combinations

1 *Compagnies à primes*. *Trans.*
2 *Combinaisons*. For the French word *combinaison*, in most cases I have used the straightforward *combination*. However, in some contexts, such as when discussing the management of multiple variables, it can also mean "strategy." In some instances I have chosen to use the latter translation. *Trans.*
3 O. Bloch and von Wartburg, *Dictionnaire étymologique*, s.v. "*risque*."
The connection Ewald highlights is between the French word *risque* and the post-classical Latin word *resecum*, the latter referring to an ocean shelf, ocean reef, or, more figuratively, any sort of pitfall of a given situation. The English word "risk" shares the same etymology as the French word. However, the connection Ewald cites between the maritime context and the word is now disputed. Other scholars point to the similarity with the Arabic *rizq*, which denotes chance by divine providence. See the *Oxford English Dictionary*, 3rd ed. (2010), s.v. "risk." *Trans.*
4 Say, "Assurance."
5 Picard and Besson, *Traité général*, 1:35.
6 Chaufton, *Les Assurances*, 1:309.
7 Coinsurance is a form of insurance where multiple contracting parties, most simply the insurer and the insured, share the risks and therefore the costs of the insurance and any claims made. Reinsurance is the insurance that insurance companies obtain to cover their own risks (of potential claims they will need to cover over a certain period of time). This ensures that a large number of claims over a short period of time will not bankrupt an individual insurance provider. *Trans.*
8 The French word is *responsabilité*, which is meant to parallel Ewald's earlier discussions of responsibility and foresight. *Trans.*
9 Chaufton, *Les Assurances*, 1:103.
10 Chaufton, *Les Assurances*, 1:216.
11 A tontine was a form of life insurance fund where each member contributed a set amount. Each year an annuity was paid to the surviving members—as members died the share of the annuity increased for those members still alive. It eventually fell into disrepute, in part because it was perceived to encourage unscrupulous members to kill off other subscribers in order to increase their own annuity. *Trans.*
12 Chaufton, *Les Assurances*, 1:303.
13 Chaufton, *Les Assurances*, 1:296.

14 Gros, *L'Assurance*, 11.
15 "How Yukong Moved the Mountains" is a Chinese folktale about an old man who moves a mountain, stone by stone, and whose work is carried on by his sons. Mao Zedong discussed the fable in his revolutionary writings as a testament to the power of collective action. Joris Ivens also used the fable to title his popular 1976 French documentary on the Chinese Cultural Revolution. *Trans.*
16 Halpérin, *Assurances en Suisse et dans le monde*, 22.
17 Halpérin, *Assurances en Suisse et dans le monde*, 28.
18 L. Richard, *L'Homme est un capital*, 6. NB: This note was left out of the 1996 French edition but is found in the longer version; Ewald, *L'État providence*, 192n16. *Trans.*
19 About, *L'Assurance*, 34–35.
20 Bergeron, *Oeuvres sur les assurances*, 9.
21 About, *L'Assurance*, 54, 55.
22 Chaufton, *Les Assurances*, 1:291.
23 Reboul, *Étude sur les assurances*, 70.
24 We still find, at the beginning of the twentieth century, accusations of immorality leveled against insurance. Thus, Georges Duhamel: "I understand that for a number of my contemporaries insurance simultaneously holds a place of conscience, as guardian angel, a place of honor, gratitude, and many things further. . . . 'Insurance will pay,' there you have it, the magical formula in that the act of faith is encapsulated. It is an act of faith and an act of contrition"; Duhamel, *Scènes de la vie future*, 100.
25 Hémard, *Théorie et pratique*, 1:171.
26 Jean-Baptiste Colbert (1619–83) was finance minister under King Louis XIV, responsible for a number of reforms in favor of centralizing state control over the economy. *Trans.*
27 Boiteux, *Fortune de mer*, 75.
28 Pothier, *Traité des contrats aléatoires*.
29 Portalis, *Discours, rapports, et travaux*, 243–46.
30 The Conseil d'État was the highest court of appeal on legislative matters under the Old Regime in France. It provided the framework for the modern Conseil d'État established in 1799 by Napoleon, which is the one that still exists today. *Trans.*
31 Juvigny, *Coup d'oeil sur l'assurance de la vie des hommes*, 72. The same argument was taken up by the administrators of the "four major companies" in response to the attorney general Dupin's 1864 condemnation: "As for the institution's morality, do we need to demonstrate it? And if we ask how the actions of the father of a family that annually sets aside provisions in order to insure the fate of his loved ones in the case of a premature death must be qualified, each of our consciences respond"; *Livre du centenaire de "La Nationale,"* 457.
32 Pardessus, *Cours de droit commercial*, 2:303.
33 "Malpractice" here should not be read as only medical malpractice. Literally, the French term *l'assurance des fautes* means "fault insurance" and is distinct from *assurance de responsibilité*, liability insurance. *Trans.*

34 Pothier, *Traité du contrat d'assurance*, 105; Émérigon, *Traité des assurances et des contrats à l grosse d'Émérigon*, 1:363. These citations are missing from Ewald's original. *Trans.*

35 Frémery, *Études de droit commercial*, cited by Pouget, *Dictionnaire des assurances terrestres*, s.v. "Faute," "Faute lourde."

36 De Courcy, *Assurances*, 22.

37 Quoted in Persil, *Traité des assurances terrestres*, 26. NB: citation for Toullier's statement is missing from the original French edition. *Trans.*

38 Pardessus, *Assurance contre les accidents de voiture*, 16.

Chapter 6. Universal Politics

1 The French term "the political" (*le politique*), a postwar French neologism, is distinct from "politics" (*la politique*). Usually, as in this case, the distinction is between the political (*le politique*) as an autonomous domain of human activity representing situations of public power struggles, deliberation, and political procedure, and politics (*la politique*) representing foundational claims to political truth. The former is primarily strategic and situational; the latter is grounded in extrapolitical values and norms. For an overview of the history of this distinction in twentieth-century thought, see Jay, *Virtues of Mendacity*, 76–129. *Trans.*

2 Leibniz, "Assurances," cited by Gurvitch, *L'Idée du droit social*, 209.

3 The history of insurance institutions is retraced in L. Richard, *Histoire des institutions d'assurance en France*; Hamon, *Histoire générale*; Sénès, *Les Origines des compagnies d'assurances*; Blum, "Les Assurances terrestres."

4 The *Prospectus de l'éstablissement des assurances sur la vie* is reproduced in *Le Livre du centenaire de "La Nationale," 1830–1930*.

5 L. Richard, *Histoire des institutions d'assurance en France*, 37.

6 Clavière would be tax minister in the Girondin ministry led by Dumouriez-Roland. He would submit to the Convention the plan for *National Administration of Popular Economy* with the goal of "cementing equality by effacing the traces of misery"; see also Bouchet, *L'Assistance publique en France pendant la révolution*, 370.

7 La Rochefoucauld-Liancourt, *Quatrième rapport du Comité de Mendicité*, cited by Lallemand, *La Révolution et les pauvres*, 123.

8 The term *caisse de prévoyance* translates as "prudential fund," or "pension fund," but literally means "foresight bank," and recalls Ewald's previous discussions of foresight. *Trans.*

9 Bibliothèque municipale d'Orléans, dossier Lavoisier, manuscript 1326.

10 Levasseur, *Histoire des classes ouvrières*, 1:108–9. NB: This citation corrects the one Ewald gives in the French original: *Histoire des classes laborieuses*, 1:156–57. *Trans.*

11 Condorcet, *Esquisse d'un tableau historique des progrès de l'esprit humain*, 342–43. *Trans.*

12 Cited by Dreyfus, *Un Philanthrope d'autrefois*, 449. La Rochefoucauld-Liancourt had developed the same position in the *Quatrième rapport du Comité de Mendicité*, 120.

13 See L. Richard, *Histoire des institutions d'assurance en France*, 26. Richard retraces in particular the history of the Lafarge tontine, about which Mirabeau would pronounce the still-celebrated formula "I will freely name thrift the second providence of the human race."

14 Thiers, *Rapport présenté par M. Thiers au nom de la Commission de l'assistance et de la prévoyance publiques*, 117.

15 Ferrouillat, *Rapport au nom du Comité du travail*, 4.

16 Deboutteville, *Des Sociétés de prévoyance ou de secours mutuels*, 9; Gérando, *Traité de la bienfaisance publique*, 3:99.

17 Deboutteville, *Des Sociétés de prévoyance ou de secours mutuels*, 24; Gérando, *Traité de la bienfaisance publique*, 3:105; Villermé, *Tableau de l'état physique et moral*, 180; Hubbard, *De l'Organisation des sociétés de prévoyance*.

18 Gérando, *Traité de la bienfaisance publique*, 3:105.

19 The result of these works was an open commission composed of economists and politicians gathered in 1844 that would serve as the basis for all later studies; see, for example, Lefort, *Les Caisses de retraites ouvrières*, 2:9.

20 The politics of mutual aid societies is systematically studied in Laurent, *Le Paupérisme et les associations de prévoyance*. For the following period, see the works of the *Congrès scientifique international des institutions de prévoyance* and Guillemaut, *La Mutualité en France au XIXe siècle*, which is a commentary on the law of April 1, 1898.

21 The Waldeck-Rousseau project, having the institution of national pension funds as its aim, Assemblée Nationale constituante, *Impressions*, no. 125 (June 8, 1848), Rouveure's proposition having the institution of mutual aid funds and prudential funds, Assemblée Nationale constituante, *Impressions*, no. 694 (December 9, 1848).

22 Rouveure's proposition introduced the principle of obligatory patrons' contributions.

23 Ferrouillat, *Rapport au nom du Comité du travail*, 2.

24 Ferrouillat, *Rapport au nom du Comité du travail*, 10. Ferrouillat continued, "Doesn't the need to know the truth lead to a sort of labor inquisition, terrible for those very people we wish to aid?"

25 Ferrouillat, *Rapport au nom du Comité du travail*, 17.

26 Ferrouillat, *Rapport au nom du Comité du travail*, 18.

27 The recognition of public utility allowed for the receipt of gifts and inheritances. Among the other specified advantages: the exemption of postage and local registration rights and the printing of books and records freely provided by the communes. The obligations were to be open to persons of both sexes, to exclude covering risks involving unemployment and retirement, to stop the right to aid to those who ceased to pay their premiums, to only be able to dissolve through the order of a prefect after consultation with the cantonal commission.

28 Ferrouillat, *Rapport au nom du Comité du travail*, 35.

29 Benoist d'Azy, *Rapport au nom de la Commission*, relating to the mutual aid societies and the creation of a general bank for retirement pensions, Assemblée Nationale legislative, October 6, 1849, 288.

30 Benoist d'Azy, *Rapport au nom de la Commission*, 292.

31 See the organic decree of March 26, 1852, and its commentary in Laurent, *Le Paupérisme et les associations de prévoyance*, 1:394. This role is the same one that was asked of patrons of big business to play regarding their personnel.

32 Ferrouillat, *Rapport au nom du Comité du travail*, 56.

33 Assemblée Nationale législative, Sessions of July 10 and 11, 1850, 458, 480, 484, 490.

34 Boudon, *Organisation unitaire et nationale de l'assurance*.

35 Assemblée Nationale constituante, Session of June 13, 1848; also P. Richard, *Histoire des institutions d'assurance en France*, 58.

36 De Girardin, *La Politique universelle*. This work went through a number of editions. I will cite the 1855 edition. This work systematizes the views that Emile de Girardin had certainly formulated over a long period, in particular in the *Journal des connaissances utiles*.

37 De Girardin, *La Politique universelle*, 17.

38 De Girardin, *La Politique universelle*, 17.

39 De Girardin, *La Politique universelle*, 19.

40 De Girardin, *La Politique universelle*, 39.

41 De Girardin, *La Politique universelle*, 40. It goes without saying that the tax would simultaneously become an insurance premium.

42 De Girardin, *Le Droit*, 587.

43 De Girardin, *Questions de mon temps*, 1:xlvi.

44 De Girardin, *La Politique universelle*, 55.

45 De Girardin, *L'Abolition de la misère par l'élévation des salaires*.

46 Reclus, *Émile de Girardin*, 198.

47 *Journal des connaissances utiles* 5 (1835): 285. Later on, he would repeat, "Insurance companies have solved the problem of the association between the insured, without carrying the most minor infringement on any of their liberty"; de Girardin *Questions de mon temps*, 12:84.

Part III. The Recognition of Professional Risk

1 On the republican philosophy, see Nicolet, *L'Idée républicaine en France*.

2 Marx, *Eighteenth Brumaire of Louis Bonaparte*, 32, trans. altered. *Trans.*

Chapter 7. Charitable Profit

1 In Anglo-Saxon common law, legal liability is treated somewhat differently than in the French law based in the Civil Code. In the Anglo-Saxon model, legal liability rests on the commission of specific wrongs; it also covers both contractual liabili-

ties and tort liabilities. The latter are harms committed against persons or goods, but the main type of tort relates to negligence. In this model, each individual tort has its own rule. As Ewald notes, the civil legal liability established by the Civil Code rests primarily on the concept of obligations. In this framework, tort liabilities are not based on individualized and specific harms, but the general concept of fault stemming from the Civil Code. For an in-depth assessment of these distinctions, see Wagner, "Comparative Tort Law," 1004–41, esp. 1005–12, 1015–20. *Trans.*

2 Imperial Court of Lyon, 13.12.1854, in *Recueil Dalloz* (1855), 2:86.

3 A synthesis of these jurisprudential decisions can be found in the article "Travail," *Supplément au Répertoire Dalloz*, 119–29.

4 This expression of Jules Favre expresses well the difficult situation in which workplace accidents would place the common law of responsibility; "Réponse à l'addresse de l'Empereur," session of January 20, 1864, *Annales du Sénat et du Corps législatif*, 161.

5 Court of Metz, 26.5.1864, Arnould v. Wendel, *Recueil Dalloz* (1869), 2107.

6 Court of Appeals, 7.1.1878, Schneider v. Boissot, *Recueil Dalloz* (1878), 1, 297.

7 Jules Favre was a French politician who headed the Republican faction of the National Assembly under the early years of the Third Republic. *Trans.*

8 Ewald is here referring to the landmark Teffaine case of 1896, in which the widow of an engineer who was fatally injured by an exploding tugboat boiler brought a case against the owners of the tugboat. See the editor's introduction for a discussion of this case. *Trans.*

9 *Recueil Dalloz* (1870), 1, 361; *Recueil Sirey* (1870), 1:9.

10 *Recueil Sirey* (1870), 1:9.

11 Article 1386 of the Civil Code states that "the proprietor of a building is responsible for the damage caused by its degradation when it is the result of inadequate maintenance or defective construction." *Trans.*

12 Conseil d'État, 21.6.1895, *Recueil Sirey* (1897), 3:33, Hariou's note.

13 *Recueil Dalloz* (1897), 1, 433, Saleilles's note; *Recueil Sirey* (1897), 1:12, Esmein's note.

14 Prior to the Teffaine case, French case law had only recognized two instances in which ownership of a thing (*chose*) could justify liability. These instances were enumerated in article 1385, which mentions damage caused by animals, and article 1386, which refers to damage caused by the collapse of dilapidated buildings. *Trans.*

15 Saleilles, *Les Accidents de travail et la responsibilité civile*; Josserand, *De la Responsabilité du fait des choses inanimées.*

16 Labbé, *Recueil Sirey* (1885), 4:25.

17 Tolain, "Rapport fait au nom de la commission," *Journal Officiel*, January 24, 1889, 21.

18 Tarbouriech, *La Responsabilité des accidents dont les ouvriers sont victimes dans leur travail*, 68, which summarizes a number of authors.

19 Girard, "Rapport," *Journal Officiel*, April 26, 1883, 1009.

20 On relief funds, one should consult Hatzfield, *Du Paupérisme à la sécurité sociale*, chap. 3, "Les attitudes patronales"; and more particularly, Bréchignac, *Les*

Caisses de secours des ouvriers mineurs dans le bassin de la Loire; Salomon, *Les Caisses de secours et de prévoyance des ouvriers mineurs en Europe*; Widmer, *Les Caisses de secours et de retraite ouvrières*, vol. 2, chap. 2; "Caisses libres ouvrières et patronales."

21 On these two experiences, see Troclet, *La Première Expérience de sécurité sociale*, and Bourgin and Bourgin, *Le Régime de l'industrie en France*, which reproduces the administrative correspondence concerning the Rive-de-Gier's fund.

22 Bourgin and Bourgin, *Le Régime de l'industrie en France*, 137 (the Loire prefect and the Minister of the Interior).

23 Analysis of the jurisprudence in Bréchignac, *Les Caisses de secours des ouvriers mineurs dans le bassin de la Loire*, chaps. 5 and 6; Salomon, *Les Caisses de secours et de prévoyance des ouvriers mineurs en Europe*, 31–45.

24 Frédéric Engel-Dollfus was a French industrialist in the Second Empire and politician of Third Republic. He was associated with the Dollfus-Mieg textile mill in Mulhouse and the Saint-Simonian school of economic and social thought. In 1867 he created the Association for the Prevention of Mechanical Accidents. *Trans.*

25 Simonin, *La Vie souterraine*, 1: "Victor Hugo had recently said of the struggle of the sea workers. What he so justly calls the obstacle, the *Ananke* of the elements, also applies to the miner. Like the marine, the miner is the soldier of the abyss, and nature inexorably puts both of them to the test."

Ananke is the ancient Greek goddess of necessity. *Trans.*

26 Simonin concludes the take of the Meons catastrophe (1835) in these terms: "Finally one of the men who descended with the master miner is discovered. He is alive! Washed away by a storm to the bottom of a cavern, he had been terribly burned, nearly blinded. Piles of rubble closed off his exit, he had no light, he did not dare to move. Not hearing any noise for fifteen hours, with no hope of seeing another day, he patiently awaited death. He consoled himself by thinking—these are his own words—"that his wife and his children would be provided for through the mine's relief fund"; Simonin, *La Vie souterraine*, 176.

27 On January 10, 1812, sixty-eight miners died in the Horloz coal mine (near Liège) when a pocket of methane gas ignited. On February 28, 1812, the Beaujonc coal mine (southeast of Brussels) was flooded by a nearby river that broke through one of the mineshafts, drowning twenty-two miners and trapping seventy more over the course of the next five days. *Trans.*

28 Guyot, *La Famille Pichot*. This work constitutes an astonishing document on the customs in the miners' companies under the Second Empire. It says much more, and much more crudely, than Zola would ever say.

Yves Guyot was a journalist, novelist, economist, and politician active in the Second Empire and Third Republic. *Trans.*

29 *Gauchisme* is a French term for extreme left-wing politics. In the years following the student and worker strikes of May–June 1968, many *gauchiste* groups occupied factories and staged protests over workers' conditions. One of the most famous of these events was the workers' show trial at the Fouquière-les-Lens

mine following a January 1970 explosion that killed sixteen mineworkers. The philosopher Jean-Paul Sartre acted as the trial judge. Two years later, the Bruay Affair occurred: the daughter of a coal miner was found dead in a vacant lot in the town of Bruay; the main suspect was a lawyer connected to local mining interests. Ewald was one of the main activists in charge of publicizing the affair and organizing responses. The practice of workers' inquests (*enquêtes*) that Ewald mentions later are another parallel. *Trans.*

30 Zola, *Germinal*, xiii, 12. *Trans.*

Chapter 8. Security and Responsibility

1 *Personne morale*: This French term translates as "legal entity," but one of the connotations lost in English translation in this instance is the fact that the person of the *patron* is being displaced by a new legal objectification of the business that now embodies the formerly personal responsibilities attributed to the *patron*. *Trans.*

2 Article 8 of the collective policy of *La Préservatrice*, cited by Tarbouriech, *La Responsabilité des accidents dont les ouvriers sont victimes dans leur travail*, 110.

3 Tarbouriech, *La Responsabilité des accidents dont les ouvriers sont victimes dans leur travail*, 158.

4 I have not been able to find the source of this quote, and Ewald does not provide a citation in the original. It does not appear in either the preceding or following references. *Trans.*

5 He concludes, "You make too much of charity; so dream of justice before dreaming of charity"; Favre, *Annales du Sénat et du Corps législatif*, May 30, 1868, 126.

6 Favre, *Annales du Sénat et du Corps législatif*, May 30, 1868, 133.

7 Favre, *Annales du Sénat et du Corps législatif*, May 30, 1868, 134.

8 Favre, *Annales du Sénat et du Corps législatif*, May 30, 1868, 134.

9 Favre, *Annales du Sénat et du Corps législatif*, May 30, 1868, 134.

10 Favre, *Annales du Sénat et du Corps législatif*, May 30, 1868, 137.

11 Favre, *Annales du Sénat et du Corps législatif*, May 30, 1868, 129.

12 La Réforme Sociale was the name given both to the journal and group started by Frédéric Le Play in the second half of the nineteenth century, taking its name from one of Le Play's works. For the sake of consistency I have given the name as the title of the group rather than the journal. *Trans.*

13 "There are some, the majority of whom have good sense, who expect a better result of the association between patrons and workers. They rely on a number of examples, notably of the dispositions taken by certain railroad companies toward their workers. By closely examining the particulars, it strikes me as impossible to take part in these illusions"; Reybaud, "Économistes anglais," 131. NB: This citation corrects the original provided: "J. S. Mill et l'économie politique anglaise." *Trans.*

14 Reybaud, "Du Patronage dans l'industrie," 747.

15 Law of June 29, 1894, on relief funds and miners' retirements. On the history of this law, see Hatzfeld, *Du Paupérisme à la sécurité sociale*, 226.

16 This argument, sketched by Amédée Burat, secretary of the Committee of French Coal Mines in his brochure *Les Grèves en 1870*, is developed by Jules Marmottan, president of the Company of the Bruay Mines, in a brochure titled *Vrai Caractère des caisses de secours instituées par les compagnies houillères*.
17 When police tried to intervene in the mining strikes at Anzin during these years, the strikers met them with considerable violence. The Black Band was a supposed anarchist group active around the area surrounding Lyons in the 1880s. They were accused of detonating bombs targeting coal mine operators, political authorities, and local religious figures. *Trans.*
18 Beau de Rochas, *Commentaire de la loi*.
19 Say, "Chamber of Deputies," *Annales du Sénat et du Corps législatif*, May 18, 1893, 314.

Chapter 9. First and Foremost, a Political Law

1 To navigate the labyrinth of the parliamentary debate, the already-cited remarkable work of Ernest Tarbouriech, and more recently, the important work of Yves Le Gall are available; Tarbouriech, *La Responsabilité des accidents dont les ouvriers sont victimes dans leur travail*; Le Gall, "La Loi de 1898 sur les accidents du travail." As for commentary on the law of April 9, 1898, refer to, in chronological order of publication, Sachet, *Traité théorique et pratique de la législation sur les accidents du travail*; Loubat, *Traité sur le risque professionel*; Cabouat, *Traité des accidents du travail*; Rouast and Givord, *Traité du droit des accidents du travail et des maladies professionelles*.
2 *États généraux*, literally "estates general," recalling the assembly representing all sectors of French society at the beginning of the French Revolution of 1789. *Trans.*
3 Nadaud, "Proposition de loi sur 'les responsabilités des accidents dont les ouvriers sont victimes dans l'exercice de leur travail,'" Chamber of Deputies, *Documents*, no. 2660 (May 29, 1880).
4 Peulevey, Chamber of Deputies, *Documents*, no. 399 (February 11, 1882).
5 Faure, Chamber of Deputies, *Documents*, no. 283 (January 14, 1882).
6 Maret et al., Chamber of Deputies, *Documents*, no. 564 (March 7, 1882).
7 Sauzet, "De la Responsabilité des patrons," 626; Sainctelette, *De la Responsabilité et da la garantie*, 133.
8 I have normally translated *accident du travail* as "workplace accident." However, in this instance, Ewald's focus is on the part of the phrase emphasizing the worker's labor, not the specific site of the accident. *Trans.*
9 Sauzet, "De la Responsabilité des patrons," 617.
10 Labbé, *Recueil Sirey* (1885), 4:27
11 *Delit. Trans.*
12 Ricard, Chamber of Deputies, *Journal Officiel*, May 18, 1888, 1445.
13 Girard, "Report," Chamber of Deputies, *Documents*, no. 694, *Journal Officiel*, March 28, 1882, 1008.

14 Say, Senate, *Journal Officiel*, March 28, 1889, 231.
15 Faure, Chamber of Deputies, *Documents*, no. 599 (February 11, 1882).
16 Peulevey, Chamber of Deputies, *Journal Officiel*, March 9, 1883, 521.
17 Le Breton, Senate, *Journal Officiel*, March 21, 1889, 301.
18 Faure, Chamber of Deputies, *Journal Officiel*, March 9, 1883, 525.
19 See, for instance, Say, Chamber of Deputies, *Annales du Sénat et du Corps législatif*, May 18, 1893, 308.
20 The first article of Felix Faure's first project stipulates, "The head of *every industrial, commercial,* or *agricultural* business." On the limitlessness of professional risk, see Lacombe, Senate, *Journal Officiel*, March 9, 1889, 219: "Isn't the principle of professional risk in reality everywhere? Really, a provision that is restricted to certain industries is a completely arbitrary one." See also Bérenger, Senate, *Journal Officiel*, March 14, 1889, 252; Sebline, Senate, *Annales du Sénat et du Corps législatif*, November 28, 1895, 153.
21 Say, Senate, *Journal Officiel*, March 12, 1889, 232.
22 See Lacombe, Senate, *Journal Officiel*, March 9, 1889, 220, and the response from Tolain, Senate, *Journal Officiel*, March 12, 1889, 238; Maze, Senate, *Journal Officiel*, March 22, 1889, 314: "I conclude that we are completely in the realm of the vague and arbitrary."
23 The French word *transaction* can mean a transaction in a financial sense as well as a compromise. Throughout the rest of the chapter Ewald plays on both meanings of the word. For the most part, I have chosen to render the word "transaction." *Trans.*
24 Girard and Nadaud, "Report," Chamber of Deputies, *Journal Officiel*, annex no. 2634, February 16, 1884, 259.
25 Faure, Chamber of Deputies, *Journal Officiel*, March 9, 1883, 528.
26 *Transaction. Trans.*
27 Thévenet, Senate, *Annales du Sénat et du Corps législatif*, March 4, 1898, 309.
28 Sauzet, "De la Responsabilité des patrons," 694.
29 Bérenger, Senate, *Annales du Sénat et du Corps législatif*, January 28, 1896, 23.
30 Also known in English as "wergild" (literally, a "man's yield"), it was the legal practice of ancient Germanic tribes of putting a set price on items and every person in the social hierarchy. In case of theft, accident, or murder, the price could be paid as reparation. *Trans.*
31 Bérenger, Senate, *Annales du Sénat et du Corps législatif*, January 28, 1896, 26.
32 Camecasse, Chamber of Deputies, *Journal Officiel*, May 17, 1888, 1423.
33 See Maillet, "Les Effets de l'assurance accidents du travail dans le champ médical."
34 Faure, Chamber of Deputies, *Journal Officiel*, May 17, 1888, 1426.
35 The first article of his 1889 counterproposal stipulated, "Every accident caused by the execution of labor known to be dangerous gives the right, to the benefit of the worker or the employee who has been a victim, or to the rights holders, to a compensation, unless it can be established that the accident had been caused by his own lack of foresight."

36 Lecomte, Senate, *Annales du Sénat et du Corps législatif*, March 20, 1896, 336.
37 Poirier, Senate, *Annales du Sénat et du Corps législatif*, July 4, 1895, 218.
38 Ricard, Chamber of Deputies, *Journal Officiel*, May 18, 1888, 1434.
39 Graux, Chamber of Deputies, *Journal Officiel*, March 11, 1883, 549.
40 Martin, Senate, *Journal Officiel*, March 19, 1889, 291–92.
41 Chimirri, "La Faute lourde dans la législation," 252.
42 De Mun, Chamber of Deputies, *Journal Officiel*, May 17, 1888, 1425.
43 De Mun, Chamber of Deputies, *Journal Officiel*, May 17, 1888, 1425.
44 Tolain, Senate, *Journal Officiel*, March 19, 1889, 286.
45 Ricard, Chamber of Deputies, "Rapports au nom de la Commission," *Journal Officiel*, impression no. 1926, February 25, 1892, 75–76.
46 Bérenger, Senate, *Journal Officiel*, March 14, 1889, 252.
47 Van Overbergh, "La Faute lourde en matière d'accidents du travail," 203.
48 Dr. Bödiker, président de l'Office impérial des assurances de Berlin, "Séance du Mercredi Après-Midi, 23 Septembre," 685.
49 Lacombe, Senate, *Journal Officiel*, March 9, 1889, 217.
50 Cheysson, "La Faute lourde en matière d'accidents du travail," 234.
51 *Transaction. Trans.*
52 A Roman jurisconsult is a specialist in Roman law. *Trans.*
53 Passy, Chamber of Deputies, *Journal Officiel*, May 22, 1888, 1475.
54 Maruéjouls, Chamber of Deputies, *Annales du Sénat et du Corps législatif*, May 18, 1893, 463.
55 Nadaud, Chamber of Deputies, *Journal Officiel*, March 13, 1883, 567.
56 Duché, "Report," Chamber of Deputies, *Documents*, no. 2150 (November 28, 1887).
57 Maruéjouls, Chamber of Deputies, *Annales du Sénat et du Corps législatif*, May 18, 1893, 318.
58 Say, Chamber of Deputies, *Annales du Sénat et du Corps législatif*, May 18, 1893, 368: "The worst type of socialism, bourgeois socialism."
59 Poirier, "Report to the Senate," impression no. 73, *Journal Officiel*, April 3, 1895, 13.
60 Poirier, "Report to the Senate," impression no. 73, *Journal Officiel*, April 3, 1895, 14.
61 The formula comes from Jean Jaurès, Chamber of Deputies, *Annales du Sénat et du Corps législatif*, July 7, 1897, 151.
62 Sarrut, Sub Court of Civil Appeals, January 21, 1903, *Recueil Dalloz* (1903), 1:105.
63 The law of April 9, 1898, would continually be extended until Social Security absorbed the question of workplace accidents (law of October 30, 1946): through the laws of June 30, 1899, December 15, 1922, and April 30, 1926, concerning agricultural accidents; the law of April 12, 1906, concerning accidents in commercial operations; the law of July 15, 1914, concerning logging operations; the law of October 25, 1919, concerning occupational diseases; the law of August 2, 1923, which extends the 1898 law's benefits to domestic servants and household staff. The law of July 18, 1907, allows employers not subject to the law to freely ascribe to it for the benefit of their personnel. The law of 1898 would be reformed through the law of July 1, 1938, which stipulates that the legislation of accidents applies "to

whoever has proven, through any means, that he has performed under any sort of contract, valuable or not, renting his services." See, for example, Rouast and Durand, *Précis de législation industrielle*, 503.

64 Faure, Chamber of Deputies, *Journal Officiel*, March 9, 1883, 527.

65 Labbé, *Recueil Sirey* (1884), 4:28.

66 According to unanimous doctrine, the employment contract is characterized by the *relationship of subordination* in which the employed is placed vis-à-vis the employer. See, for example, Camerlynck, *Traité de droit du travail*, 1:47. The article by Savatier, "Louage d'ouvrage et d'industrie," 830, specifies that "these are the social laws that have brought out this last meaning, since they only take wage earners under their protection, on account of their dependence."

67 The provisions for reparation in the 1898 law were revised in 1938. *Trans.*

BIBLIOGRAPHY

Government and Legal Publications

Annales du Sénat et du Corps législatif. Paris: Moniteur universel.

Assemblée Nationale constituante (France). *Comte rendu des séances de l'Assemblée nationale.* 10 vols. Paris, 1848–49.

Assemblée Nationale constituante (France). *Impressions.* Paris: 1848–1849.

Assemblée Nationale législative (France). *Comte rendu des séances de l'Assemblée nationale législative.* 17 vols. Paris, 1849–51.

Journal Officiel. Paris.

Le Moniteur universel. Paris.

Recueil Dalloz. Paris: Bureau de la jurisprudence générale.

Recueil Sirey. Paris: Librairie du Recueil Sirey.

Supplément au Répertoire Dalloz. Paris: Bureau de la jurisprudence générale.

Books and Articles

About, Edmond. *L'Assurance.* Paris: Hachette, 1865.

Baccou, Philippe, et le Club de l'Horloge. *Le Grand Tabou: L'économie et le mirage égalitaire.* Paris: Michel, 1980.

Baker, Tom, and Jonathan Simon, eds. *Embracing Risk: The Changing Culture of Insurance and Responsibility.* Chicago: University of Chicago Press, 2002.

Bastiat, Frédéric. *Harmonies économiques.* Vol. 6 of *Oeuvres complètes.* Paris: Guillaumin, 1864.

Bastiat, Frédéric. *Justice et fraternité.* Vol. 4 of *Oeuvres complètes.* Paris: Guillaumin, 1864.

Beau de Rochas, Alphonse. *Commentaire de la loi portant création d'une caisse d'assurance en cas d'accidents resultant de travaux agricoles et industriels, etc.* Paris: Lacroix, 1868. https://papers.ssrn.com/sol3/papers.cfm?abstract_id=2142163

Becker, Gary S., François Ewald, and Bernard E. Harcourt. "Becker on Ewald on Foucault on Becker: American Neoliberalism and Michel Foucault's 1979 'Birth of Biopolitics' Lectures." 2012. https://papers.ssrn.com/sol3/papers.cfm?abstract_id=2142163.

Behrent, Michael. "Accidents Happen: François Ewald, the 'Antirevolutionary' Foucault, and the Intellectual Politics of the French Welfare State." *Journal of Modern History* 82 (September 2010): 585–624.

Bénéton, Philippe. *Le Fléau du bien*. Paris: Laffont, 1983.
Bergeron, Louis. *Oeuvres sur les assurances*. Paris: Warnier, 1891.
Bidiss, Michael. *The Age of the Masses*. New York: Penguin, 1977.
Bloch, Camille. *L'Assistance et l'état en France à la veille de la révolution (généralités de Paris, Rouen, Alençon, Orléans, Châlons, Soissons, Amiens) (1764–1790)*. Paris: Picard, 1908.
Bloch, Oscar, and Walther von Wartburg. *Dictionnaire étymologique de la langue française*. 4th ed. Paris: Presses universitaires de France, 1964.
Blum, Edgar. "Les Assurances terrestres en France sous l'Ancien Régime." *Revue d'histoire économique et sociale* 8, no. 1 (1920): 95–104.
Bödiker, Dr. Anton, et al. "Séance du Mercredi Après-Midi, 23 septembre." In *Congrès international des accidents du travail, 2e session tenue à Berne du 21 au septembre 1891*, 681–92. Berne: Staempfli, 1891.
Boiteux, Lucas Alexandre. *La Fortune de mer: Le besoin de sécurité et les débuts de l'assurance maritime*. Paris: S.E.V.P.E.N., 1968.
Bouchet, Michel. *L'Assistance publique en France pendant la révolution*. Paris: Jouve, 1908.
Boudon, Raoul. *Organisation unitaire et nationale de l'assurance: Mémoire addressé à l'Assemblée nationale*. Paris: Libraire agricole, 1848.
Bouget, Denis. "Movements by the Unemployed in France and Social Protection: The *Fonds d'urgence sociale* Experience." In *Changing Labor Markets, Welfare Policies and Citizenship*, edited by Jørgen Goul Andersen and Per H. Jensen, 209–34. Bristol: Policy, 2002.
Bourgin, Georges, and Hubert Bourgin. *Le Régime de l'industrie en France de 1814 à 1830*. Paris: Picard, 1912.
Bréchignac, Victor. *Les Caisses de secours des ouvriers mineurs dans le bassin de la Loire, étude critique des usages et de la jurisprudence*. Saint-Étienne: Chevalier, 1869.
Bronstein, Jamie L. *Caught in the Machinery: Workplace Accidents and Injured Workers in Nineteenth-Century Britain*. Stanford, CA: Stanford University Press, 2008.
Burat, Am. *Les Houillères de la France en 1866*. Paris: Baudry, 1867.
Burlamaqui, Jean-Jacques. *Élémens du droit naturel*. Lausanne: Grasset, 1783.
Cabouat, Jules. *Traité des accidents du travail*. Paris: Bureaux des Lois nouvelles, 1901.
Camerlynck, Guillaume Hubert. *Traité de droit du travail*. Vol. 1, *Contrat de travail*. Paris: Dalloz, 1968.
Castel, Robert. *La Gestion des risques: De l'anti-psychiatrie à l'après-psychanalyse*. Paris: Minuit, 1981.
Castel, Robert. *L'Ordre psychiatrique: L'Âge d'or de l'aliénisme*. Paris: Minuit, 1976. Published in English as *The Regulation of Madness: The Origins of Incarceration in France*. Translated by W. D. Halls. Berkeley: University of California Press, 1988.
Castel, Robert. "'Risquophiles' et 'risquophobes': L'individu selon le Medef." *Le Monde*, June 7, 2001, http://www.lemonde.fr/acces-restreint/archives/article/2001/06/07/499547452672odeb55f43f87ac9d1719_4202584_1819218.html.

Chaptal, Jean-Antoine. *Essai sur le perfectionnement des arts chimiques en France, an VIII.* Paris: Déterville, An VIII [1800].
Chaptal, Jean-Antoine. *De l'Industrie française.* Paris: Renouard, 1819.
Chaptal, Jean-Antoine. *Mes souvenirs sur Napoléon.* Paris: Plon, 1893.
Chaptal, Jean-Antoine. *Quelques réflexions sur l'industrie en général.* Paris: Corréard, 1819.
Chateleux, P. J. L. de, and J. P. van Rooijen. *Le Rapport de Johan de Witt sur le calcul des rentes viagères.* The Hague: Nijhoff, 1937.
Chaufton, Albert. *Les Assurances, leur passé, leur présent, leur avenir, au point de vue rationnel technique et pratique, moral, économique et social, financier et administratif, légal, législatif et contractuel, en France et à l'étranger.* 2 vols. Paris: Chevalier-Maresq, 1884, 1886.
Chevallier, Émile. "Assistance" and "Paupérisme." In *Nouveau dictionnaire d'économie politique*, edited by Léon Say and Joseph Chailley-Bert, 1:69–83. Paris: Guillaumin, 1893.
Cheysson, Émile. "Le Devoir social et la formation sociale du patron." *La Réforme Sociale* (July 1905): 48–67.
Cheysson, Émile. *L'Économie sociale à l'Exposition universelle de 1889: Communication faite au congrès d'économie sociale, le 13 juin 1889.* Paris: Guillaumin, 1889.
Cheysson, Émile. "La Faute lourde en matière d'accidents du travail." *Bulletin du Comité permanent du Congrès des accidents du travail.* Vol. 1. Paris: Comité, 1890.
Cheysson, Émile. *Oeuvres choisies.* 2 vols. Paris: A. Rousseau, 1911.
Chimirri, Bruno. "La Faute lourde dans la législation relative aux accidents du travail." In *Congrès international des accidents du travail et des assurances sociales, 4e session, tenue à Bruxelles du 26 au 31 juillet 1897*, 245–75. Brussels: Weissenbruch, 1897.
Le Club de l'Horloge. *Les Racines du futur: Demain la France.* Paris: Masson, 1977.
Comité des Houillères du Nord et du Pas-de-Calais: Réponse au questionnaire adressé aux compaginas houillères par les Commissions d'enquête parlementaire sur le régime économique. Douai: Crépin, 1870.
Condorcet, Jean-Antoine-Nicolas de Caritat, marquis de. *Esquisse d'un tableau historique des progrès de l'esprit humain.* Paris, 1794.
Condorcet, Jean-Antoine-Nicolas de Caritat, marquis de. *Mathématique et société.* Edited by Rushdi Rashid. Paris: Hermann, 1974.
Congrès international des accidents du travail et des assurances sociales: Quatrième session tenue à Bruxelles. Brussels: Weissenbruch, 1897.
Congrès scientifique international des institutions de prévoyance, tenu à Paris du 1 à 7 juillet 1878. Paris: Ministère de l'Agriculture et du Commerce, 1881.
Costaz, Claude-Anthelme. *Essai sur l'administration de l'agriculture, du commerce, des manufactures et des subsistances.* Paris: Huzard, 1818.
Costaz, Claude-Anthelme. *Les Lois et instructions ministérielles sur les manufactures, les ateliers, les ouvriers et la propriété.* Paris: Didot, 1819.
Cournot, Antoine Augustin. *Exposition de la théorie des chances et des probabilités.* Paris: Hachette, 1843.

Cousin, Victor. *Du Vrai, du beau et du bien*. Paris: Didier, 1853.
Cousin, Victor. *Justice et charité*. Paris, 1848.
Crozier, Michel. "Western Europe." In *The Crisis of Democracy: Report on the Governability of Democracies to the Trilateral Commission*, edited by Michel Crozier, Samuel P. Huntington, and Joji Watanuki, 11–58. New York: New York University Press, 1975.
Deboutteville, Lucien. *Des Sociétés de prévoyance ou de secours mutuels*. Paris: Guillaumin, 1844.
de Courcy, Antoine. *Les Assurances*. Paris: Comité des publications politiques, 1886.
Defert, Daniel, Jacques Donzelot, François Ewald, Gerard Maillet, and Catherine Mevel. *Socialisation du risque et pouvoir dans l'entreprise: Histoire des transformations politiques et juridiques qui ont permis la légalisation du risque professionnel*. Paris: Collège de France, 1977.
de Girardin, Émile. *L'Abolition de la misère par l'élévation des salaires*. Paris: Administration de librairie, 1850.
de Girardin, Émile. *Le Droit*. Paris: Librairie Nouvelle, 1854.
de Girardin, Émile. *La Politique universelle, décrets de l'avenir*. 3rd ed. Paris: Librairie Nouvelle, 1855.
de Girardin, Émile. *Questions de mon temps, 1836–1856*. Paris: Serrière, 1858.
de Jouvenal, Bertrand. *Napoléon et l'économie dirigée*. Paris: Toison d'Or, 1942.
Deleule, Didier. *Hume et la naissance du libéralisme économique*. Paris: Aubier, 1979.
Deleuze, Gilles. "Écrivain non: Un nouveau cartographe." *Critique* 242 (December 1975): 1215.
Denord, François. "La Conversion au néo-libéralisme: Droite et libéralisme économique dans les années 1980." *Mouvements* 35 (2004–5): 17–23.
Desrosières, Alain. *The Politics of Large Numbers: A History of Statistical Reasoning*. Translated by Camille Naish. Cambridge, MA: Harvard University Press, 1998.
Donzelot, Jacques. *L'Invention du social: Essai sur le déclin des passions politiques*. Paris: Fayard, 1984.
Dreyfus, Ferdinand. *Un Philanthrope d'autrefois: La Rochefoucault-Liancourt, 1747–1827*. Paris: Plon-Nourrit, 1903.
Dubreuil, Henri. "Le patronage." *La Réforme Sociale* 7 (1884): 465–71.
Duchâtel, Charles Marie Tanneguy. *Considérations d'économie politique sur la bienfaisance ou de la charité dans ses rapports avec l'état moral et le bien-être des classes inférieurs de la société*. 2nd ed. Paris: Guiraudet et Jouaust, 1836.
Duhamel, Georges. *Scènes de la vie future*. Paris: Fayard, 1934.
Dutton, Paul V. *Origins of the French Welfare State: The Struggle for Social Reform in France, 1914–1947*. Cambridge: Cambridge University Press, 2002.
Duxbury, Neil, "Juridicity as a Theme in French Legal Philosophy." *International Journal for the Semiotics of Law* 2, no. 4 (1989): 85–95.
Émérigon, Balthazard-Marie. *Traité des assurances et des contrats à la grosse d'Émérigon*. Vol. 1. Paris: Béchet, 1827.
Ewald, François. *L'État providence*. Paris: Grasset, 1986.

Ewald, François. "Foucault et l'actualité." In *Au risque de Foucault*, edited by Dominique Sauche, Sabine Prokhoris, Yves Roussel, and Roger Rotmann, 203–12. Paris: Centre Georges Pompidou, 1997.

Ewald, François. *Histoire de l'état providence*. Paris: Librairie Générale Française, 1996.

Ewald, François. "Norms, Discipline, and the Law." Translated by Marjorie Beale. *Representations* 30 (Spring 1990): 138–61.

Ewald, François. "La Providence de l'état: Interview with François Ewald." *Revue Projet*, March 2, 2000. http://www.revue-projet.com/articles/la-providence-de-l-etat/.

Ewald, François. "The Return of Descartes' Malicious Demon: An Outline of a Philosophy of Precaution." In *Embracing Risk*, edited by Tom Baker and Jonathan Simon, 273–301. Chicago: University of Chicago Press, 2002.

Ewald, François. "Risk, Insurance, Society: Interview with Paul Rabinow and Keith Gandal." *History of the Present* 3 (1987): 1–2, 6–12.

Ewald, François. "Risque, assurance, sécurité." PhD diss., Institut d'études politiques de Paris, 1986.

Ewald, François. "Two Infinities of Risk." Translated by Brian Massumi. In *The Politics of Everyday Fear*, edited by Brian Massumi, 221–28. Minneapolis: University of Minnesota Press, 1993.

Ewald, François. "What Do You Want Me to Regret? An Interview with François Ewald by Johannes Boehme." *Los Angeles Review of Books*, November 3, 2017. https://lareviewofbooks.org/article/what-do-you-want-me-to-regret-an-interview-with-francois-ewald/.

Fenet, Pierre-Antoine. *Recueil complet des travaux préparatoires du code civil*. Vol. 13. Paris: Videcoq, 1827.

Ferrouillat, Jean-Baptiste. *Rapport fait au nom du Comité des travailleurs, sur des articles supplémentaires au décret relatif aux Conseils de Prud'hommes, par le citoyen Ferrouillat*. Paris: Imprimerie de l'Assemblée nationale, 1849.

Finkel, Alvin. "Workers' Social Wage Struggles during the Great Depression and the Era of Neoliberalism: International Comparisons." In *Workers in Hard Times: A Long View of Economic Crisis*, edited by Leon Fink, Joseph A. McCartin, and Joan Sangster, 113–40. Champaign: University of Illinois Press, 2014.

Fishback, Price V., and Shawn Everett Kantor. *A Prelude to the Welfare State: The Origins of Workers' Compensation*. Chicago: University of Chicago Press, 2000.

Foucault, Michel. *The Birth of Biopolitics: Lectures at the Collège de France, 1978–1979*. Edited by Michel Senellart. Translated by Graham Burchell. New York: Palgrave Macmillan, 2008.

Foucault, Michel. "L'Extension sociale de la norme." In *Dits et écrits*, edited by François Ewald and Daniel Defert, 3:74–79. Paris: Gallimard, 1994.

Foucault, Michel. *Histoire de la folie à l'âge classique*. Paris: Plon, 1961. Published in English as *History of Madness*. Edited by Jean Khalfa. Translated by Jonathan Murphy and Jean Khalfa. London: Routledge, 2006.

Foucault, Michel. *The History of Sexuality*. Vol. 1. Translated by Robert Hurley. New York: Pantheon, 1978.

Foucault, Michel. *Security, Territory, Population: Lectures at the Collège de France, 1977–1978*. Edited by Michel Senellart, François Ewald, Alessandro Fontana, and Arnold I. Davidson. Translated by Graham Burchell. New York: Palgrave Macmillan, 2007.

Foucault, Michel. *Society Must Be Defended: Lectures at the Collège de France, 1975–76*. Edited by Mauro Bertani and Alessandro Fontana. Translated by David Macey. New York: Palgrave Macmillan, 2003.

Foucault, Michel. *Surveiller et punir: Naissance de la prison*. Paris: Gallimard, 1975. Published in English as *Discipline and Punish: The Birth of the Prison*. 2nd ed. Translated by Alan Sheridan. New York: Vintage, 1995.

Gérando, Joseph-Marie, Baron de. *Traité de la bienfaisance publique*. 3 vols. Paris: Renouard, 1839.

Gibon, Alexandre. *Des Divers modes de rémunération du travail*. Paris: Guillaumin, 1890.

Gounot, Emmanuel. *Le Principe de l'autonomie de la volonté en droit privé: Contribution à l'étude de l'indiviualisme juridique*. Paris: Rousseau, 1912.

Gouraud, Charles. *Histoire du calcul des probabilités depuis ses origines jusqu'à nos jours, avec une thèse sur la légitimité des principes et des applications de cette analyse*. Paris: Durand, 1848.

Grégoire, Mathieu. *Les Intermittents du spectacle: Enjeux d'un siècle de luttes (de 1919 à nos jours)*. Paris: La Dispute, 2013.

Gros, Ferdinand. *L'Assurance, son sens historique et social*. Paris: Bureau d'organisation économique, 1920.

Guéneau, Louis. "La Législation restrictive du travail des enfants: La loi française du 22 mars 1841." *Revue d'histoire économique et sociale* 15, no. 4 (1927): 420–503.

Guérin, Urbain. "Du Salaire et des moyens d'existence des familles ouvrières." *La Réforme Sociale* 4, no. 9 (July–December 1887): 117–25.

Guillemaut, P. *La Mutualité en France au XIXe siècle: Histoire et législation des sociétés de secours mutuels (loi du 1er avril 1895)*. Paris: Rousseau, 1899.

Gurvitch, Georges. *L'Idée du droit social: Notion et système du droit social; Histoire doctrinale depuis le 17e siècle jusqu'à la fin du 19e siècle*. Paris: Recueil Sirey, 1932.

Guyot, Yves. *La Famille Pichot: Scènes de l'enfer social*. Paris: Rouff, 1882.

Guyot, Yves. "La Question des accidents de travail et le Congrès de Milan." *Revue politique et parlementaire* 2 (1894): 281–302.

Hacker, Jacob S. *The Great Risk Shift: The New Economic Insecurity and the Decline of the American Dream*. Oxford: Oxford University Press, 2008.

Halbwachs, Maurice. *La Théorie de l'homme moyen: Essai sur Quetelet et la statistique morale*. Paris: Alcan, 1912.

Halpérin, Jean. *Les Assurances en Suisse et dans le monde*. Neufchâtel: Baconnière, 1946.

Hamon, Georges. *Histoire générale de l'assurance en France et à l'étranger*. Paris: L'assurance moderne, 1897.

Harrison, Barbara. "Are Accidents Gender Neutral? The Case of Women's Industrial Work in Britain, 1880–1914." *Women's History Review* 2 (1993): 253–75.

Hatzfeld, Henri. *Du Paupérisme à la sécurité sociale: Essai sur les origines de la sécurité sociale en France, 1850–1940*. Paris: Colin, 1971.

Hayek, Friedrich A. von. *Law, Legislation, and Liberty: A New Statement of the Liberal Principles of Justice and Political Economy.* Volume 1, *Rules and Order.* Chicago: University of Chicago Press, 1973.

Hayek, Friedrich A. von. "Résultats des actions des hommes et non de leurs desseins." In *Mélanges Rueff: Les Fondements philosophiques des systèmes économiques; Texte de Jacques Rueff et essais rédigés en son honneur.* Paris: Payot, 1967. Published in English as "The Results of Human Action but Not of Human Design." In *The Collected Works of F. A. Hayek*, vol. 15, *The Market and Other Orders*, edited by Bruce Caldwell, 293–303. Chicago: University of Chicago Press, 2014.

Hegel, G. W. F. *La Phénoménologie de l'esprit.* Translated by Jean Hyppolite. 2 vols. Paris: Aubier, 1960. Published in English as *Phenomenology of Spirit.* Translated by A. V. Miller. Oxford: Oxford University Press, 1977.

Hémard, Joseph. *Théorie et pratique des assurances terrestres.* 2 vols. Paris: Recueil Sirey, 1924.

Horwitz, Morton. *The Transformation of American Law, 1870–1960.* Oxford: Oxford University Press 1992.

Hubbard, Nicolas Gustave. *De l'Organisation des sociétés de prévoyance.* Paris: Guillaumin, 1852.

Humboldt, Wilhelm von. *Essai sur les limites de l'action de l'état.* Translated by Henri Chrétien. Paris: Baillière, 1867.

Jay, Martin. *The Virtues of Mendacity: On Lying in Politics.* Charlottesville: University of Virginia Press, 2010.

Josserand, Louis. *De la Responsabilité du fait des choses inanimées.* Paris: Rousseau, 1897.

Jourdan, Alfred. *Le Droit français: Ses règles fondamentales, ses rapports avec les principes de la morale, avec l'économie politique et avec l'utilité générale.* Paris: Plon, 1875.

Juvigny, Jean-Baptiste. *Coup d'oeil sur l'assurance de la vie des hommes.* Paris: Renard, 1818.

Kant, Immanuel. *Doctrine du droit.* Translated by A. Philonenko. Paris: Vrin, 1971. Published in English as "The Metaphysics of Morals." In *Practical Philosophy*, translated by Mary J. Gregor, 353–603. Cambridge: Cambridge University Press, 1996.

Kant, Immanuel. *Idée d'une histoire universelle au point de vue cosmopolitique.* In *La Philosophie de l'histoire: Opuscules.* Translated by Stephane Piobetta. Paris: Aubier, 1947. Published in English as *Idea for a Universal History from a Cosmopolitan Perspective.* In *Toward Perpetual Peace and Other Writings on Politics, Peace, and History*, translated by David L. Colclasure, 3–15. New Haven, CT: Yale University Press, 2006.

Kelsen, Hans. *Introduction to the Problems of Legal Theory: A Translation of the First Edition of the Reine Rechtslehre or Pure Theory of Law* [1934/1960]. Translated by Bonnie Litschewski-Paulson and Stanley L. Paulson. Oxford: Clarendon, 1992.

Klein, Jennifer. *For All These Rights: Business, Labor, and the Shaping of America's Public-Private Welfare State*. Princeton, NJ: Princeton University Press, 2003.
Kolboom, Ingo. "Patron et patronat: Histoire sociale du concept de patronat en France au 19e et 20e siècle." *Mots* 9 (October 1984): 89–112.
Kotkin, Stephen. *Magnetic Mountain: Stalinism as a Civilization*. Berkeley: University of California Press, 1997.
Lallemand, Léon. *Histoire de la charité*. 4 vols. Paris: Picard, 1902–12.
Lallemand, Léon. *La Révolution et les pauvres*. Paris: Picard, 1898.
Land, Hilary. "Women, Work and Social Security." *Social Policy and Administration* 5, no. 3 (1971): 183–92.
Laurent, Émile. *Le Paupérisme et les associations de prévoyance*. Paris: Guillaumin, 1860.
Lefevre, Henri. *The Urban Revolution*. Translated by Robert Bonnono. 1970. Minneapolis: University of Minnesota Press, 2003.
Lefort, Joseph Jean. *Les Caisses de retraites ouvrières*. 2 vols. Paris: Fontemoing, 1906.
Le Gall, Yves. "La Loi de 1898 sur les accidents du travail." In *Histoire des accidents du travail* 10, 11. Paris: C.N.R.S., 1981.
Lenoir, Rémy. "La Notion d'accident de travail: Un enjeu de lutes." *Actes de la recherche en sciences sociales* 32–33 (1980): 77–88.
Lepage, P. *Éléments de la science du droit: À usage de toutes les nations et de toutes les classes de citoyens, ou sources de devoirs de l'homme social, tant dans le for intérieur que dans le for extérieur*. Paris: Hubert, 1819.
Le Play, Frédéric. *L'Organisation de la famille selon le vrai modèle signalé par l'histoire de toutes les races et de tous les temps*. 3rd ed. Tours: Mame, 1884.
Le Play, Frédéric. *L'Organisation du travail*. Paris: Mame, 1870.
Le Play, Frédéric. *Les Ouvriers européens*. Vol. 1, *Études sur les travaux, la vie domestique et la condition morale des populations ouvrières de l'Europe, précédées d'un exposé de la méthode d'observation*. Paris: Imprimerie impériale, 1855.
Le Play, Frédéric. *La Réforme sociale en France*. 4th ed. Tours: Mame, 1872.
Le Roux, Alfred. *Exposition universelle de 1867, à Paris Jury spécial*. Paris: Dupont, 1867.
Leroy, André-Louis. *David Hume*. Paris: Presses universitaires de France, 1953.
Leroy-Beaulieu, Paul. *La Question ouvrière au XIXe siècle*. Paris: Charpentier, 1872.
Leroy-Beaulieu, Paul. *Traité théorique et pratique d'économie politique*. Vol. 4. Paris: Guillaumin, 1896.
Levasseur, Émile. *Histoire des classes ouvrières et de l'industrie en France de 1789 à 1870*. 2nd ed. 2 vols. Paris: Rousseau, 1903–4.
Le Livre du centenaire de "La Nationale." Paris: Morancé, 1930.
Locré, Jean-Guillaume. *Législation sur les mines*. Paris: Treuttel et Würtz, 1828.
Loubat, Guillaume. *Traité sur le risque professionel*. Paris: Maresq, 1899.
Machiavelli, Niccolò. *The Prince*. Translated by Peter Bondanella. Oxford: Oxford University Press, 2009.
Maillet, Gerard. "Les Effets de l'assurance accidents du travail dans le champ médical." In *Assurance-Prévoyance-Sécurité: Formation historique es techniques de*

gestion sociale dans les sociétés industrielles. Paris: Ministère du travail et de la participation, 1979.
Mamy, H. "Mesures préventives prises contre les accidents." In *Congrès international des accidents du travail*, edited by Edouard Gruner. Paris, 1889.
Marmottan, Jules. *Vrai Caractère des caisses de secours instituées par les compagnies houillères*. Paris: Guillaumin, 1870.
Marx, Karl. *The Eighteenth Brumaire of Louis Bonaparte*. In *Later Political Writings*, edited by Terrell Carver, 31–127. Cambridge: Cambridge University Press, 1996.
Marx, Karl, and Friedrich Engels. *Manifesto of the Communist Party*. In *The Marx-Engels Reader*, 2nd ed., edited by Robert Tucker, 469–500. New York: Norton, 1978.
McGarity, Thomas O. *Freedom to Harm: The Lasting Legacy of the Laissez Faire Revival*. New Haven, CT: Yale University Press, 2013.
Ménard, Claude. "Trois formes de résistance aux statistiques: Say, Cournot, Walras." In *Pour une histoire de la statistique*, vol. 1, *Contributions: Journées d'études sur l'histoire de la statistique, 23–25 Juin 1976*, 417–29. Paris: Institut national de la statistique et des études économiques, 1977.
Mettler, Suzanne. *Dividing Citizens: Gender and Federalism in New Deal Public Policy*. Ithaca, NY: Cornell University Press, 1998.
Michel, Georges, and Alfred Renouard. *Histoire d'un centre ouvrier (la Compagnie d'Anzin)*. Paris: Guillaumin, 1891.
Montesquieu, Charles de Secondat, Baron de. *The Spirit of the Laws*. Edited by Anne Cohler, Linda Miller, and Harold Stone. Cambridge: Cambridge University Press, 1989.
Moses, Julia. *The First Modern Risk: Workplace Accidents and the Origins of European Social States*. Cambridge: Cambridge University Press, 2018.
Murard, Lion, and Patrick Zylberman. *Ville, habitat et intimité*. Fontenay-sous-Bois: Centre d'études, de recherches et de formation institutionnelles (CERFI), 1976.
Nelson, Barbara. "The Origins of the Two-Channel Welfare State: Workmen's Compensation and Mothers' Aid." In *Women, the State, and Welfare*, edited by Linda Gordon, 123–52. Madison: University of Wisconsin Press, 1990.
Nicolet, Claude. *L'Idée républicaine en France, 1789–1924: Essai d'histoire critique*. Paris: Gallimard, 1982.
O'Malley, Pat. *The Currency of Justice: Fines and Damages in Consumer Societies*. New York: Routledge-Cavendish, 2009.
O'Malley, Pat. *Risk, Uncertainty, and Government*. London: Glasshouse, 2004.
Oudot, Julien. *Conscience et science du devoir: Introduction à une explication nouvelle du Code Napoléon*. Paris: Durand, 1855–56.
Palier, Bruno. "De la Crise aux réformes de l'état-providence: Le cas français en perspective compare." *Revue Française de Sociologie* 43, no 2 (2002): 243–75.
Pardessus, Jean-Marie. *Assurance contre les accidents de voitures*. Paris: Guyot, 1860.
Pardessus, Jean-Marie. *Cours de droit commercial*. 4 vols. Paris: Garnery, 1814–16.
Passy, Hippolyte. *Des Causes de l'inégalité des richesses*. Paris: Pagnerre, 1848.

Pauly, Mark V. "The Economics of Moral Hazard: Comment." *American Economic Review* 58, no. 3 (1968), 531–37.
Pedersen, Susan. *Family, Dependence, and the Origins of the Welfare State: Britain and France, 1914–1945*. Cambridge: Cambridge University Press, 1993.
Persil, S. *Traité des assurances terrestres*. Paris: Alex-Gobelet, 1835.
Picard, Maurice, and André Besson. *Traité général des assurances terrestres en droit français*. 4 vols. Paris: Librairie générale de droit et de jurisprudence, 1938–45.
Picot, Georges. "Les Institutions patronales." *Académie des Sciences Morales et Politiques: Comptes Rendus* 40 (July 1893): 290–302.
Plantier, Alexandre. *Le Livret des ouvriers*. Paris: Jouve et Boyer, 1900.
Portalis, Jean-Étienne-Marie. *Discours, rapports, et travaux inédits sur le Code civil*. Paris: Joubert, 1844.
Pothier, Robert Joseph. *Traité des contrats aléatoires*. New ed. Paris: Debure, 1777.
Pothier, Robert Joseph. *Traité du contrat d'assurance*. Paris: Sube et Laporte, 1810.
Pouget, Louis. *Dictionnaire des assurances terrestres: Principes, doctrine, jurisprudence, statistique, économie de l'assurance; Concordance des polices françaises avec les polices et les codes étrangers; Analogie avec les assurances maritimes et fluviales*. Paris: Durand, 1855.
Procacci, Giovanni. *Gouverner la misère: La question sociale en France, 1789–1848*. Paris: Seuil, 1993.
Proudhon, Pierre-Joseph. *Les Confessions d'un révolutionnaire* [1849]. Paris: Lacroix, 1876.
Pufendorf, Baron Samuel de. *Les Devoirs de l'homme et du citoyen*. London, 1741.
Quadagno, Jill. *The Color of Welfare: How Racism Undermined the War on Poverty*. Oxford: Oxford University Press, 1994.
Quetelet, Adolphe. "De l'Influence du libre arbitre de l'homme sur les faits sociaux et particulièrement sur le nombre des mariages." *Bulletin de la Commission centrale des statistiques* 3 (1847): 135–55.
Quetelet, Adolphe. *Du Système social et des lois qui le régissent*. Paris: Guillaumin, 1848.
Quetelet, Adolphe. *Études sur l'homme*. Brussels: Wouters, Raspouet, 1842.
Quetelet, Adolphe. *Lettres à S. A. R.: Le duc régnant de Saxe-Coburg et Gotha: Sur la théorie des probabilités, appliquée aux sciences morales et politiques*. Brussels: Hayez, 1846.
Quetelet, Adolphe. *Physique sociale ou Essai sur le développement des facultés de l'homme*. 2 vols. Brussels: Muquardt, 1869.
Quetelet, Adolphe. *Recherches sur le penchant au crime aux différens âges*. Brussels: Hayez, 1831.
Quetelet, Adolphe. *Sur l'homme et le développement de ses facultés; ou, Essai de physique sociale*. 2 vols. Paris: Bachelier, 1835.
Reboul, Eugène. *Étude sur les assurances: Les Assurances sur la vie*. Paris: Dubuisson, 1863.
Reclus, Maurice. *Émile de Girardin, le créateur de la presse moderne*. Paris: Hachette, 1934.

Reybaud, Louis. "Du Patronage dans l'industrie." *La Revue des Deux Mondes* 3 (1867): 737–51.
Reybaud, Louis. "Économistes anglais: M. John Stuart Mill et l'économie politique en Angleterre." *La Revue des Deux Mondes* 4 (1855): 117–48.
Reybaud, Louis. *Le Fer et la houille suivis du canon Krupp et du Familistère de Guise: Dernière série des études sur le régime des manufactures*. Paris: Lévy, 1874.
Richard, Louis. *L'Homme est un capital*. Paris: Derenne, 1876.
Richard, Pierre Joseph Élisée. *Histoire des institutions d'assurance en France*. Paris: Argus, 1956.
Rigaudias-Weiss, Hilde. *Les Enquêtes ouvrières en France entre 1830 et 1848*. Paris: Presses universitaires de France, 1936.
Ripert, Georges. *La Règle morale dans les obligations civiles*. Paris: Librairie générale de droit et de jurisprudence, 1949.
La Rochefoucauld-Liancourt, Frédéric Gaétan. *Premier rapport du Comité de Mendicité*. Paris: Imprimérie nationale, 1790.
La Rochefoucauld-Liancourt, Frédéric Gaétan. *Quatrième rapport du Comité de Mendicité*. Paris: Imprimerie nationale, 1790.
Rosanvallon, Pierre. *La Crise de l'état-providence*. Paris: Seuil, 1981.
Rouast, André, and Paul Durand. *Précis de legislation industrielle, droit du travail*. Paris: Dalloz, 1955.
Rouast, André, and Maurice Givord. *Traité du droit des accidents du travail et des maladies professionelles*. Paris: Dalloz, 1934.
Rouff, Marcel. *Les Mines de charbon en France au XVIIIe siècle, 1744–1791*. Paris: Rieder, 1933.
Rousseau, Jean-Jacques. *Discours sur l'origine et le fondement de l'inégalité parmi les hommes*. Paris: Garnier, 1962. Published in English as *Discourse on the Origin and Foundations of Inequality among Men*. Edited and translated by Helena Rosenblatt. New York: Bedford/St. Martin's, 2011.
Sachet, Adrien. *Traité théorique et pratique de la législation sur les accidents du travail*. Paris: Larose, 1899.
Sainctelette, Charles. *De la Responsabilité et de la garantie*. Paris: Chevalier-Maresq, 1884.
Saint-Léger, Alexandre de. *Les Mines d'Anzin et d'Aniche pendant la Révolution*. 2 vols. Paris: Leroux, 1939.
Saleilles, Raymond. *Les Accidents de travail et la responsabilité civile: Essai d'une théorie objective de la responsabilité délictuelle*. Paris: Rousseau, 1897.
Saleilles, Raymond. "Le Code civil et la méthode historique." In *Le Code civil, 1804–1904: Livre du Centenaire*, 1:95–129. Paris: Duchemin, 1969.
Salomon, Georges. *Les Caisses de secours et de prévoyance des ouvriers mineurs en Europe*. Paris: Guillaumin, 1878.
Sauzet, Marc. "De la Résponsabilité des patrons vis-à-vis des ouvriers dans les accidents du travail." *Revue critique de législation et de jurisprudence* (1883): 596–640.

Sauzet, Marc. "Essai historique sur la législation industrielle de la France: La police des manufactures de papier." In *Revue d'économie politique* 6, no. 1 (1892): 1097–1135.

Sauzet, Marc. *Le Livret obligatoire des ouvriers*. Paris: Pichon, 1890.

Savatier, René. "Louage d'ouvrage et d'industrie." In *Nouveau dictionnaire pratique de droit*. Paris: Dalloz, 1933.

Sawyer, Stephen W., and Daniel Steinmetz-Jenkins, eds. *Foucault, Neoliberalism, and Beyond*. Lanham, MD: Rowman and Littlefield, 2019.

Say, Jean Baptiste. *Cours complèt d'économie politique pratique*. 3rd ed. 2 vols. Paris: Guillaumin, 1852.

Say, Léon. "Assurance." In *Nouvelle Dictionnaire d'économie politique*, edited by Léon Say and Joseph Chailly. 2 vols. Paris: Guillaumin, 1900.

Schaller, François. *De la Charité privée aux droits économiques et sociaux du citoyen: Un aspect du nouveau courant social*. Neufchâtel: Baconnière, 1950.

Sénès, V. *Les Origines des compagnies d'assurances soit à primes, soit mutuelles fondées en France depuis le XVIIe siècle jusqu'à nos jours*. Paris: Dulac, 1900.

Simonin, Louis. *La Vie souterraine; ou, Les mines et les mineurs*. Paris: Hachette, 1867.

Smith, Adam. *The Theory of the Moral Sentiments*. Edinburgh: Kincaid and Bell, 1759.

Société des Mines de Lens et de Douvrin (Pas-de-Calais). *Habitations ouvrières: Monographie de l'ouvrier mineur*. Lille: Danel, 1900.

Steinhouse, Adam. *Workers' Participation in Post-Liberation France*. Lanham, MD: Lexington, 2001.

Tarbouriech, Ernest. *La Responsabilité des accidents dont les ouvriers sont victimes dans leur travail: Histoire, jurisprudence et doctrine, bibliographie, travaux parlementaires jusqu'à la date du 24 mars 1896*. Paris: Giard et Brière, 1896.

Thiers, Adolphe. *Du Droit de propriété*. Paris: Pagnerre, 1848.

Thiers, Adolphe. *Rapport présenté par M. Thiers au nom de la Commission de l'assistance et de la prévoyance publiques dans la séance du 26 janvier 1850*. Paris: Paulin, 1850.

Trempé, Rolande. *Le Mineurs de Carmaux, 1848–1914*. Paris: Éditions ouvrières, 1971.

Troclet, Leon-Eli. *La Première Expérience de sécurité sociale: Liège; Décret de Napoléon de 1813*. Brussels: Éditions de la Libraire encyclopédique, 1953.

Troplong, Raymond-Théodore. *De la Propriété d'après le code civil*. Paris: Pagnerre, 1848.

Turgot, Anne Robert Jacques. "Fondation." In *Encyclopédie, ou dictionnaire raisonné des sciences, des arts et des métiers, etc.*, edited by Denis Diderot and Jean le Rond d'Alembert, 7:72–75. Paris, 1757.

Vailland, Roger. *Choderlos de Laclos par lui-même*. Paris: Seuil, 1963.

Van Overbergh, Cyrille. "La Faute lourde en matière d'accidents du travail." In *Congrès international des accidents du travail et des assurances sociales, 4e session, tenue à Bruxelles du 26 au 31 juillet 1897*, 193–226. Brussels: Weissenbruch, 1897.

Viennet, Odette. *Napoléon et l'industrie française: La crise de 1810–1811*. Paris: Plon, 1947.

Villermé, Louis-René. "Sur l'hygiène morale." *Annales d'hygiène publique* 4 (1830): 25–47.

Villermé, Louis-René. *Tableau de l'état physique et moral des ouvriers employés dans les manufactures de coton, de laine et de soie*. Paris: Renouard, 1840.

Wagner, Gerhard. "Comparative Tort Law." In *The Oxford Handbook of Comparative Law*, edited by Mathias Reimann and Reinhard Zimmermann, 1004–41. Oxford: Oxford University Press, 2006.

White, G. Edward. *The Constitution and the New Deal*. Cambridge, MA: Harvard University Press, 2000.

Widmer, Georges. *Les Caisses de secours et de retraite ouvrières: Thèse de doctorat soutenue à la Faculté de droit de Paris*. Alençon: Guy, 1899.

Wilkinson, Frank, and Simon Deakin. *The Law of the Labour Market: Industrialization, Employment, and Legal Evolution*. Oxford: Oxford University Press, 2005.

Witt, John Fabian. *The Accidental Republic: Crippled Workmen, Destitute Widows, and the Remaking of American Law*. Cambridge, MA: Harvard University Press, 2004.

Zamora, Daniel, and Michael Behrent, eds. *Foucault and Neoliberalism*. Cambridge: Polity, 2016.

Zola, Émile. *Germinal*. Introduction by David Baguley. Translated by Raymond MacKenzie. Indianapolis: Hackett, 2011.

INDEX

CPSIA information can be obtained
at www.ICGtesting.com
Printed in the USA
BVHW041201110920
R11198100001B/R111981PG588309BVX1B/1